# The Kiss of Sweet Scottish Rain

*A Walk from Cape Wrath to the Solway Firth*

# The Kiss of Sweet Scottish Rain

*A Walk from Cape Wrath to the Solway Firth*

## ROBERT MCWILLIAMS

Homebound Publications

*Ensuring that the mainstream isn't the only stream.*

Published in 2018 by Homebound Publications
Front Cover Image © Claudine Van Massenhove | Shutterstock.com
Interior Maps by © Robert McWilliams
Cover and Interior Designed by Leslie M. Browning
ISBN 978-1-947003-62-0
*First Edition Trade Paperback*

Homebound Publications
*Ensuring the mainstream isn't the only stream.*
WWW.HOMEBOUNDPUBLICATIONS.COM

10 9 8 7 6 5 4 3 2 1

For Charissa

*It would have been impossible otherwise.*

*1*

# Turning Point

There is, boot rubber aside, just one means of transport to Cape Wrath. And this tourist excursion—a ferry across the kyle[1] and then a minibus over the moors—runs at the mercy of tide, storm, and the Ministry of Defence. Two days before, at the end of a faint and crackling telephone line from my hostel in Inverness, ferryman John Morrison appeared to confirm that his first crossing on Saturday morning would leave at 9:30, as advertised. I planned to hike 14 miles that first day over rough and mostly trackless country south from the cape, and was anxious to reach my starting point with as much daylight left as possible.

I spent Friday night in Durness, a village strung out along cliffs, the nearest settlement to Cape Wrath. My room in the Ben View[2] bed & breakfast looked out at the rounded, bare hills of the country toward the cape, and to the Atlantic Ocean where they ended abruptly. It was unmistakably the very edge of Scotland. I looked at my gear spread about the neat bedroom and felt the weight and imminence of my adventure. I went out in search of supper. The evening was blustery, and gusts of mild Atlantic air shoved me through the village to the Sango Sands pub. It was spacious, echoing, and close to empty. I took my pint to the big windows that looked out over the ocean. The bar livened up after supper. There was football[3] on TV—England versus Bulgaria. But the drinkers—locals, German tourists, me—paid it scant attention, and raised no cheer when England scored.

Until a few months ago, at around this time on a Friday evening, I would have been tidying my desk after a week of conference calls and corporate dysfunction. Or I might have been facing the long journey home from Hong Kong or Chile in Seat 37C. But I have put an end to all that, resigning in pique when the carpet was pulled from beneath yet another carefully constructed project. The heaving of the carpet—and with it the meaninglessness of successive presentations, discussions, and agreements—was announced in an e-mail that arrived in my inbox in our overheated New York offices one morning in March. The mail made me mad, but I wasn't helpless. I had known the moment would come, and for years a plan had grown unobtrusively in the back of my mind, a plan for a new direction that would begin with an adventure. It was the prospect of the adventure, as much as the visceral urge to escape this job, that emboldened me to answer the e-mail with my resignation. But now, fighting the gale back to the Ben View, I felt more trepidation than excitement. What sort of new start would it be if I fell at the first fence, if the adventure defeated me?

Tracy Mackay served my breakfast at 7:30, bringing coffee and chatter, then porridge and more chatter, into the dining room of the Ben View. There were no other guests. Tracy was a young mother, neat and proper. She was self-conscious about the chatter. "Och, I talk too much. It must be a nuisance for you," she said after each burst and scurried back to the kitchen. It wasn't a nuisance at all. But I felt fidgety and confined after three days of sedentary travel, and as soon as my coffee was gone and the last bits and pieces zipped and clipped into my pack, I unlatched the Ben View's small iron gate, and set out for the ferry pier and the Cape Wrath excursion. The wind had died down, leaving behind a gray and wet morning. Even so, it was a relief to be outside, cooling off from Tracy's steaming porridge.

The pier lay two and a half miles away at Keoldale, off the road south. The road was a single lane, empty of traffic, lined by dry stone walls that wrapped pastures of deepest green. A few white-faced sheep looked up at me inquisitively. Most, unmoved, grazed on. Halfway to the pier, the daily minibus from Durness to the outside world broke the all-embracing silence. The driver sounded his horn and waved as he overtook me. It was Neil. My journey up from Inverness yesterday had involved first a train to the inland village of Lairg, and then Neil's minibus to Durness. We had talked on and off for most of the two-hour trip. There was only one other passenger, a vagrant-looking man who sat right at the back, and said nothing at all, until his thanks when he got off in Kinlochbervie. Neil was from the Midlands of England; in his early 30s, I assumed, until he said he had been up here for 20 years. He gave no indication he would ever leave, and driving among the austere hills and shining lochs that bright afternoon I could not blame him.

"Do you get to do this every day?" I asked.

"Nah, I'm just standing in while my mate's away."

"So what's your normal job?"

"I've got an arts and crafts shop. Do my own stone-carving for it." He had mentioned earlier helping out with sheep-shearing.

"You're a busy man," I said.

"I'm a volunteer fireman too!" Neil was also hoping to start a micro-brewery. We talked about names for his brews. I thought "Hops of Wrath" but kept it to myself. In Durness, he called several B&Bs on my behalf before taking me to Tracy. I wanted to buy him a pint that evening for his help.

"I'd like to," he replied. "But I'm the community development officer, and there's a meeting tonight."

Seeking reassurance, I had asked Neil about the Cape Wrath excursion too, and he had agreed that the first run in the morning would depart at 9:30. So, turning now onto an even smaller road, I expected to be bouncing over the moor in an hour. The road ran beside the pebbly and seaweed-strewn shore of the Kyle of Durness to parking spaces for the pier. They were empty. It was still before 9:00, I told myself, and the last thing I wanted to see, anyway, was a host of other passengers. It was September 3rd. The summer holidays were over, but I still feared being bumped to the next excursion, hours later or even tomorrow, by the tourists who were still about. Near the top of the pier, there was a small yellow notice, next boat sailing to connect with minibus 11 am.

Almost as soon as I arrived at the pier and took off my pack, the rain stopped and the last of the wind died. This brought out midges[4], not in maddening swarms but enough to keep you moving about. Otherwise, the wee pier at Keoldale was not a bad place to kill a few hours. A kyle is usually a strait but the Kyle of Durness is an estuary, and the incoming tide was flowing over its yellow-brown sands before my eyes. Looking south over the shifting waters, the first of the bens that would accompany my walk were touching a base of low cloud. Even with map and compass, it is not always obvious which hill is which. Summits hide in cloud and behind each other. Distance deceives. But I was fairly sure that it was Beinn Spionnaidh and Cranstackie, six miles away, with the mist drifting over their tops, and Foinaven fully shrouded behind them. The names are from Gaelic[5] and mean, the experts say, the strong mountain, rugged stack, and wart mountain, respectively.

As I paced the cul-de-sac by the pier to keep one step ahead of the midges, other would-be passengers came by—and went as quickly away when they read the notice board. I was content to stay put and keep my place in line. I tried sitting on the rocks

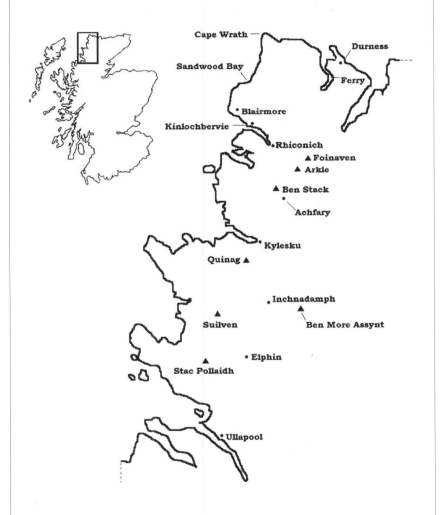

Map 1: Cape Wrath to Ullapool

above the pier to study the day's route on my map, but sharp rock underneath, and gathering midges above, set me pacing again. A weather-beaten German in bike leathers came by, said he could only speak a little English, and painstakingly photographed a single wildflower.

Soon passengers were arriving steadily and, knowing it was first-come-first-served, sticking close to the pier. Three years ago I took the cape excursion on a family vacation, and I recognized the ferryman and minibus driver when they too arrived. I think ferryman Morrison was also in the Sango Sands pub last night. Now he clambered over seaweed-covered rocks to pull a small boat to shore, cutting himself on a lost fishing hook lodged in the rope. "Happens all the time. Bloody fishermen's hooks!" he muttered to the assembled trippers. It was hard to gauge the mix of humor and real annoyance in the remark. After patching himself, he started the outboard on the small boat and putt-putted out to a slightly larger one riding out in the kyle. We watched anxiously as its motor failed to start on the first few pulls, but before long eight or nine of us were stepping gingerly down into its wobbling hull at the head of the pier.

Crossing the kyle took all of ten minutes, just long enough for John to collect fares. Mine was the only one-way ticket. As we waited on the far shore for the ferry to fetch more passengers, a clean-cut, military-looking Englishman asked where I was heading.

"Well, today from Cape Wrath to Sandwood Bay and Blairmore, but eventually to Portpatrick near Stranraer," I said, naming the village in the far southwest of Scotland that was my final destination.

"How's the hike going?" he asked.

"Oh, today's the first day. I'm starting at Cape Wrath."

"How are you feeling about it? Ready to go?" His question gave me the opportunity to confess my fears.

"I'm glad to be underway at last. I just hope I see it through. It's a long time away from family and the comforts of home." Then I came to the crux of the matter.

"I'm afraid I'll jack it in if the going gets too tough." I made a similar confession at the dinner table at home before leaving for Scotland. My middle daughter, nearly 16, said, "Somehow I don't think that will happen. When dad says he's going to do something, he usually does it." My anxiety, now, was about failing that confidence, about returning home early and foolish, without new ideas or stories.

"I'm sure you'll make it," the Englishman said and seemed to mean it. Neil said the same thing yesterday. I wondered how they could possibly be sure. I suppose they could have said, "I'm sure you'll be OK for a while, until you get blisters or fall in a stream. A lonely night in a wet sleeping bag might finish you off too." I was grateful they had not.

It was also around the family dinner table, a week or two after handing in my notice, that I told my daughters that I would be leaving my job, and leaving them for a while too. I said that I wanted to find a better way of making a living now that I was in my 50s, one with more time for things I really cared about. I wanted to assure them that, apart from the weeks I would be away in Scotland, they would see more of me, and nothing about my plans would mean big changes for them. In particular, Katie, 18 in four months, would start at the University of Connecticut in August with all the financial support that we—mom and dad— had promised. I had expected Katie, Caroline, and Marjorie to understand why I was doing this, even to be pleased (after all, isn't a dad on a solo trek infinitely more interesting—infinitely *cooler*—than one who snores on the 5:40 from Grand Central?); but they seemed genuinely excited for me and for themselves, and that added to the sense of rightness I felt about my decision. They had no questions about my destination. My little plan may have grown unobtrusively, but my dream of hiking across my country of birth was no secret in our family.

By the time the minibus was climbing the west shore of the kyle the sun was out, bringing the primary colors of the country into sharp focus—blue estuary and ocean; yellow sandbars and beaches; green pasture. We swung away from the kyle, crossed a burn[6] on a narrow wooden bridge, and set out across ten miles of moor. This most northwesterly corner of Britain is uninhabited and treeless, an expanse of detached hills, lochans[7], streams, and sky. It is also a bombing range and army training ground, and the occasional military buildings and vehicles take something away from its feeling of wilderness. The bus clunked slowly over the potholed and overgrown track, stopping now and then for views and sightings—the sea unbroken to the northern horizon; a buzzard; a huddle of red deer does; and, just possibly, a young golden eagle. A walker was lazing in the heather where a track forked down to Kearvaig Bay. There is a bothy[8] by the bay, a place to sleep by the cliffs and waves. I remembered a sad tale about it.

In December 2002, two shepherds bringing in sheep for the winter noticed that the bothy door was open. Inside they found an emaciated and semi-conscious woman. She was airlifted to hospital in Stornoway in the Western Isles but died two days later of hypothermia. Margaret Davies was a 39-year-old painter and traveler, an experienced outdoorswoman with a taste for solitude. She had trekked alone in Afghanistan, Nepal, and other remote places. This time she left her parents' home in the south of England in late September, apparently in pursuit of isolation. As she had done before, she told them she might be out of touch for some time and would return after Christmas. What happened will never be known for sure, but it seems likely that Margaret caught a debilitating bug, and then discovered just how hard it was to find help. She left notes in the bothy window asking for food, but no one came by. Even if she had had a cell phone, there was no signal. The Cape Wrath excursions would long ago have ended for the season, and to walk out from the bothy to the nearest house would be a tough day's work, even for the healthy. It was a useful reminder that you can walk yourself beyond the reach of help even on the crowded island of Great Britain.

Mather stopped his minibus at the cluster of buildings around the Cape Wrath lighthouse and kept the passengers on board to explain the sights and safety tips. I was impatient and felt like interrupting, "This doesn't apply to me. Please let me out!" but of course I didn't. Cape Wrath—400 feet above the sea at the light—is mainland Britain's most northwesterly point. If you sailed straight west you would make landfall in the tundra of Labrador, 1,000 miles north of New York City. No land separates the cape from the North Pole, something over 2,000 miles away. The cape's name has nothing to do with the anger of sea and storm. It was bestowed by the Vikings who used its high cliffs to navigate their sailing ships on voyages of raid and settlement along the west coast of Scotland. *Wrath* is derived from *hvarf*, their word for a turning-point.

I wanted this journey to be a turning point for me too, but for now, Cape Wrath was just my starting place. I turned my back on its attractions—its nesting seabirds; its vertigo-inducing cliffs; and the lighthouse built by the grandfather of Robert Louis Stevenson, author of *Kidnapped*, *Treasure Island*, and much-loved children's poems. The attractions did not include a loo[9], so I took a quick pee behind a wall, and then walked southwest to the edge of the cliffs. There, heading in roughly the right direction, the faintest trace of a path could be seen. I paused to look back at the lighthouse, whitewashed on its green cliff top, and turned south for good just after midday.

# 2

# *Rough Edge*

The trace of path soon faded completely into rough grass and bog cotton, but there was no mistaking the way ahead. Follow the cliffs to Sandwood Bay! I could not see the sands of the bay yet, but could just make out the sea stack at its southern end—seven miles south as the puffin flies, where the rocky islets called Am Balg stood offshore. It was a bright afternoon of broad views to land and sea, and I was underway at last. My trepidation vanished amid high spirits. Not that following the cliffs was easy. Their line was broken by wave-gouged inlets called geos[10]; and valleys and ravines carried burns down from the moor. These obstacles forced me off the cliff tops—down to sea level and back up; inland and back to the waves; along the banks of the burns to find stepping-stone crossings.

For several hours I made these detours, advancing fitfully south. Where one burn debouched into a narrow cove the foaming surf had deposited a selection of colorful debris—gasoline cans; water bottles; buoys of various sizes and shades of red; a soccer ball. The junk lay about this barren edge like enigmatic evidence of a distant and unknown civilization. Looking inland from this cove, the winding line of the burn led all the way to a hill with a sunlit crown of rocks. At the cliff edges the show was the boiling sea, surging and crashing to enlarge the geos and its own domain. By mid-afternoon, I was climbing over bare rock around a pink-hued geo and came to a cluster of boulders, a good place to rest. The geo was *Geodha Ruadh na Fola* on my map. *Geodha* is the Gaelic form of geo. But Gaelic and English are both imitations of a Viking word, *gjá*. It was another illustration of the layers of language laid down in Scotland, a topic that was to absorb me all the way to the Solway.

I ate nuts, oatcakes[11], and a tortilla with little hunger, but sucked from my reservoir with greater enthusiasm. Back toward the cape the moorland lay bright green in the sunshine—the few miles of Scotland I was done with. But a cold mist, called a *haar* locally, was sweeping in from the sea to shroud the cliff tops and hills of the way ahead. Drizzle touched my face. Sharp rocks put a small tear in my waterproof pack cover as I worked it over my pack. Furthermore, I had thought that a burn and ravine I recently crossed with considerable effort was the Keisgaig River and that Sandwood Bay was now just two miles off. But a quick read of my map burst the bubble. The Keisgaig was still nearly a mile away. As the rocks dampened in the mist so did my mood, elation evaporating with the awareness of the long walk still between me and rest. Cold now from the mist and inactivity, I put on a rain jacket and heaved on my pack ("Come on you big bastard!"). Then I set off up the cliffs again, hoping it would not turn out to be a bad haar day.

Once the initial anger and sore feelings of my resignation had subsided, my boss and I agreed we would both be better off if I stayed on part-time for a while. Despite this gentle separation, I sometimes woke in the night and felt a knot in my stomach. I had cut myself loose and faced an uncertain future. In spite of the power games, mine had not been such a bad job. My colleagues were mostly good people, a multinational assemblage not much given to corporate norms or bullshit. I disliked the airplanes, but not the places to which they flew me. Sometimes I had to spend a weekend in Hong Kong, a city whose odorous streets and joking people I loved. I had found the trails that wound along the mountain ridge behind the harbor-hugging skyscrapers and would work up a Saturday sweat on them before cooling off with beer in the hotel bar. Hardships like this brought in an income, one that gave us our life in a spacious Connecticut suburb. "What about money, Rob?" the big boss had asked when I confirmed my resolve to go. I told him what I told myself: "I'm not rich enough to retire, but I can take a risk." My fear now was not about money, but about my place in the hurly-burly of the world. I wanted to step back from it, but not to be in the wilderness—real or metaphorical—forever. My nocturnal knot was worry that having left a niche in the big world I might not easily find another.

The drop to the Keisgaig River was precipitous, and soon left the cold mist far above. I descended by making zigzags, fearful of turning an ankle where the thick heather hid holes and ruts. The river marked the end of the army training ground, although nothing since the cape had hinted at its existence. It could, apparently, have been otherwise. A notice facing south read:

> *Cape Wrath Training Centre. Troops may be training in this area and it may not be obvious where they are. This could include ambushing, blank-firing, and tactical manoeuvres. Warning: sudden noise, smoke or illumination possible. This could include gunfire and the use of pyrotechnics, including thunder-flashes, trip-flares and smoke emissions.*

Given the possibilities, it had been a peaceful afternoon.

I scrambled up the far bank of the river, rested briefly at a broken-down turf-roofed stone hut, and trudged up a long slope of cropped grass to the edge of another spectacular geo. The fissured rock gave me the uneasy feeling that everything could slide at any moment into the sea. It seemed that even the sheep gave these 500-foot cliffs a wide berth[12]. Then, a mile on, at five o'clock, rounding a hill named in Gaelic for the "red-brown" geo now behind me, Sandwood Bay appeared below. Waves were breaking on its gently sloping beaches. The sea stack was now sharply defined against a steel-gray ocean, like a lone Easter Island moai staring out to sea.

Getting down to the bay took some time. At the Strath Chailleach river there was no obvious place to cross. Impatient at the thought of taking off my boots, I tried to pick my way over on stones. But it became clear, on a midstream islet above a waterfall, that this burn would demand wet feet. I took off my pack, boots, and socks; rolled my pants to my knees; and put on sandals, stepping into the cold current with my sock-stuffed boots tied around my neck by their laces. Using my trekking poles for balance, I waded cautiously across on big smooth pebbles. With a safe route established, I returned to the islet for my precious pack. It would be unfortunate to soak the clothes I wore, a disaster to immerse the pack. By the end of the second crossing my feet stung from the icy water. Dried off, they were refreshed for the short walk to the beach.

Sandwood Bay is extravagantly praised, rated Scotland's most beautiful beach, and among its loveliest sights of any kind. Its peace is preserved by the four-mile walk from Blairmore, the only way in, other than the route I had come by. Even in my growing tiredness, its beauty was undeniable. The sand was freshly washed, unadorned with weed or driftwood, as smooth as new snow. The only footprints upon it were the lonely ones behind me, which quickly flooded and lost shape. A thin veil of sea-spray blurred the southern headland. At its end, the sea stack stood guard—*Am*

*Buachaille*, the herdsman. The whole bay appeared deserted, until I caught sight of figures moving away in the dunes, two human and one canine—my first company since Cape Wrath. A burn meandered through the beach to meet the crashing surf between two piles of rock marooned on the expanse of sand. To my dismay, it was too wide to jump and too deep and stone-less to cross booted. I followed it to the surf hoping it would spread and become crossable, but all I did was tire myself more by walking in wet sand. Returning along the burn toward the dunes, I realized there was no alternative but to pull my boots and socks off again.

The soggy sand in the bottom of the burn, and then the loose stuff in the grassy dunes behind the beach, made for tough walking. By the time I was climbing out of the bay, up a slope generously dotted with sheep droppings, I was done in. It was not only today's exertions catching up with me. I had arrived in Glasgow two days before after a sleepless flight from New York. Leaving home had been delayed when Hurricane Irene came through on the last Sunday in August. After the airports reopened I left my family still without electricity four days after her visit. Traveling north to Durness took two days by train and on Neil's bus, but I still did not catch up on sleep. The Inverness youth hostel dormitory was stiflingly warm and full of snoring, not all of it mine. At the Ben View I woke in pitch darkness in the middle of the night without a clue where I was. Here, among the dunes, an absent tribe of campers had hidden their squat tents. I could have done the same. I was not on a firm schedule but had long planned that "Day One" would end at Blairmore. Meeting that target was important for my morale at this stage of the journey, when I had so many doubts about my ability to complete the task. So I pressed on, past Sandwood Loch and its derelict cottage and sheepfold. Then the flat, maintained track to Blairmore began, and the weather switched again. The dull moor became bright—a landscape of lochan and bog stretching away to hills in the east, all cast in the orange light of a sinking sun.

My reservoir was empty, half a gallon of Ben View water sucked up and gulped down at the brows of hills as greedily as the accompanying lungfuls of breath. I knelt now at a trickle of a trail-side burn to refill it and popped in two iodine tablets. I hemmed and hawed about those tablets throughout the journey. My father used to say proudly that Scottish water was so pure you could put it straight into the car battery, in contrast to the distilled stuff needed in England where we lived. On vacations "up north" we drank freely from streams. Scotland's water has not gone bad in the 45 years since, but our times are fussier. The official message now is that even water from Highland burns should be purified, especially if livestock is nearby. I decided that the taste of iodine and disloyalty was better than the risk of a debilitating belly bug on a lonely ben, and for the most part used the tablets. There were, however, no ill effects when, judging the sheep and cattle too few or faraway, I rebelled and drank the stuff neat.

The last miles to Blairmore yielded my first conversation since the cape—a short exchange with two gentlemen heading out to a bothy on the Strath Chailleach River. They were cheerful and shabby, looking like they would be at home on stools in the public bar. They might indeed have been intent on a Saturday night booze-up under the stars. But I was judging books by covers and told myself they could be going into the wild for simple peace and quiet, companionship, or even prayer. It was nearly eight o'clock, but the sun was still hanging over Loch na Gainimh, one of the larger lochans strewn across the moor—the "sandy loch". The amount of daylight varies enormously in Scotland over the year. If it had been June, there would still have been three hours of daylight ahead of me. By December, it would be dark here well before four. Even in the course of this six-week journey, the days would shorten by more than three hours. But this evening the sun was just beginning to set when the scattered white cottages of Blairmore, at last, came into view.

The cell phone signal had returned and I texted my wife to say I was well and had survived the rough edge. On the day I resigned, I had not called Charissa to ask if I should go ahead. I didn't feel I had to. She knew there were problems, and she knew all about the plan that was hatching in the back of my mind. People often say trite things they don't really mean. Charissa had often said, "I just want you to be happy". She meant it. It was, I think, a simple equation. If I were happier, our whole family would be. She saw other benefits in the plan, as well. If I spent less time away for work, I would be a bigger presence in our daughters' lives. I am sure my chances of staying healthy were a factor for Charissa, too. I walked plenty. Even on the days I commuted into New York, I hoofed it from Grand Central to our Union Square offices and back, except in the foulest weather. But the business trips, more often than not, involved sedentariness, overeating, and overdrinking. Despite this, cutting myself loose meant an uncertain future for Charissa too. It did not seem to put a knot in her stomach. She had made her own leaps into the dark, and they had worked out. In her 20s, she left Michigan for Japan, alone, and made a life there. It was in Tokyo that we met, started a family and married before we knew one another well at all. Now Charissa was backing me in this adventure. It would have been impossible otherwise.

Blairmore, or more precisely the small parking area of the John Muir Trust estate, met my every need. They were admittedly few. A tap of delicious cold water allowed me to ditch the iodine brew. There was a level grassy area to pitch my tent at one end of the unpaved car park, and a telephone box which appeared to work. Finally, there was excellent company. Andrew walked over from his van as I prepared to put up my tent, and offered a cup of tea, quickly accepted. My little tent takes only minutes to erect, and the job was done and my gear thrown higgledy-piggledy inside by the time he returned with a cup of lukewarm, milky tea, and his partner. You could wish that the world was peopled with Andrews and Rebeccas, for they were easy company—outgoing, funny, and knowledgeable. As the moon rose in the sky, our talk ranged effortlessly. They had a long-distance relationship. He lived in France, she in Beauly—a small town near Inverness where my train had stopped on the way to Lairg the day before. They were on a weekend outing to what Andrew called "the real Highlands", condemning Beauly by implication. Both were Scots, with the light accents that often signify private education and decent means. They were young and appeared in love.

My journey naturally turned our talk to travel. Rebecca had recently returned from donkey-trekking in France. "In the Cévennes, by any chance?" I asked, thinking again of Robert Louis Stevenson. One of his first works was *Travels with a Donkey in the Cévennes*, an account of a 12-day hike through the mountains in 1878 in the company of a "lady friend". Of Modestine, he wrote, "Her faults were those of her race and sex; her virtues were her own". Modestine, let it be said, was his donkey.

"Yes!" said Rebecca. But I was already turning away from her. There was a scraping noise coming from behind. In the fading light I saw a tail, waving briskly as its owner grubbed in a hole.

"What's that?" I said, and added stupidly, "Is it a skunk?"

"No, no, that's my dog," said Andrew. Its head was buried in a rabbit hole, and its rear-end looked a bit like a skunk's, at least in the moonlight; and if you are myopic and without your glasses, and so very tired you forget there are no skunks in Scotland. Then it transpired that Andrew, Rebecca, and their dog were the figures on the dunes at Sandwood Bay. "We saw you on the beach, crossing the burn," they said, and I was glad they had been too far off to hear my mumbled curses at having to take my boots off again.

My time with Andrew and Rebecca was running out. They wanted to find a lonely place to spend the night. Now, we weren't exactly in Piccadilly Circus right here, but there were a few cars and cottages, and now a small blue and yellow tent. Why settle for that if you can have a whole coast to yourselves? So, alone now, I called home from a phone box encrusted with dead insects and old spider webs, then zipped myself into my sleeping bag, and fell asleep to BBC Radio Scotland's weekly pipe music program on my radio.

# 3

## Rounding the Stack

I woke from my best sleep in days. A calming roar of breaking waves was rising from the shore. The sky looked auspicious when I zipped open a bit of tent flap and peered out. The clouds were high and revealed abundant blue. I packed up quickly and took the single-track road that wound east. From the first rise I looked back at good Blairmore. It seemed still asleep, nobody about among its half-dozen slate-roofed cottages or in the rough fields marked out with dry stone walls. Then, from the next hill, I saw Ben Stack ahead, a distant, conical silhouette in the early-morning light. It was the southernmost of three prominent hills, farther off than the long ridge of Foinaven and the lump of Arkle. Through the clear air I soon saw mountains yet farther south, marking out my route for the days to come. But for now, I walked the empty, rolling road to Kinlochbervie.

The road passed the neighboring hamlets of Oldshorebeg and Oldshoremore. These names were more evidence of the linguistic history of Scotland, and in particular of Sutherland, this most northwesterly corner. They invite a digression. The names have nothing to do with "old" or "shore". "Oldshore" is a corruption of *Àisir*, a Norse-origin[13] word meaning a path or pass[14]. Versions of "beg" and "more" litter the map of most of Scotland. They are but the Gaelic words for small and big. So what were the Norse up to naming places in Scotland? The Pictish[15] tribes living in this part of what is today called Scotland 1,500 years ago spoke a Celtic language closer to modern Welsh than to Gaelic (in the 500s AD the Gaelic-speaking Saint Columba, in search of converts, needed an interpreter to speak with a Pictish king in the Highlands). The Picts shared this "British" with the other peoples of the island of Great Britain at the time when the Roman legions were withdrawing from the imperial province they called *Britannia*. Gaelic—close to Irish but not to Welsh—was spoken by a people that the Romans called *Scotti*. These Scotti were settled on the central west coast of Scotland by the 400s, probably having sailed from Ireland. That corner of Scotland is still called Argyll—*Earra-Ghàidheal*, "the coastland of the Gaels". From the 500s on, Gaelic spread from Argyll, contributing to the extinction of Pictish over the coming centuries.

The Norse were late-comers, but by all accounts, their appearance around 800 was traumatic ("… *men of terrible wickedness and unheard-of bravery*" as a later chronicler put it). They came first as raiders, heathens sailing from Norway on voyages of plunder and extortion. But they stayed to farm, and indeed to rule, in Sutherland and other parts of the north and west. The Norwegians who settled in Sutherland would have found themselves among people speaking Pictish or Gaelic or both. Relinquishing their swords for hoes, the Norse became the new neighbors. Norse and Celt[16] would have traded goods, but also genes and language, and begun to name (or rename) their shared landscape with words from their very different tongues. In some places in Scotland the Norse were so dominant that their language for a time replaced all others. But here their presence was lighter and more fleeting, and their imprint in place-names more scattered. The imprint was on my map—Durness ("deer headland"), Cape Wrath, Sandwood ("sand water"), and Sutherland itself (a "southern land" from their far-north perspective). The Norse tongue died out in most of Scotland within a few centuries, to be replaced by all-conquering Gaelic. It survived as Norn[17] until the 1700s in Orkney and Shetland.

Shortly after walking through Oldshoremore ("the big path" or "the big pass"), the road left the John Muir Trust estate. The land from Sandwood Bay to Blairmore, and for some distance east along the shore and onto the moors, is owned by the Trust. It was good to see Muir recognized in his native land, his inspiration protecting its wild country. Little-known in Britain, at least during the years of my education here, the patron saint of wilderness and founder of the Sierra Club was nevertheless a proud Scot. Muir was born in 1838 in Dunbar, 30 miles east of Edinburgh and far from the wild Highlands. He sailed to New York from Glasgow at the age of 11, and returned to Scotland but once. On July 6th, 1893, he wrote to his wife from Dunbar, referring to the publisher David Douglas who had shown him around Edinburgh on the days before: *"From feeling lonely and a stranger in my own native land, he brought me back into quick and living contact with it, and now I am a Scotchman and at home again."* It takes more than half a century in a strange new land to knock the Scotchman out of a boy.

Now the road ran across rough pasture, skirted lochs, and finally cut through low, craggy hills by the shore. My arrival at the edge of Kinlochbervie set farm dogs barking, the only disturbance of the Sabbath silence. The village, population 500, is big by Sutherland standards, but I stumbled upon its hotel straightaway. Well-scrubbed German tourists were loafing in the car park, and I became unsure of the welcome awaiting a grubby backpacker. In reception, a stout woman appeared, eventually, behind the counter.

"Good morning! Do you do breakfast for non-residents?" I asked, trying to sound as pleasant a customer as you could wish for.

"I'm sorry, but our breakfast room only serves guests." But her tone was sympathetic, then conspiratorial.

"Take a seat in the lounge," she said, handing me a menu. And I did, taking care to thoroughly dust the seat of my pants before sitting on her cream sofa.

I ordered a bacon roll and coffee, and when the stout receptionist brought them in, she stayed to chat. We began, naturally, with the weather. The wind that buffeted my outing to the Sango Sands pub on Friday evening had pummeled Kinlochbervie too. It was, she said, the leftovers of Hurricane Irene, reaching Scotland five days after sending my family and I scurrying to our basement for shelter. I congratulated myself on being, surely, one of the few to greet Irene on both sides of the pond.

I went down to the harbor in search of provisions. Sunday in the Highlands is observed more traditionally than in most places, but exception is often made for tourist services, and I thought the store might be open. It wasn't. "Bervie Stores" would not open until lunchtime. It didn't seem a big problem. Much of the food I bought in Inverness was still in my pack. And since there was nothing else about Kinlochbervie's bleak commercial fishing harbor to detain me, I set off through the drawn-out village toward Rhiconich. I passed the Free Presbyterian Church. It was as closed as the grocery store ("Sabbath 11:30 a.m."). Then, beyond the last of the cottages, the road began to climb straight and steep toward the hamlet of Badcall. It was a two-laner now but just as empty as before. The sun was up and there was no wind or shade, and soon I was peeling off layers to stem my sweat.

The brow of the hill brought a view worth the perspiration. The landward end of Loch Inchard—the half-mile-wide sea loch[18] that juts four miles inland from Kinlochbervie—lay 250 feet below. Beyond the silver loch were dark gray-green hills, including Arkle and Ben Stack, now close enough to make out the ruts in their rocky peaks. Close enough, but Ben Stack was still nine miles away even by line of sight. Above the hills were flat-bottomed, light gray clouds. The rest of the sky was blue except for white wisps here and there. In the foreground the rocky slopes were dressed in fern, heather, and lush grass. I stopped often as the road descended through the dispersed cottages of Badcall, Inshegra, and then Achriesgill, and each time the scene was magnificent. At Inshegra, there was a seaward view of Loch Inchard, as calm and shiny as a mirror all the way to its narrow opening to the Atlantic. Its southern shore looked wild and deserted compared to this gentle country beside the road. The sky over the distant sea was almost perfectly cloudless.

Past Achriesgill there was a parking area that looked over an arm of the loch to the hamlets and the crags behind them. It had a picnic table. I was not weary, but this was an irresistible rest stop. I sat on the bench, and the table behind my back took the weight of my pack. I slipped my shoulders easily from its straps. This was so much better than wrestling it off, and from then on I never walked past a picnic table without easing my shoulders a while. I sat here in the sun for 15 minutes, and thought what fun this journey across Scotland was going to be! In the final analysis, I had left my job for it. Back in April, I told a co-worker that I was quitting because I was fed up with power games and dysfunction. "You're lucky, the rest of us just have to suck it up," he replied. I could have sucked it up some more too, but I didn't need to. I had my plan. By far the most alluring part of the plan was the adventure to kick it off. My life had seen plenty of travel, and some of it had crossed the ill-defined line into adventure, where challenge, risk, and the out-of-the-ordinary take over. When I was 19, a friend and I set off from England for Spain. We hitchhiked through France, then walked, rode slow trains, and hitched some more down to southernmost Andalucía, crossing briefly to Africa! We slept rough, woken by thunderstorms, or in cheap *pensiones*, and once on the roof of a Moroccan inn. We had no contact with home at all. I liked this first adventure very much, my satisfaction boiling down to seeing what the world looked like along a winding line between one point on the map and another, a line in part designed by my friend and I, in part set by the haphazard events of the journey itself. I liked the experience so much, in fact, that two years later, after university, I returned to Iberia and, alone this time, traced another line for a month and a week. Now, 30 years later, I recognized the thread connecting those first adventures and this one.

I slid back into my pack and returned to the road. Soon white buildings at the very end of the loch came into view. An elderly man approached from their direction, moving slowly but not unsteadily, warmly dressed in the sunshine. We exchanged pleasantries, and I was struck by something uncommonly gentle about him. He was friendly, but undemonstratively so, radiating a serene self-confidence. He said his words in a soft Highland voice, and set off with a short-paced gait along the sparkling shore.

About 11:30 I reached the main road at Rhiconich, and crossed over to the hotel with hamburger and chips in mind. My next chance for hot food would be 20 miles on. The signs, quite literally, were promising. Out on the road, for the negligible traffic traveling up or down between Durness and the south, stood one; *Rhiconich Hotel, Non-Residents Welcome, Open All Day*. At a front door stood another; *Bar Meals 12.30 - 2.30*. This door was locked, so I followed a sign to reception, peering into vacant, unlit rooms along the way. Reception was locked up too. 'Open all day' probably means 12:30 on a Sunday, I told myself, and was happy to sit out front to wait and look around. Apart from the hotel, Rhiconich boasted a public loo, an unmanned police station, and a red phone box. I did not need the first, and hoped to have no need of the second (or it of me), but I strolled over to the phone box to kill time by calling my sister. Jackie was 670 miles away near

London, and it seemed astonishing that the crowded southeast of England could be on the same island as Rhiconich.

I returned to my post outside the hotel before 12:30. A few drivers pulled up, nosed around, and went away. There were no cars in the car park, and my doubts grew that there were guests or workers in the hotel. But sounds came from within that seemed to be of cleaning, and eventually I saw a young woman at an upstairs window. I waved to her, and she pushed the window open.

"Will you be opening for lunch?" I called up.

"I think we *should* be," she said very hesitantly, and closed up. Knowing that not everything happens punctually in the Highlands (and remembering the old joke that there is no word in Gaelic to convey the urgency of *mañana*), I waited a little longer, and tried the doors one last time. Finally I decided that trail rations would have to do, and set off along the path by the Rhiconich River thinking "a pox on that hotel".

There was reason to expect the next four miles to be tough. My map showed the dashed line of a path only for the first mile and a half. Thereafter it would be heather-whacking to the next path beneath Arkle. The mood of the day changed swiftly with my first steps along the path and away from the coast. The sun withdrew, the last hint of a breeze faded, and the air took on a buggy feel. Ben Stack disappeared as lesser hills closed in. My euphoria faded into a practical frame of mind. From now on, my gaze was directed at the ground right in front, looking for even, dry places to put my boots down. The path was a foot wide, with stretches that were swampy and overhung with undergrowth. The comfortable three miles per hour since Sandwood Bay was over. Near where the river flowed out of slender Loch a' Garbh-bhaid Beag, a fisherman in yellow wellington boots was casting into the stream.

"How's it going? Any luck?" I asked amiably, working on an invitation to admire his catch. I like looking at fish, dead or alive.

"No! They're *in there*. But not so much as a bite."

"Maybe it'll get better later," I soothed.

"Well, it will have to get better with the next two casts, because then we're going home!" "We" was he and the dog who had come to greet me on the footpath. I thought of asking if the banana-colored wellies might be tipping the fish off, but he did not seem in the mood for a joke. I wondered only later if he was leaving to unlock a hotel. Now I pressed on along the marshy lochside to the Garbh Allt. "Allt" means stream in Gaelic; "Garbh" is a word of warning. It means "rough". Later in the journey, an outdoorsman put it to me this way: "The Highlanders who named these places were nae softies so, when you see 'garbh' on the map, you pay attention". I looked at this burn, and gave it my undivided attention.

Garbh Allt is a product of the huge rainfall that drenches Foinaven and Arkle, moist Atlantic air that rises and condenses on contact with their slopes. It was a more substantial stream than those by Sandwood Bay yesterday. I walked upstream to find a place where the banks were low and the crossing looked least risky—and then followed my routine. I took off my boots and socks for the trial run and, this time, as the stream was deeper and there was certainly nobody about, I took off my pants too and wrapped them around my neck. Near the far bank, the *allt* ran fast and deep, and its weight pressed on my legs as I picked over its slippery bed rocks. I never got to welcome these wet crossings, but always felt a sense of achievement when everything was safely on the other side. The cold wash always gave my feet new life for the next stretch too. It turned out I was lucky to be crossing the *allt* now. A few days later, in Ullapool, a German hiker told me she had that morning given up at the Allt Garbh and returned to Rhiconich. By then more rain had fallen on the bens, and the stream was rough indeed.

The walk to and along Loch a' Garbh-bhaid Mòr was grueling—slick, rocky, waterlogged, and hummocky by turns, and all trackless. After two miles I reached a small beach at the end of the loch, and sat down on a bleached tree trunk to drink and eat. It was 3:30. The next trail was half a mile away as the grouse would fly (no puffins in this landlocked place), but the ground offered no clues for a route to it. The moor was furrowed with peaty canyons and, on lower ground, covered in several inches of water. I climbed a rocky hillock for a better view, and decided to head straight for the steep slopes of Arkle, knowing this line would have to hit the trail before hitting the mountain. Sure enough, a rough vehicle track soon came into view, looking akin to heaven after the miles from Rhiconich. But between me and it was a ditch with steep, peaty sides. I leaped as best one can with a 40lb pack, but my left foot landed short on slick peat. I fell forward onto the track, kissing the heather between its ruts somewhat less decorously than His Holiness pecks a foreign runway.

No harm was done, and I got moving along the fine track. On a brighter day it would have been a magnificent walk among the bens and lochans. This afternoon's gray skies and thick air took something away from it. Or maybe it was that, around this time, I felt the first burn of blisters on my heels. A covey of grouse flapped noisily into the air when I startled them, startling me back. Presently I heard voices, and soon saw at a distance two luminously clad hikers coming from the opposite direction. The path made a 90-degree turn to the southwest, and we met on a sliver of land between lochs. They were European, one with an Inspector Clouseau moustache. I was, they said, the first person they had seen in days. They seemed indeed to be hiking to Cape Wrath by a particularly remote route, bypassing even the few villages along the way. They asked about the path ahead, and one of them (not the Inspector) looked despondent at my description of the terrain. So I added, encouragingly but possibly deceptively, "You'll have earned a beer at the Rhiconich Hotel tonight!". From the top of the next rise, I watched their green and orange jackets disappear into the vast landscape. Their chatter had ceased.

The track ended at the A838 road. Ben Stack rose abruptly from the shore of its namesake loch, its summit a mile off and a half-mile up. I found a rock that looked good to rest on. But no sooner had I put my pack down and stuck my poles into the earth than a swarm of midges appeared from nowhere, settled on my hands and face, and drove me on. The hamlet of Achfary lay three miles away by road, a little more by footpath around Ben Stack. The path would be wet and steep, so the choice was easily made, and I set out down the same single-track road that Neil had driven me up two days before. Then the sun had been out, and the wind whipping up spray on Loch Stack. Now it was overcast and still, gloomy in the shadow of the ben. I began to fear what pitching a tent would be like on such a bug-infested evening. Although I had put up a tent in the teeth of swarming midges before—leaping in and zipping up so fast that few could follow—it was not an entertainment I wished to repeat. To add to my worries, somewhere along the lochside it began to rain. I heaved off my pack once more, and put waterproofs on myself and on it. As soon as this was done, the shower stopped as abruptly as a tap turned off, and I was left to walk on, overheating, certain that taking my waterproofs off again would bring back the rain. Just short of Achfary, sticky and footsore, I reached a milestone of sorts, and took a measure of comfort from packing away my first used-up map ("Cape Wrath") and unfolding the next ("Loch Assynt")[19].

I asked myself what I would do if Achfary had a B&B. It was the opening shot in a sporadic but enduring conflict between my desires for comfort and roughing it. In my heart I knew it was a pointless question here. Passing through on Neil's bus, Achfary had seemed a sleepy estate community, a minute cluster of neat buildings. Now smoke was rising from the chimney of the largest building, and my hopes for a cozy inn rose. But close up I saw that the smoke was coming from the estate offices and sheds. I wandered around them hoping to fill my water reservoir and ask about a place to camp. But it was like poking around the *Marie*

*Celeste*—a smoking chimney, humming machinery, open doors, but not a soul anywhere. Across the road there was a row of cottages, and sounds of activity within. I knocked on a door, and a young Englishman came out. Midges instantly surrounded his bald head like dirt about Pig-Pen in a Peanuts strip. He flapped at them calmly and took my reservoir inside to fill. When he returned, I asked where I could camp.

"Anywhere really. Where are you going?"

"Kylesku, tomorrow," and I gestured at the ridge behind the cottages where the path to Kylesku lay.

"You might want to go up tonight. There could be a breeze and not so many midges." I thanked him, but I was much too tired for that. It had been 18 miles from Blairmore, and a long uphill slog was not in my plans. I decided to take the path toward Kylesku, but put my tent down at the first suitable spot, breeze or no breeze. On my way out of Achfary, I tried its only public service—a call box which did not work.

Scottish footpaths are often not well signposted, and I walked right by the start of this one, inexplicably failing to notice how it set off from the backyard of a private home. Once I realized I had gone too far along the road, a bit of map-reading sent me back to nose around the house and its outbuildings, and soon I was climbing gently through mixed woodland. Maybe half a mile in and 150 feet up there was a patch of ground to the right of the path. It was just about the right size for my tent, dry, and mostly free of roots and rocks. I stood still for a time to see if the midges would attack. When they did not, I said to myself "this is the place" and spread out my tent footprint.

Before leaving home I dithered over whether to buy a new, lighter tent. At length I decided that the pound or two it would take off my load would be offset by lost space. My tent might weigh 5lb, but my pack fitted inside it with me, a definite advantage in Scottish weather. So, in a few minutes, the tent was up and nearly all my stuff inside it. I sat down to arrange things. I lay the pack down one side, and blew up my sleeping mat to fill the other. Boots and socks, too aromatic to sleep with, were put outside under the fly. I laid out my sleeping bag, and made a pillow of its stuff-sack filled with clothes. Food I placed near to hand, next to nighttime accessories—watch, headlamp, book, wooly hat[20]. The next task was my feet, which I examined for nascent blisters. I found them on the backs of my heels, and stuck on moleskin patches. My options for supper were limited. Another cause for dithering had been whether to carry a stove (and, consequently, utensils and gas). A trailside cup of tea or soup sounded appealing, but I thought cooking and washing-up would be a bother more often than not, and never regretted the decision. I have already mentioned nuts, tortillas, and oatcakes, and some combination of these, plus dried fruit and granola bars, was my sustenance that night. Then I slid into my sleeping bag, and drowsily read a few pages of Rudyard Kipling. *Kim* was the only book in my pack, except a guide or two. I had given careful consideration to its selection. It had to be light in weight; heavy enough in content to last six weeks; and it had to have nothing whatsoever to do with Scotland or walking. It failed on the last point, when Kim's peregrinations with his lama became too like a hike, and pertinent messages were delivered. "We must not always delight in soft beds and rich food" admonished the lama. I fell asleep to the sound of an owl screeching in the woods.

The new day was calm, gray, and humid, uncharacteristically unchanged from the evening before. A fleeting shower spattered the tent as I lay in my sack after waking. I walked farther than planned yesterday, and today's hike could, therefore, be short, just seven miles over the hills to Kylesku. There was a hotel in Kylesku. A reservation would not be needed on a September Monday, and I was greatly looking forward to soft beds and rich food. Now my task was to climb to the *bealach*[21]. It is Gaelic for a pass, an ancient traverse of the hills for travelers and their cattle. Bealach nam Fiann lay 1,200 feet above Achfary. The ascent began in the mixed woodland of my camp, and continued through pine plantation and then open moor. (I am not good at trees, and "pine" here means the pine family. They were more likely spruce or larch.) Soon small flies were settling on me in considerable numbers, but they did not bite. Perhaps they were after my sweat. They were indestructible. I picked them off, crushed them between finger and thumb, and then saw them fly off when I let go. Then, where the trees gave way to moor, I startled a group of deer, and watched them dash back into the forest.

The path was steep now, and I stopped often to "admire the view". To force the pace, I set short-term goals—"I'll go 100 full paces before stopping again" or "Let's reach that tree" (or rock or tuft of coarse grass). The views *were* worth stopping for. They were to the north here, from where I had come. Ben Stack and Arkle were topped with cloud, drifting ever so slowly this still morning, trailing out of the corries[22] like smoke from a wildfire. The low ground was dotted with lochs and lochans. It was the same country as yesterday evening, in the same weather, but now it was awe-inspiring. Maybe it was the elevation of my vantage point, or just a good night's sleep. At the bealach there was a ruined shieling[23] and a palpable sense of boundary between one country and another. I turned my back on Ben Stack and the other hills that had accompanied me for two days, and walked toward a whole new land.

# 4

# The Kylesku Hotel

The path from the bealach to Kylesku was broad, dry, and mostly downhill. But it was composed of rubbly stones, which made for awkward footing and aggravated my blisters. The view was southeast now, high over silver-gray lochs to even wilder country. Too bad it is forever associated in my mind with pain. I could not get my clothing right either. Changing altitude, and the sun forever coming out or going in, meant I was constantly taking off my pack to shed or restore a layer of clothing. I made one such change beside a burn and took the opportunity to refill my reservoir and stick more moleskin on my heels. At mid-morning Kylesku appeared below—a few white houses on a promontory amid sea lochs. It took another two hours to reach it, a time I spent reflecting on my relationship with this country, and what it was that brought me to try to walk across it.

I was born in Glasgow in 1960, in the hospital on a street called Rotten Row. My father's newspaper job took him to London, and all of us to Surrey, when I was three years old. Our ties to Scotland stayed strong enough for a few years after that. There were relatives to visit around Glasgow, and summer vacations on the Isle of Arran and, once, in the Cairngorm Mountains. These fresh-air holidays made a big impression on me, my imagination stirred by the steep hills, basking sharks glimpsed in the Firth of Clyde, and hints of wildcats in the Caledonian forest. For an imaginative boy, it was plain more exciting than Surrey. But the ties then became tenuous. I worked out on this descent that I visited Scotland just four times between the ages of ten and 30; going north for a football match, a grandmother's funeral, a political march, and my dad's retirement party. It could have ended there, the relationship no more than cheering for Scotland when the football World Cup came around. I was moving away physically too. I left Britain entirely after graduation from Oxford and, except for a 20-month stay during which I started work at Reuters news agency in London, have never returned to live in the 30 years since.

Two events rekindled the relationship. First, my mother and father retired to the Ayrshire coast. By this time I was with Reuters in Hong Kong and Tokyo, but it meant that when I came "home" I came to Scotland. Then, a few years later, Charissa and I started our family. There is something about that, at least for a wanderer, that promotes a sudden interest in roots, and an odd desire to do with your kids what your parents did with you. We used generous expatriate home leave to spend long summer breaks in Scotland and kept up shorter visits even after I fell into the miserly vacation regimes of American companies. I don't know what these holidays will do for my daughters, but in me they provoked a thirst to know my birth-land, to make up for my years of ignorance of its history and ways. P.J. Kavanagh—a poet of Irish roots born and brought up in England—said in his memoir, *The Perfect Stranger,* that he fell in love with England as an adult "with a passion that wouldn't have been possible if I'd felt myself a native". It happened differently with me. I did not fall in love with England, and never felt—or perhaps wanted to feel—a native. But I did fall for Scotland, my half-native, familiar-but-foreign country. I think it is a grown-up love—smitten by beauty and character but eyes open to flaws.

Three years ago, a dozen miles southwest from where I was walking now, on a sunny, breezy vacation walk with Charissa and the girls, I had the idea of hiking from one end of Scotland to another—one day, when I had time, maybe. Well, here I was now, trudging with blistered feet toward Kylesku. The closer the hamlet came, the more its dramatic location revealed itself. Kylesku stands at the head of Loch a' Chàirn Bhàin, four miles from the open ocean, on a short, narrow strait between that loch and two others that probe even farther inland. Its name—no surprise—means "the narrow strait". Seen from a distance, Kylesku was dwarfed by the modern bridge that carries the north-south road over the strait, and across which I would have to walk. I reached the shore at Kylestrome, another impeccably tidy and seemingly deserted estate village. I plodded to the main road and saw how it curved up through a cut to the bridge. I was weary and the gradient might as well have been the north face of the Eiger. I baulked at it. By the side of the road, a patch of ground overlooked the sea loch and the peaks of Quinag beyond. I put my pack down and lay back against it. Feeling the sea breeze and the sun on my skin, I looked close-up at the thistles and other wild flowers about me, then shut my eyes.

I might not have actually slept, but when I got up I strode to the bridge as if there were no hill at all. There was a sign by the roadside that welcomed the traveler, in English and Gaelic, to Assynt, and invited him to use Kylesku's tourist services. You bet.

I rang the bell at the front desk of the Kylesku Hotel. A pretty young woman came out to help me—the first person I'd seen all day.

"I'm looking for a single room, one night. Do you have anything?" She looked down at the register.

"Hmm, we're booked tonight. We have vacancies tomorrow and ..." But I wasn't really listening any more. I was fighting disappointment. What about my cozy room, my steaming shower, the big dinner, company? I composed myself and asked if she knew somewhere else nearby. Nearby mattered. The Kylesku Hotel had the only restaurant and bar for miles. She mentioned two B&Bs, and we went through to the bar to call them. I listened as she spoke on the phone, and could tell from her tone and pained expression that the news was bad even before she said they were full too. Feeling grubby and ungainly with my pack in the tight bar, I asked if I could have lunch outside while I thought about what to do. Of course, she would bring a menu right out.

I sat at a weathered picnic table beside the hotel. There isn't much to Kylesku, but the hotel and the small pier in front of it are its "Plaza Mayor". There were a few knots of people at the tables, drinking, chatting in Scottish and English accents, restraining their dogs. My pack excited interest, and my plight became at once a public matter. "You'll find accommodation in Lochinver," said a Scotsman, naming a village 20 miles away, and well off my planned route. I knew it from a family vacation, and it had the added advantage of a bank and food store. I could ride there, and ride back tomorrow to resume the walk here.

"Is there a bus?" I asked.

"Oh, you don't have a car?" Everyone agreed that not having a car was a handicap when it came to getting to Lochinver, and having a big pack would be a handicap for getting a ride if I felt like sticking my thumb out. I would not have been loath to try if there were a fair prospect of success. I hitched a ride with a charming

old couple from Mississippi at a Great Smoky Mountains trailhead eight years ago and surely looked more harmless now at 51
than then at 43. Then the pretty receptionist came out with the
menu, and I ordered fish & chips and two diet cokes.

Someone mentioned the hotel at Inchnadamph, a hamlet on
my route. It was eight miles ahead, but over an 850-foot pass even
on the road. I did not feel up to it. My fish & chips arrived, and
I gave up pondering my options to enjoy a first hot meal since
Durness. When the girl came back to clear away my plate, she
asked if I had worked out what to do. I had not.

"Do you have a tent?" she asked.

"I do."

"You may not want to do this, but there's a place to camp back
there." She pointed to a little path going into the trees behind the
hotel. "It's under the bridge. We often send hikers there when
we're full."

"And I could use your bar and restaurant this evening?"

"Best to book for the restaurant. We have tour groups coming
in." So it was that simple! I had resigned myself to another night
in the tent already but was looking forward neither to finding a
campsite nor to the isolation afterward. This "official" site, practi-
cally in the hotel's backyard, made all the difference. I'd get everything except the hot shower and soft bed. "Thank you so much," I
said, with a lot more feeling than the words usually carry.

The footpath climbed through woods and descended to open
ground near the bridge. This is not a modest structure. Its span is
80 feet above the kyle, and huge legs are planted on both shores.
But it is handsome enough, and may even add to the beauty of the
place. As I walked downhill to pass beneath it, the air filled with
a powerful stench. The source soon became apparent. A sheep lay
underneath the span as if it had jumped to an ovine suicide, its
carcass now in an advanced state of decay. I held my breath and
walked around it. The camping site was undeniably good. There

was a fine view down the loch, and a breeze to keep the midges down. But I did not fancy passing that carcass several more times, especially not after dark and a beer or two. There had been an area of grass and heather farther back, and I returned for a closer look. The margins were squelchy, but next to a hummock there was ground that was dry and flat enough for my tent. So, my lodgings arranged, I went back to the hotel and booked a table for dinner, and for good measure called the Inchnadamph Hotel and reserved a room there for tomorrow night.

I had a few hours to fill before what I thought would be the right time to pitch my tent. Across the road from the hotel there was a patch of grass, and for the second time today I lay against my pack and shut my eyes. This time, my rest was interrupted by a heart-stopping hazard of the glens and lochs—the Royal Air Force on low-level flying practice. It started as a low drone, like traffic on a distant highway, but intensified at amazing speed until the world was filled with an ear-splitting racket, and my heart rate doubled. As the din faded, I saw the dark, rolling shape of the jet disappear into the landscape, and I returned to my rest. Afterward, restored, I felt as though I could have made it to Inchnadamph after all, but I trekked no farther than the post office. I had nothing to mail but was low on money and food. Highland post offices often provide other services (or these days it may be a store that hosts the post office). But any hope of finding much of anything was dashed when I saw the place—a hut smaller than my garden shed set in the garden of a cottage. It was unattended, but the cottage door was open. I peered inside and called out a hello. An old woman came out, inevitably accompanied by a dog. The woman exuded unrushed calm. Her looks reminded me of a late aunt of mine. I would need to go to Scourie for a cash machine and store, she said, and then showed me how to use the latch to get back through the garden gate.

"He's very clever, so it has to be a bit difficult," she said, looking at her dog with admiration. My route had bypassed Scourie by going inland to Achfary. Scourie was ten miles back up the coast. I'd have to get by with the cash and food I had.

At five o'clock I went back to my spot, put up my tent, and arranged my gear for the night. It is hard to dress elegantly inside a small tent. Trousers and boxers demand a lie-back-sit-up-lie-down-again maneuver to change, and shirts have you smacking the sides of the tent as you push arms through sleeves. But I replaced every stitch of my trail clothes for clean garments and felt reasonably fresh and sharp as I set off through the heather for a night out.

I ordered a pint of Tennent's lager.

"You'll be taking that outside?" inquired the barman. He was probably remembering that I ate lunch outside, but I wondered if it was a hint that I was too stinky for his bar. Anyway, I took the beer no farther than the phone in the porch and called home for Labor Day. Everyone there seemed very cheerful, which made me even happier than I had been. Then I did go outside. The evening was mild and calm, and I was alone but for seals snorting and whimpering on rocks out in the loch. During my afternoon siesta, a few had broken the surface and looked about with their big sad eyes. Soon the midges were out too, and I was driven back inside, grubby or not. Anyway, it was time for dinner, and this tramp sat down to Mediterranean tomato soup, venison with a herb crust on risotto, and finally Lanarkshire blue cheese with more oatcakes.

I went back to the bar in search of company. Just as I arrived, someone got up from a corner barstool and left. I grabbed it, saying aloud "that was good timing".

"I was just about to take that!" said a ruddy, middle-aged man standing at the bar. He was obviously joking, but I made as if to get up.

"No, no. Take it. I was just kidding." This was James, half of the evening's double-act. James was from Derbyshire, and tonight was celebrating the sale of his home there and his permanent re-settlement in Scourie. He was clearly a frequent and well-liked guest at the hotel, and the liking was mutual. He was a gourmet and *bon viveur* and rated the hotel's food very highly.

The other half of the act was a younger James. James the bar-man was from Edinburgh, and his accent confounded Derbyshire James from time to time. I asked barman James if he was a Hearts or Hibs fan, naming the big football teams in the capital. His look of utter distaste at the mere mention of Hibernian revealed him as a Jambo, that is, a supporter of Heart of Midlothian Football Club. And quite a fervent one apparently. One of the staff said she had once been with James and his family as they watched a Hearts game on television, and had become quite alarmed at the level of passion.

"What about you?" asked James.

"Celtic," I replied, naming the Glasgow team I have supported for over 40 years.

"Nobody's perfect." I chatted with Derbyshire James while Jambo James served his customers. He had once walked from Land's End to John o' Groats; that is, from the far southwest of England to the extreme northeast of Scotland, a far greater distance than my hike.

"On my last day I did 35 miles, and could've kept on going," he said.

"Thirty-five miles!" I was astonished.

"I wasn't carrying a pack." Even so. I wondered if I would be as supercharged when I neared my finish line. An oxtail stew, especially cooked for James, now came from the kitchen. He switched from ale to French wine, and everyone toasted his move to Scourie.

As he slurped his stew and wine, barman James asked me about my route to Kylesku.

"Oh, so you came in past the chookie's hydro scheme." I hadn't heard of any scheme but was tickled that he said "chookie" unselfconsciously. I thought it was something only comedians said when they parodied Scottish speech. It's slang for a Duke, as in "Chookie Embra", who is, of course, the Queen's husband, Prince Philip, duke of Edinburgh. The chookie with the scheme was the Duke of Westminster, one of Britain's richest men. It was probably not exactly *his* scheme, but it was on his property, the 96,000-acre Reay Forest Estate that I had been crossing more or less since kissing the trail to Ben Stack. James was unenthusiastic, giving the impression that the scheme was just another act of landlord rapaciousness that would blight the land. It seemed innocuous enough—a weir, some buried pipes and cables, and a powerhouse to harness the waters of the Maldie Burn.

On Saturday, James and James were going to drive the 90 miles to Inverness to watch the Inverness Caledonian Thistle versus Hearts football game. Had it not been for Hurricane Irene, I might have been there too. I had thought that, after reaching the railway at Achnashellach after ten days on the trail, it would be nice to take a ride to Inverness for a rest, provisions, and football. But I wouldn't make it now. I tried to picture gourmet James among the hardcore fans up from Edinburgh. Then barman James said that jam tarts liked to take their shoes off and wave them to show their enthusiasm.

"Jam tarts?" enquired gourmet James.

"Another name for a Jambo," said Jambo James.

"I think you're more of a jam tart," said a waitress pensively, addressing herself to gourmet James. He feigned bafflement. He was switching now to champagne and asked Jambo James if he'd like a glass.

"That's what Jambos drink!" I quipped and imagined the two of them in the stand at Inverness, shoe aloft in one hand and a champagne flute in the other.

By the time most customers had gone, the whole staff had joined James' party. I was made to feel welcome but did not want to intrude. I said my goodbyes and went through the darkened wood to my tent in the heather as content as any chookie to his castle. But you don't drink pints of good ale and then sleep uninterrupted through the night. If anyone had been around in the small hours, they would have heard my tent unzip, and seen a groggy figure emerge to totter into heather that was quivering in a freshening breeze.

# 5

## Sweet Scottish Rain

I don't know what time it was when wind and rain began to lash my tent, but sometime between my night foray and first light a squall pattered and buffeted the fabric. It was followed by others. I felt cozy listening to the wild weather outside, though anxious lest it break in. The gusts shook the tent, caving its west-facing side toward my bed. But there were lulls, and I used the first to walk to Kylesku's public conveniences for morning ablutions. During the next blast I sat in the tent and packed my gear. When the next lull came, I swung into action, quickly putting my pack outside, covering it, and taking the tent down. I was soon walking up the A894, feeling rather smug about the efficiency of my striking of camp.

The storm had taken me by surprise. Throughout the journey I sought out the weather forecast and usually had some expectation—no matter how false—for the conditions to come. My source was often local people, better plugged into media than I. But I hadn't talked weather since Kinlochbervie, nor been able to pick up stations on my radio. In Kylesku barman James mentioned, in passing, that today would be "breezy". Certainly the forecasts I had heard since arriving in Scotland were dismal. On a crowded train between Glasgow and Perth, I read about the long-range forecast in the newspaper. It had been the coldest summer in years, the article said, but the weathermen were dashing any hope of an Indian summer. The first autumn Atlantic storm was on its way and would bring "gale force winds and heavy rain" on Monday. October looked diabolical, with a risk of tornados and early frost. Well, Monday had been a nice day, and I forgot all about the forecast gale.

There was no footpath out of Kylesku, no real alternative to the four-mile road-walk to the gap between the mountains of Quinag and Glas Bheinn. It was an uphill slog through driving rain, but I wasn't bothered. I felt strong, maybe from the good food and company of Kylesku. And even if I took the longest route to Inchnadamph today, the walk would be another short one, with guaranteed indoor comforts at the end of it. On another day there would have been a fine view as the road climbed, but this morning the sky, hills, and Loch Glencoul all merged into scarcely varied shades of gray. Some clouds were edged with yellow and the lighter shades of gray to show that the sun had not forsaken the earth altogether. I turned over plans in my mind. Tomorrow, I intended to walk east from Inchnadamph, over a bealach beneath Ben More Assynt[24]. I'd camp somewhere in the hills. On Thursday I'd hike into Ullapool, my first big milestone and a planned day off. But the closed store in Kinlochbervie was catching up with me. I was short of food. One guide in my pack said there was a small store in Inchnadamph, the other that there was none.

I stopped in the hairpin bend beneath the pass and ate a tortilla smeared with beef paste. The unappetizing goo would have stayed in my pack if my supplies were not so depleted. A mile to the west stood the massive slopes of Sail Gharbh—that *garbh* word again, the "rough spur". They rose gently enough at first but straightened into a rock wall that ended in a flat, misty, lost-world summit. Sail Gharbh is one of the three peaks of Quinag. That name comes from the Gaelic for a milking pail, which the range supposedly resembles. At the pass, I set out to follow a backcountry route that would take me past Scotland's highest waterfall, 658-foot Eas a' Chual Aluinn. The trail departed across the boggy, outflow end of a loch. The storm had turned merely soft ground into an impassable quagmire. Well, perhaps not impassable; but the way ahead looked so tiresome, and the rewards of hill-walking today so uncertain, that I turned back in favor of a more direct route to Inchnadamph. It was a rational decision, but it left me feeling that I had copped out, traded adventure for ease.

The Marble Road quickly dispelled those feelings. It was anything but a road, and today more like a burn than a trail. It made for stepping-stone hiking, a futile attempt to keep boots out of deep water. A mile from the loch the "road" reached its summit, 1,100 feet up on the exposed slopes of Glas Bheinn. The southwest gale now struck head-on. A bone-chilling wind and horizontal rain sent me diving into my pack for more layers. The rain's sting mysteriously pulled from my subconscious some words of "Scotland the Brave", the anthem once sung before Scotland's international football matches, and presumably in my head because of last night's football talk. My parents owned at least one version of the song among their 33 rpm records, which Jackie and I took out when we were bored. One verse has sad-faced exiles "yearning to feel the kiss of sweet Scottish rain". "Kiss?" I thought, "More like a smack in the mouth." I put on a wooly hat under my hood and pulled on gloves. Of such weather is hypothermia made. But the high ground also revealed new scenery. Loch Assynt, six miles long and 300 feet deep, lay down to my right, and beyond it rose the mountains of Canisp and Suilven, as weirdly formed as their names.

These mountains of Assynt are inselbergs, meaning they are isolated, rising abruptly and alone from the surrounding lowlands. Suilven is the flagship, 2,400 feet of sandstone sitting on a boggy moor. From my vantage point, seven miles to its northeast as the golden eagle would fly, I saw the full length of its ridge, a jagged blade rising to a dome. But Suilven looks quite different from other angles. The Vikings saw it from the sea, and gave it the first part of its name—*sula*, a pillar. The Gaels added their word for mountain, *Sula-bheinn*[25]. I have sometimes puzzled why Scotland's mountains are so impressive. "Mountains" may not even be the right word. Scottish outdoor types are just as likely to talk of "the hills". The top of the highest ben is a meager 4,406 feet above sea level, roughly on a par with the highest points of Vermont and Georgia. The Assynt peaks are lower still. Now, I have hiked in the Appalachians and Rockies, traveled in the Andes and the high sierras of Spain, and gazed at the perfect cones of mounts Fuji and Mayon, but the Highlands still take my breath away. I don't think it is just that they are the "hills of home". Their impact is increased by the ever-present sea and lochs, ideal foreground for the bens to rise behind. Then, unlike mountains in the Rockies viewed from land that is already thousands of feet up, when you look at Ben Nevis you can see every inch of those 4,406 feet. The Highlands are mostly bare too. The full drama of rock, corrie, gully, scree, and lochan are unobstructed by forest (if often enough by cloud). Add to all this the ever-changing weather drifting over summits reaching to the most distant remoteness, and you have a scene more stirring than mere statistics can suggest.

Those travels in the Andes and volcano-gazings in Asia were not part of grand adventures. Soon after my second loop around Spain after university, I took a job as a tour guide in the south of France, then a similar job in Spain, and finally worked as an English teacher in the city of Zaragoza. The purpose of these dead-end jobs was to keep me abroad, a place of poetic unfamiliarities, and especially appealing when you have no idea what you might do at home. The jobs gave me a chance to explore—the dry mountains standing forgotten behind Spain's teeming tourist coast were a favorite on days off—but I did not "adventure". Before I went back to Britain after four years away, I managed two more grand circuits of Spain and Portugal, but by then what unfolded along my winding lines was familiar to me—loved, but no longer extraordinary. Over the quarter-century that followed, I acquired first a "proper" job, then a family, and finally a mortgage. I tried to recapture the flavor of adventure now and again. It proved elusive. The problem was not a lack of new territory to explore. Reuters sent me to live and work in Hong Kong, then Japan. These were adventures in themselves, but not of the roaming sort. I roamed on my vacations, but found that the comforts I could now afford spoiled the dish. So too did the required itineraries, reservations, and hard stops to get back to the office. Occasionally, the recipe felt about right; like the bus ride, contorted on a hard seat above the wheel well, through guerilla-afflicted south Luzon to view Mount Mayon, or struggling with my poor Japanese to make my way back to Tokyo on buses, trains, and an empty ferry across the cold Tsugaru Strait from Hokkaido.

On the descent to Achmore Farm, the flooded, stony, but non-slip trail at the pass gave way to a steep, greasy slope. If I were not careful I would end up seated in sheep droppings. The wind subsided, and I overheated in my upland layers. I passed the farm buildings and reached the farm track. Halfway down the track a Land Rover and trailer approached. When it passed, I saw that the trailer contained the bloody heads of four deer, a reminder that this was stalking season. Then the track rejoined the main road near parking spaces for Ardvreck Castle. I rested here, not bothering to walk the few yards to the ruin on the shore of Loch Assynt. A handful of visitors came and went. Two, who I took as mother and grown-up son, spent a minute outside and scurried back to their car. "Ooh, fancy a hot cup of coffee?" said she to him in a London accent. "Ooh, yes please!" I thought, and strapped on my pack for the last mile to Inchnadamph. The heavens opened, and the mile was like five. I passed the time worrying about my reservation. I imagined a Basil Fawlty figure eyeing me from dripping cap to soaked boots, and saying "Hmm, I'm sorry, sir, but we can't seem to find your booking". I stepped on to the porch of the Inchnadamph Hotel about mid-afternoon.

Leaving my pack and poles under cover on the porch, I went inside. There was no one about. I rang the reception bell, and looked around at the mounted fish and weighing scales. A man in his 30s came out and introduced himself, with an English accent, as Richard. His welcome was matter-of-fact and reassuringly informal, in line with his sweatshirt and jeans. Here was no Basil Fawlty. I said I would take my boots and waterproofs off. "No, don't worry, this is a fishermen's hotel," he said, handing me a big plastic basket to put my wet gear in when I was ready. As we went up to the room, the hotel struck me as dim, cavernous, and cold. Perhaps reading my mind, Richard pointed to some big closed doors. "Through there's the bar. It's open from 5:00, and meals are served from 6:30."

My room was simple but a treat, and I set about using it to the full. But first I took my tent downstairs, where Richard showed me to the coal shed behind the hotel where I could hang it to dry. It was a precarious job, standing on a wobbly log, pegging tent sheets to a big loop of line as the wee birds who lived there darted about. In my room, I spread my gear on the floor, including maps (to be studied and dried) and remaining food (for inventory). The shower was cramped and the flow weak, but it was steamy hot, and it felt wonderful to be clean again. Possibly for the first time in my life I used the little kettle, tubes of instant coffee, and tubs of long-life milk you are given in British hotels. I ate the plain digestive biscuits. I tended to my feet. I lay on the crisp white duvet, but saved the luxury of bed-sleep for later. Finally, I washed my quick-drying shirts and boxers in the scalding water of the sink with the hotel's perfumed soap, making a mental note to use my own soap next time, the better to smell as a trail-hardened hiker should.

All this was fine, but I needed to make a plan. I went to the shed to check on the tent, and had to dash through the rain that was still bucketing down. Back inside, I saw that Richard had opened the bar, and I asked if he had seen a weather forecast. He directed me to the print-out of the Northwest Highlands forecast from the Mountain Weather Information Service pinned up in reception. From then on I was to use the MWIS forecast whenever I could get it. It focuses on conditions at 3,000 feet, but you can infer what it might be like lower down. It begins with a map of the whole British Isles showing areas of high and low pressure, then moves on to the nitty-gritty of how windy, wet, misty, sunny, and cold it is going to be in the northwest Highlands. It did not look promising. The isobars were packed tight, and strong west winds were shown. Reading on, the good news was that I need fear neither freezing temperatures nor sunburn. The other elements were problematic. There would be frequent showers, sometimes merging together, and the wind would be particularly strong in them. But most significant for me was the low cloud. If I followed my intended route, I would cross 1,700-foot Bealach Trallgil. The chances of its being misted in looked very good. I sought out Richard.

"How far is it to Ullapool along the road?" I had a good idea, but wanted him to confirm it.

"A bit less than 24 miles."

"So walkable in a day."

"A very long day."

The backcountry route to Ullapool was not appealing in this weather. I envisaged a drenching grind to a boggy and trackless pass where a fierce wind would be channeling cloud through the invisible mountain walls. This would be followed by a soggy night camped somewhere on the other side and, judging by Thursday's forecast, an equally soaked walk into Ullapool. If I put my back into the road tomorrow I could be in Ullapool ahead of schedule, and save the joys of the hills for better weather. I announced my decision to Richard.

"I am sure someone will be going into Ullapool tomorrow and could give you a lift," he said. I thanked him, and explained that I was committed to walking every foot of the way to the end of Scotland. Then I went into the phone cupboard and made a reservation at the Ullapool youth hostel for two nights. I didn't even look around tiny Inchnadamph for the food store. The pangs of guilt returned.

By early evening the Inchnadamph Hotel was transformed. The bar was open, coal and wood blazed in the grate, and other guests were making an appearance. There were two "munro-baggers" from the north of England, men about my age. A munro is a Scottish mountain over 3,000 feet, and a bagger a fool who aims to climb all 283. It's the kind of insane obsession I could easily fall into. Three Scots fishermen were playing pool and nipping outside to smoke. A Spanish threesome looked at their warm, dark beer with mistrust. After dinner—a mountain of smoked salmon and an enormous lamb casserole—a couple came in from outside. The man was a geologist, in Assynt, he said, to get close to some extremely old and well-exposed rock. He wandered the bar studying the photos of scenery and the framed geological maps, and muttered "inselbergs" to himself. He also wanted to get close to the fire. When he and his wife pulled their chairs right in front of it, and the glow and warmth faded for the rest of us, I decided it was time for bed.

I would have liked to set off at sunrise—6:30 around here in early September—but breakfast was served at 8:00, and it would set me up for the day. The same crowd as last night was in the dining room. The munro baggers told me they would take a low-level hike today as conditions on Ben More Assynt were too hazardous. I had slept long and deep, my pack was ready, and Richard had dried my waterproofs and boots. All that remained was to consume a Full Scottish Breakfast—cereal, baked beans, sausage, bacon, black pudding, and fried tomato and mushrooms. No eggs for me as I watch my cholesterol (a joke, I don't like them). Afterward, on the porch, one of the fishermen was having a smoke. He showed me a brown trout, unwrapping it delicately from foil. It was a good size, the red spots on its flanks beautiful and brilliant. It would, he said, be cooked at home in Stirling tonight. It was not raining right now, but I put my waterproofs on. And, since I would walk on tarmac all day, I stuffed my heavy boots into my pack and put on lighter ones, saving my feet at the expense of my shoulders.

I came to two idyllic places on the edge of the strung-out village of Elphin—one for this world and one for the next. It had been a two-hour walk to reach them. The river Loanan stayed on my right all the way to Loch Awe, in which there were tiny islands, each wooded with a handful of trees. Near the loch I stopped at a group of cows and got into a staring contest, judging myself the winner when they went back to chewing. A van passed, bragging on its side "World's Favourite Haggis", and I thought "some boast!". Showers came and went, and I had to press against a powerful wind on turning west at Ledmore Junction. I was grateful not to be up in the bealach. I came to the first idyllic place—a vivid scene at the bridge over the Ledmore River. The sun was temporarily out, and reflecting brightly off the river and blacktop. Brown and white cattle were grazing the deep green grass along the riverbank. In the surrounding hills there was the purple of heather and the green of planted conifers. Overhead the clouds were sharply either white or black, driving rapidly toward the mountains. A little farther on was a most beautiful graveyard, a perfect place to think your bones would one day rest. A low stone wall surrounded about a dozen headstones planted in lush grass. Two small evergreens stood in one corner of the enclosure, sharply defined against a backdrop of Suilven and Canisp across the choppy waters of Cam Loch.

A sign at Ledmore Junction had reminded me that Ullapool was still 18 miles away, so I left the river and the graveyard, and pushed on through Elphin, gaining some shelter from the wind from the mountain of Cul Mor now to my right. At the Elphin Tea Room I bought a soda, and took it outside to a table. As a squall approached and I got ready to leave, a fat Englishman stopped on his way in.

"You walk fast! We saw you walking back there!" he said cheerily, and pointed his thumb behind his shoulder, north up the road. Then he added, chuckling, "Are you running away from something?"

"Always!", I replied, and walked off into the developing rain.

But I wasn't running away. I was trying to repeat a trick. All the best things in my life have flowed from fits of imprudence. A degree from Oxford University is supposed to lead smartly to the top echelons of this or that. But in my final year of university, I shunned the careers office, and in return got to know Spain inside out. When Reuters hired me five years later, they liked the languages I had learned by fleeing abroad, and then sent me to places more exciting than the top echelons of anything. When Charissa and I fell in love in Tokyo, we would have been well advised to take it slowly, to get to know each other. We did no such thing, and it may have fallen apart if we had. Apart from anything else, I was her boss. As it was, in short order we were living together, then imprudently but intentionally pregnant. Unconnected to this relationship with an American woman, Reuters sent me next to New York. Three months after we arrived—married now—so did Katie. We started house-hunting with her, and all looked fair for a suburban life in New Jersey.

Although I was based in New York, I was working for Reuters' Latin American division, and spent significant parts of Katie's first winter—a notably bitter and snowy one—flying away to balmy places. At home, Katie sat bundled up on piles of snow watching mom shovel. I came home from a mid-February trip with the news that I'd been offered a job in Venezuela. I had told the manager that I would talk to my wife and we would think it over, but I gave him half an answer just by mentioning our baby. Caracas was a violent, polluted city, with tropical diseases and an unpredictable supply of Huggies. Reuters had a shabby office in a dodgy part of town. I do not recall how long Charissa and I talked it over, but I do remember her unequivocal "Let's go!". The burbs beckoned, safe and convenient, but they did not exert the pull on us that we had imagined they would. Latin America—first Venezuela, then Brazil—cemented our marriage with the trials and joys of raising a child, then children, in chaotic places full of surprises. Fits of imprudence had worked out well for me. I hoped this walk would prove no different.

The next ten miles were smooth, and took me within striking distance of Ullapool by mid-afternoon. You lose a sense of adventure following a road, but a compensation is looking more at what is around you and less at where you are putting your feet. I climbed out of Elphin in a downpour and stopped for a stormy view of Cul Mor, Cul Beag, and the glen between them. "Cul" means "back". You know already what "mor" and "beag" mean. When I was planning this journey I hoped to walk through Sutherland in particular in bright weather, to see its rugged wide-open landscapes at their best. But as I looked at the mist constantly dressing and undressing the hills, I wondered if I really wanted a bright blue sky. As Richard had said, dark brooding is part of the Highland atmosphere. While I was looking at the moody scene on Cul Beag a car pulled up and the driver jumped out to admire it with me. He struck up a conversation with an Australian accent. It turned out we were both toddler emigrants from Glasgow, he to Tasmania and I to southeast England. We didn't speak for long. It was, he said, far too bloody cold to hang about.

There is a monotony to walking country roads that does not exist on trails. Maybe it is that the mind is freed not only from looking for footing but also from the tasks of way-finding and even survival. Tarmac is the human world, and you take more for granted. Instead of burn-crossings, bealachs, and bogs, I remember trivia from these miles—a broken down van, a dead sheep in a ditch, counting roadside snow poles to pace myself up a long hill. On the long descent to Drumrunie—a place little more than a T-junction—I was pleased that my only discomfort after 14 miles was a dull ache in the ankles and behind my knees and calves. Beyond the junction, Stac Pollaidh[26] appeared five miles northwest. It is a famous hill, beloved of calendars, but today the points of its rocky pinnacles were hiding in cloud. At the next pullout, I took off my pack, and began a break. A car pulled up. This time two middle-aged men came out, New Yorkers. After we spoke, they offered me a ride, which I declined with the same speech I gave Richard. Then I crossed the wind-whipped strath[27] of the River Canaird and put away another used-up map, opening the "Gairloch & Ullapool" sheet in its place.

I left Sutherland and Assynt behind on the stretch from Elphin too. Scotland presents the visitor with a bewildering variety of regions to which signs welcome him or bid her return. In truth most now have little meaning beyond the sentimental. The only region I have passed through so far on this journey that is actually in the business of government is that of the Highland Council, a big area that I would not leave until well south of Fort William. The historic counties of Sutherland and Ross and Cromarty have insignificant real functions today, but they are how people refer to the places. Indeed even older and smaller subdivisions are common throughout Scotland. I might have been entering Ross and Cromarty now, but most locals would call where I stood Wester Ross, or even Coigach, the small coastal region north of Ullapool.

I hope it has been obvious from this narrative that Sutherland is a very sparsely populated place, and not only by the standards of Great Britain. Scots as a whole have six times more elbow room than the English, living on average a little less tightly packed together than Michiganders. Scots living in the Highland Council area, however, bump into one another less frequently than Nebraskans, while Sutherland is scarcely more crowded than Montana. The Highlands have never teemed with humanity, but they are emptier now than 150 years ago, a fact not unconnected with the vexed question of land ownership. When the Highlands began to enter a money economy from the 1600s, the Gaelic chiefs who controlled the land would still have followed old clan-based understandings of who could live on it, and in return for what duties. The motivation of the chiefs changed in the 1700s, and especially 1800s, when profit became the main consideration. The quest for income drove the adoption of commercial sheep farming and, in turn, the infamous Clearances of the population.

The Highland Clearances—the eviction of whole communities by landowners intent on the maximum commercial exploitation of their estates—are easy to mythologize. My own mental picture is of a stalwart, be-tartaned people driven from their ancestral glens as their houses are burned behind them. The cold shores of Canada beckon. This may not be such a mistaken picture of what happened at least here in Sutherland in the 1810s, except for one detail. Eviction at that stage of the Clearances was more likely to be to new coastal crofting communities than to the colonies. Crofting—a livelihood organized around an individual smallholding and common grazing land—has a cozy ring, and it is often assumed that the Gaels lived thus from time immemorial. In fact, the crofting townships were created by landlords as places to relocate cleared populations, places where arable land would intentionally be so scarce that the people would have no choice but to work part-time in the landlord's fishing and kelping[28] industries. Thus the inhabitants of Sutherland, cleared from fertile glens in the interior, became crofters on the barren coast. On shores like that between Lochinver and Kylesku, they scraped a living from land and sea, and ventured farther afield to seasonal jobs, or in the King's army. Depopulation certainly followed as they sought a better life overseas and in Scotland's booming industrial cities. As for the cleared land, when sheep became less profitable much was given over to deer forest and other sporting uses, and ownership became ever more concentrated. By 1900, half the Highlands were owned by just 15 landowners.

The last miles to Ullapool were harder. Pounding the tarmac with a heavy load was taking a toll on my ankles and shoulders. And whenever the shelter of the hills fell away, the west wind caught my pack side-on, jolting me as if I were a high-sided vehicle. The road went through a gorge, a place of bumptious nature. The wind huffed constantly, a burn to my right prattled, the waterfall across the road smacked gleefully down onto rock. Cars were like timid gate-crashers. The evening grew warm and bright, and gave me the confidence to peel off my waterproofs. As I was doing so a car came from a driveway, and I declined the afternoon's second offer of a ride. Walking without waterproofs felt good, the wind flapping my clothes dry. At Ardmair, the road joined the shore, and I rested on rocks at the entrance to a campground. It was an exposed spot, and I fancied my chances of seeing a tent kite by into the hills.

The road wound over a rocky hill and descended to a bridge across a burn. The parapet was of perfect height to support my pack a while without my having to take it off. There was a half-mile, 300-foot climb ahead to a small conifer wood. This *must* be the last hill, I thought, and dutifully set off. Halfway up, I heard a motor behind me. It seemed to be struggling even more than I. Then an old blue camper van belched past at twice my speed. The young guy at the wheel gestured to ask if I wanted a ride. He was probably relieved not to lose his momentum when I shook my head and waved thanks. Rounding the bend at the crest of the hill, about 6 p.m., Ullapool appeared below, white walls and gray roofs on a square promontory in Loch Broom. It was a grand sight.

On the way down, I saw rain sweeping briskly across Loch Broom toward the road, and launched Operation Restore Waterproofs. But then the shower fizzled after a few desultory drops. Footsore and pack-weary, every step to the youth hostel was now a burden. I reached the buildings of Ullapool and was struck by how urban the village felt after six rural days. Ullapool may have only 1,300 inhabitants, but it boasts street lamps, sidewalks, and pedestrian crossings. I knew the hostel was on the waterfront and remembered it toward the west end. But I did not find it there among the pretty cottages, and had to trek back the full length of Shore Street. It was a cruel half-mile. All pangs of guilt for shortcutting were gone.

I had walked 72 miles from Cape Wrath. Today I would rest my legs and do errands. I stepped out onto Shore Street, bought *The Scotsman*, and went to the Tea Store café to read it over coffee and a bacon roll. The newspaper was reporting the rhetoric from the start of the new term of the Scottish Parliament. Alex Salmond, First Minister and nationalist, had strong words:

> "Independence, he said, was 'the opposite of dependence, of limited ambition, of negativity, caution and pessimism'. And he said backing for an independent country would be to reject the arguments of 'those who tell us we are too lazy and too poor'".

We'll return to the question of independence. For now, I went back to my bacon roll, and turned to the sports pages.

I took the short walk along Argyle Street to the bank, then doubled back to the post office to mail home my used-up maps. As I look at the stack of maps from the journey on my desk now, they are, like an ice core drawn from a glacier, a record of weather past. The Cape Wrath sheet is in good condition, but Loch Assynt, taken out on the Marble Road and along the road to Ullapool, is ripped and frayed. The maps corresponding to the coming days of the journey are trashed. I'd had only one serious run-in with midges but, anxious my luck might run out, headed now for Lochbroom Hardware. It was on the corner of Quay and Shore streets, a minute from the post office. There I stocked up on repellent and even bought a net to cover my head. I replenished my blister supplies at Boots pharmacy.

Last night a friend back home had texted that he'd googled Ullapool and it seemed "a small place". Reveling in its amenities and bright lights, I had replied: "Feels like Paris to me!" But now I was standing outside Boots wondering what to do until the hostel reopened. An obvious answer lay back on Quay Street—The Chippy. Every visitor to Ullapool, it seemed, went to this fish & chip shop, and Ullapool gets a lot of tour buses. It was low season, but I still had to wait for the line to subside to sneak in before the next bus unloaded. I took my meat pie and chips outside to eat sitting on a low window sill. Around the corner was another chip shop. It had no customers at all. I took an after-lunch stroll on West Shore Street, looking out across Loch Broom to the hills I would walk into tomorrow, and then set about the arduous business of time-killing. I sat in the ferry terminal and worked on my notes. I wrote a postcard to Katie at UConn. I got hungry again and bought a stale sandwich to eat with the fat gulls on the quay. I went to the Frigate Café for a cup of coffee. I even went to the museum, but could not muster the interest to enter. On the way back, a group of tourists was waiting for their coach by The Chippy. A chorus of "here he comes!" in Yorkshire accents went up as a Shearings bus rounded the corner. When the door of the hostel opened at 4:00, it was like the power coming on after a long outage. I could get busy again.

I would stay, by the end of my journey, in seven Scottish Youth Hostel Association (SYHA) hostels. "Youth" is a great misnomer. Most guests were middle-aged English walkers and cyclists, assorted continental tourists (mainly German, all grown-up), retired Aussies on car tours of the old country, and a sprinkling of Scottish munro-baggers in just a few locations. The hostels were all clean, well-run, inexpensive, and often in prime locations. I don't know what a hotel on Shore Street costs but it is not £17.50 a night. The hostels had the added advantage of laundry facilities, and the MWIS forecast was always posted. The staff, too, were a good source of knowledge, often outdoor types themselves. In Ullapool, it was Tam. He was behind the counter at reception when I went to buy laundry soap. He said he had walked the Way of Saint James in Spain. He did it in sandals, bruising his feet. I wondered if this had a religious motivation, but did not ask. He said he was disappointed that there were long stretches of the Way that ran through cities, and he had now learned that the very best hiking was right here at home!

The washing machines were in the drying room, as hot as a greenhouse but smelling of sweaty socks and wet boots. On the trail, when socks became too wet or smelly to wear any longer, I sealed them in a Ziploc bag. I now had the pleasure of opening a bag of fermenting wool. I was in the middle of this fragrant task when the German hiker told me her tale of defeat at the Garbh Allt. She seemed sweet at that moment, but I saw her outside the hostel later, dressed all in black, smoking, giving someone a very hard time in German on her cell phone. By then I was about as prepared as I could be for an early start tomorrow. The grocery store would open at 7 a.m., and I'd buy food then. So now it was back to the slow round of Ullapool—a pint at the Ferry Boat Inn, pizza at the Frigate again, a call home from the same puddled call box as yesterday. It was my third visit to the Frigate in 24 hours. The waitress said, "You like it here!" It's a small place is Ullapool.

# 6

## The Great Wilderness

Before leaving home I planned the walk as far as Ullapool quite thoroughly. I did not stick to the plan, of course. Had I done so I might be feeling my way about Bealach Trallgil on hands and knees to this day. But I knew throughout those first days more or less the route I wanted to follow and where I might spend each night. I had no plans like that for after Ullapool. I knew only that there was the "Great Wilderness" to cross, and that deer stalking might present an added complication. It was the time of year when red deer are culled—for herd management as well as sport—and estates sometimes close off land. The Great Wilderness was a patchwork of estates.

Once upon a time there was a passenger-ferry across Loch Broom. If it had still been running, it would have made possible a direct, backcountry route to the Great Wilderness. As it was, I had no alternative but to start today with another seven miles of the A835. A steady rain fell as I walked. Shrouded peaks and mist-filled corries now seemed the eternal order of things. At Leckmelm, I breakfasted under sturdy trees growing along a low stone wall, and looked down over cattle and pasture to Loch Broom. At Inverlael, the loch ended at a flat-bottomed strath. I left the main road for a narrow lane and, reviewing a guard of thick trees to either side, presently came to the handful of cottages called Crofton.

I turned onto a faint trail beside a stone wall. It looked in the right place to be the path across the hills to the Dundonnell River. It led through an overgrown field to a pasture. But there was so much fence, wall, and gate between the pasture and open hillside that I thought this could not possibly be the way. I went back to the cottages and tried the opposite direction. A genteel-looking woman glided by in a luxury car. She smiled at me. She was snug and knew where she was going, and briefly I felt forlorn. Soon this way did not seem right either, and I returned to the pasture, looking fruitlessly on the way for someone to ask directions. This time I climbed a gate, and then a wire fence. I was about to climb the final gate too, but on an impulse tried the bolt. It opened, but there was no path on the other side. I was standing on a steep and slimy hillside, the goo underfoot half earth, half sheep shit.

I inched cautiously up for a better view and decided to follow the edge of the wood above Crofton until, with luck, I would find a path. It was steep, rough, sodden ground. Near a fallen branch, I found antlers in the mud and wondered if their owner had perished looking for a route into the hills. Then I found a gravelly path above the trees, which soon began to climb the escarpment in earnest. The oily green pasture gave way to the brown grasses of open moor. It was a steep ascent, rising in a mile from the sea-level strath to a lochan-strewn plateau 1,350 feet up. The plateau summits were called *meall* on my map, "lumpish hills". The closest was Meall Dubh29—the black lumpish hill. Somewhere up here the path came to slabs of rock piled to make a dam. The structure had

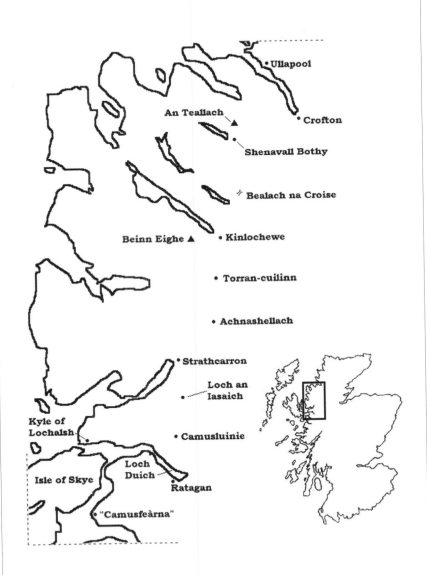

Map 2: Ullapool to Ratagan

crumbled, but purple heather grew lavishly on the ruin, bright and beautiful even in the gloom. I stopped here despite a cold wind. In Ullapool, knowing I would eat nothing but the food in my pack for two days, I had bought perishable luxuries, and now enjoyed bread, cheese, and a pork pie. I pushed on across a dismal moor. The Scots have a word for this kind of scene and weather, *dreich*—dreary, cheerless, bleak. Approaching the final descent to the Dundonnell River, I stopped above a swollen waterfall, and realized late that the burn that fed it would have to be waded. Then getting down to the valley floor proved every bit as steep and awkward as the climb above Crofton, and I arrived at the river worn out. There was a short walk along a deserted road to the trailhead for the Great Wilderness. It had been 13 miles from Ullapool. There were just four more to the bothy where I planned to spend the night, and relatively easy ones too. Or so I thought.

I don't know how I got the idea that these miles would be easy. It might have been because of the vehicle track shown on my map for half the distance. Or maybe it was that the peaks of An Teallach[30], the 3,500-foot mountain that the path would skirt, were hidden from me all day by gloom. Whatever the reason, I did not notice that the map contours showed another climb to 1,350 feet, followed by a 1,000-foot drop to the bothy. The vehicle track grew in steepness through woods of silver birch. Where the birch ended, a white cascade poured from a craggy ridge. Here, the Great Wilderness began. The falls fed a clear burn, and in it I filled my reservoir. Then I left the track for bona fide footpath, and expected the bothy to appear before long. Instead, the ground, weather, and light worsened progressively. On the exposed spur of Sail Liath—one of An Teallach's ten peaks—dusk gathered early and the rain came on. I began to fear a walk in the dark. Two miles seemed endless. I thought I saw a building down in the mist to the south, but it was in the wrong place for Shenavall bothy. I descended a rocky chasm, scrambling as much as walking. Finally, with self-pity looming, I saw the bothy below, sharply defined in a patch of green. It was larger than I expected. A five-star hotel could not have looked more inviting.

Back at the hostel I had asked Tam about the bothy, seeking reassurance it would not be overcrowded. He said the bad weather would keep climbers out of the hills, but warned the bothy might be dirty at the end of the season. You are meant to carry out what you take in, he said, but not everyone does. Shenavall, like many Scottish bothies, is maintained by the Mountain Bothies Association. Maintained, not owned. The owner is the local estate, which has first call on it (for stalking, for instance). The MBA is a volunteer group that keeps the bothies in good condition for the free use of those in the hills. Amenities are correspondingly basic. As the MBA puts it, users should expect "no tap, no sink, no beds, no lights, and, even if there is a fireplace, perhaps nothing to burn." Furthermore, "few bothies have toilet facilities apart from a spade". Shenavall made this demanding grade, but it wasn't dirty. It was quite a substantial cottage too, and it appeared I would have it to myself. I began to wish I had noted where other bothies stood along my route before I left home. I poked around downstairs. There was indeed a fireplace but, kindling or no, I had no intention of building a fire. Walkers had left odds and ends behind that might be of use to others—candle stubs, newspaper for drying boots, tea bags. To judge by the many bottles converted to candlesticks, it was not unknown for a dram or two to be drunk at Shenavall. Liquor itself was not among the odds and ends left behind. This was Scotland after all.

I climbed the stairs to the loft where I thought there'd be less chance of rodents. It was dim, clean-swept, and empty apart from a few rickety wooden chairs. But it was out of the storm, and

I set about making myself comfortable. I put on dry socks, my wooly hat, a warm shirt, and a pair of long johns. I spread out my sleeping pad and bag. I put food, map, and radio within reach and squirmed into the sack, going from despondency to fair purring with contentment in the space of an hour. Here I was, a week and 90 miles into my journey, alone in the Great Wilderness with a storm raging outside. It was very likely there was no one else in the 40 square miles around me. After a supper of assorted trail food, I hung my grub bag on a peg in the wall out of reach of mice, and wriggled back into the down. I needed an early start tomorrow. Given the immense walls of sandstone surrounding the bothy, I was surprised to pick up Radio Scotland. Last Saturday at Blairmore, it was pipe music; tonight a "celebration of the blue-grass of Bill Monroe", whoever he was.

I had switched off the radio and begun to doze when I heard a bang downstairs. Raising myself onto an elbow, I called out. There was no answer. In ordinary circumstances I would now have spooked myself. Goodness knows the material was there. Shenavall was surely history-haunted. It means "the old farm" in Gaelic, and must have witnessed its share of bloody clan warfare, famine, and wretched clearance. I could have conjured up the phantom of a wounded clansman stumbling through this cottage door on a fruitless journey to die among his own people. Or a ghostly waif of a girl climbing to the attic with the body of her child in her arms, starved when the blight turned the potato crop to a foul-smelling mush. But I was too used up for that sort of nonsense, and fell asleep without even an inspection downstairs. There was another bang in the night, but I barely stirred.

When I did wake there was a pale gray light in the skylight above me. Together with my bladder, it said it was time to get going. It was about 6:00 a.m. I slipped into boots and went downstairs. I saw that I did not properly latch the door last night, and it must have been caught by gusts of wind. When I opened it now, a group of deer, cropping the grass around the bothy, recoiled, eyed me, and took off into the dawn. The rain had stopped and I looked out over broad Strath na Sealga as I relieved myself. There was some lighter gray cloud in the sky now, but the massive bens that enclosed the valley were a dim dark green. There were scattered trees down by the stony riverbed, dwarfed by the landscape about them. An Teallach rose directly behind the bothy, its 3,000-foot peaks hidden by lesser but closer ridges, and by ghostly mist. It was hard to articulate the feelings of being here. Awe, privilege, calm were among them. And a chilly willy. It was time to zip up and go.

Levity apart, when the memory of this walk begins to fade, I believe that Shenavall will linger longest. It was the essence of the experience I sought. After my youthful adventures in Spain, and my attempts to rekindle them hemmed in by the timetables of work, the focus of my wanderlust gradually changed. In South America, I still pored over maps, imagining grand sweeps of journeys on the continent's beat-up roads. I managed only a few, and only in miniature. After we came back to the New York area when the girls were five and three, I—often we—began to hike. A yearning for the woods and hills began to outpace that for open road. Simple visibility played a part. Some of the places I had lived for 20 years certainly boasted woods, hills, and trails, but mostly they remained off the radar of this fleeting, city-bound resident. In Connecticut, we lived enveloped in trees, and trails were effortlessly discovered. Of course, not all of them were challenging or isolated, but something that even tame trails provided whetted my appetite. I am not sure when I became irretrievably hooked, but the summer of 2006 is a good candidate. We took a family vacation to Grand Teton, Yellowstone, and Glacier national parks. We camped and hiked, and—in Yellowstone—rose before dawn to watch wolves from the side of the park road. But it wasn't enough. I wanted to walk into the backcountry. I took Katie—nearly

13—with me. Charissa and the other girls dropped us off at the trailhead, and we turned our backs to them and to the road, and walked into the wilds. We walked through pinewoods, through wide meadows where we circled chewing buffalo, and climbed to the top of a peak. We made camp among dirty snowbanks and swarming mosquitos. I slept only fitfully, thinking how we were lying down in bear country with only an unfamiliar can of pepper spray for protection. But it felt good to have reached this place under our own steam, nature sharpening our wits to look out for ourselves far from the reassurance of people. There were no bears around Shenavall, but what felt good here was essentially the same—smallness beside nature, autonomy, separation. That I was feeling it in my Scotland made it unforgettable.

I was apprehensive about today's hike, more on account of the terrain than the miles. There would be no road, the paths might be poor where they existed at all, and there would be heather-whacking for sure over Bealach na Croise, at 1,400 feet my highest pass yet. At least I had seen no evidence of stalking. I have used the name "Great Wilderness", as I imagine most people must, somewhat tongue-in-cheek. It covers 180 square miles of uninhabited mountain and loch. The Great Smoky Mountains National Park is four and a half times larger. Still, it is broad and desolate enough—without visitor center, rangers, or (Shenavall aside) shelters—and I was not about to disrespect it. My first task was to find, hidden among the hillocks of grass and heath-er around the bothy, the path that led up Strath na Sealga. This proved easy enough, and for a mile or two the path was distinct, flat, and dry. It passed a ruin called Achneigie, which must have been the false Shenavall I spied last night. The strath ended at cliffs, and I turned south and took a path along the Abhainn Loch an Nid[31]. Finding, and then keeping to, this path was not simple. It was at best a broken line of flattened vegetation or an inches-wide break in the heather. Where it did exist as a definite path, it was eroded and cut by many step-over burns. But the difficulty underfoot was offset by the views.

The best views were behind my back as I walked, back toward An Teallach. They got better all the way to the pass, giving me ample excuse to stop and turn around. When I first turned I saw a green line of birch filling the river gully that ran down the glen. The massive cliffs of An Teallach—three miles off—rose behind a closer slope. An hour later, viewed from a platform of white rock sprouting mauve heather from its fissures, the mountain was all dark, jagged peaks swept by translucent mist. Finally, as a little sun broke through to paint the grassy slopes of the closer hills a light green, even An Teallach—six miles downriver now—shed a fraction of its darkness. There were waterfalls this morning too. The wet summer and recent rain had put them in full spate, their crackling the soundtrack to my walk. There was one beside the path that was four delicate, vertical lines of white water. They had washed the black rock they tumbled over to brown. When they reached the glen floor, the lines merged to make just another burn I had to leap.

Loch an Nid was a half-mile of pale blue water at the base of grass-and-rock slopes. And a half-mile beyond it I left the path, such as it was, and struck out over tussocky ground into the steep-sided entrance to Bealach na Croise. There, among the hillocks ahead, I saw a blue-clothed figure, the first person I'd seen since Ullapool, at least the first on foot. He or she was heading my way, and I looked forward to a chin-wag when we met. But the stranger dropped from sight behind some bumpy topography, and never reappeared. The 500-foot climb from the loch to the pass proved easier than expected, and I reached the saddle at midday. It was an enclosed place compared to the pass above Achfary. Steep, craggy bens guarded it west and east. But again a whole new landscape was revealed to the south. I was elated, and stopped for lunch at this beautiful frontier.

In this case it was exhilaration, mixed maybe with just a little pride, that came before a fall. Starting down from the bealach, I slipped on a peaty bank and, falling backwards, came to rest after a few feet when the side of my chest slid into a rock. There was no pain right away, but I knew from falls past that bruised ribs take time to feel; and just how uncomfortable they can be, and for so very long. I picked myself up and set course for, I thought, the little loch that would guide me down to the good path at Lochan Fada. As I edged my way down I breathed deeply in from time to time to see if I felt the first signs of bruising. My morale since leaving Cape Wrath had generally been good. The only persistent difficulty had been believing that the journey was not just for today or this week, but would be my life for a month and a half. At a time when my hike plan still seemed daunting, a part of me whispered now and then that something would intervene to force me to change it. I think that whisper was a way of dealing with my fear that I myself would end the walk if it became too tough. The whisper said, "You won't have to end it. Something will do it for you". But now that an injury threatened to do exactly that, I did not like it. Pride was one reason. I imagined people saying "Old fool! Couldn't stay upright for one week". It was my judgment in their mouths. But my worry was about more than failing in a much-advertised venture. Mentally, I had built the next decade of my life on this trek. It was to be a clean break, a clearing out of the mind, a high from which to start working life anew. The acts of imprudence that had served me well had not all been committed with confidence, and this one had been no exception. Trying to feel if there was a pain in my side as I came down this mountain, I knew that if my carelessness caused this walk to end prematurely, my feelings of rightness about my decision to resign would evaporate, and my fears for my place in the world would return redoubled. In short, a crisis of confidence would follow. For this reason, and for the better one of wanting more Shenavalls, I felt now how deeply I wanted to see the endeavor through.

I also wanted to see little Loch Meallan an Fhúdair, but it did not show. I took out my map and, as it flapped in the wind, could see that I had drifted too far east, following a burn down rather than maintaining height to the loch. I risked walking through miles of trackless glen instead of hitting good path. There was nothing for it but to point myself southwest. I'd pick up the path a little farther east than intended. Unfortunately this meant slogging over moor, and climbing again when I had thought I was done with it for the day. And slogging it was. I took aim at rocks or other features on the moor, and walked as directly as possible toward them. It was not usually all that directly. Mini Grand Canyons etched in the peat, burns great and small, and abundant surface water made sure of that. But, despite sweat and frustration, there was something fulfilling about using map and compass in the wind and rain to find myself on the landscape and steer a course. No one else would get me to Kinlochewe. There were no signs to the car park, no well-trod trail, no voices in the landscape. There was something very special about that.

My navigation brought me to a rocky plateau of tiny lochs, but still, I could not make out anything in the scene below to tell me where the path might be. Still steering by map and compass, I started to descend. Suddenly there was movement on the far right of my field of vision, and I turned to see a red deer stag just at the moment he saw me. He had every reason to be nervous, and threw his rack and head back to trot away. He moved almost silently, just a dull plopping of hooves on waterlogged moor. I wished I could cover the ground half as easily as he. Then deliverance came quickly. I picked out silvery Lochan Fada below and the

wee lochs at its outflow, dropped down an escarpment, and saw a
soaked tent with two mountain bikes strewn outside. I knew the
path could not be far beyond. What should have been a two-mile
descent from the bealach ended up taking almost three hours. I
sighed deeply, and felt a small sharp pain in my left ribs.

Mishaps and wrong turns were always going to happen on
a walk like this. Hiking with a partner would have reduced the
chances of serious consequences coming of them, but I never considered it. I wanted to set my own pace, follow my own nose. On
this hike, more than any other, I wanted to look outward at the
countryside and people, and that argued for going solo. Besides, I
didn't know anyone who would want to come with me. There were
risks to going it alone, I knew, and fretted about them perfuncto-
rily before leaving home. One guidebook I looked at stated that
*obviously* "it would be most unwise to do a walk like this alone".
To put my resolve to the test, I reread the parts of Bill Bryson's *A
Walk in the Woods* where he graphically sets out the horrors that
can befall those who venture into the great outdoors. Analyzing
them, I decided that I need not lose sleep over wild beasts or toxic
plants. As for crazed hillbillies, Scotland exported all she had to
the North American colonies. Tick-borne diseases are a greater
threat raking leaves in my backyard. I was sufficiently knowledgeable and cautious to mitigate the limited risks of Scottish autumn
weather, which are principally those of melancholy, Vitamin D
deficiency, and trench foot. I did not fear getting seriously lost.
The Highland scene is full of feature and mostly unobstructed by
forest, so competence with the excellent OS maps and a compass
would see me through. This left accident and medical emergency
as the real dangers—a twisted ankle miles from anywhere, my
head bashed on boulders crossing a burn, a heart attack caused
by excess of Full Scottish Breakfast. All I can say is that I did my
best to minimize these risks with common sense. I kept my phone
charged. Coverage was not ubiquitous, but I had a decent chance

of signal bars if I was up to my waist in mud and sinking. I went to the doctor for a check-up before I set out, and was in good fettle. And I never, *ever*, ate haggis *and* black pudding at breakfast.

Kinlochewe was still six miles away, but at least the path was firm and dry. I had the Letterewe Estate to thank for that. Not all landowners are villains. The estate, which I entered at Bealach na Croise, covers the greater part of the Great Wilderness. It was acquired in 1977 by Paul van Vlissingen, a wealthy Dutch businessman and environmental philanthropist. He also appears, to judge from his obituaries, to have been a most interesting man. "A powerful walker, he strode over every yard of his huge domain, and learnt the Gaelic names of every loch and burn, every corrie, ridge and ben," wrote *The Independent* in August 2006. It went on "'I don't call myself the owner,' he said of Letterewe. 'You can't own a place like this. It belongs to the planet. I'm only the guardian of it.'" Van Vlissingen floated the idea, not entirely a dead letter yet, of reintroducing wolves to his estate. They have been extinct in Scotland for 300 years but would, he argued, help to keep the deer population healthy. From the walker's point of view, van Vlissingen is celebrated for the 1993 "Letterewe Accord", an agreement signed with outdoor organizations that gave responsible walkers the right to roam the Letterewe Estate. The accord was a direct precursor of the enactment, ten years later, of the legal right of the public to access any land in Scotland for non-motorized recreation. There are some obvious exceptions—your wee back garden, farmyards, sown fields, airfields, and the like—but it is still a remarkable prioritization of public rights over private. In return for access, walkers must use the land responsibly, as defined in the Scottish Outdoor Access Code. It is what most decent folk would do anyway.

In spite of the good works of the van Vlissingen family, for me the trail was a slog, a weary postscript to the adventure from Shenavall. I just wanted to cover the miles to the bunkhouse I'd booked. When Jackie and I were little our parents took us on Sunday walks in the rain ("We're not sugar, we won't melt!"). On the way home, we kids amused ourselves by mimicking an ad of the day. It was a sort of hushed chant, "hot chocolate, drinking chocolate". We hoped, I suppose, to be given some when we got home. Now I adapted it—"cold lager, drinking lager, cold lager, drinking lager", and looked forward to some in Kinlochewe. Then I was ambushed by sheep, unprovoked. I admit to reminding sheep of the impending pot by calling out "mint sauce" or "rosemary and garlic" in their direction, but on this occasion had done no such thing. Suddenly, there was a loud baa behind me, and I turned to see a big ewe coming directly toward me off the hillside at a fair canter. She veered sharply away, but continued to trot parallel to me behind bracken. Then she exploded out of the ferns onto the track ahead, and turned as if to confront me. Again she turned away, and trotted along the track a few yards in front of me. She baa-ed incessantly, drawing all the sheep of the neighborhood to her. Soon it looked as if I were herding them to market, or they were a posse bringing me to justice.

A jogger came up the track from the direction of Kinlochewe, soon followed by a holidaying couple on bicycles. Seeing them was like seeing land birds in the rigging after a long ocean voyage, a sign of approaching safe haven after the void. Beinn Eighe was straight ahead now, the latest great hill to dominate a segment of my walk. I was not destined to see much of Beinn Eighe. I hobbled into Incheril and put my pack down on a big tree stump, intent on a rest before taking on the half-mile to Kinlochewe. There was an ATV parked close by, and a stout, older man out in a field. He came toward the ATV, and me, looking very much as if someone had stolen his toffee apple. When I greeted him, he replied gruffly. But he turned out to be a nice fellow. He asked where I had walked from, and knew the lochs and passes when I told him. He said there was a hurricane coming, *from America*. Many British people pick up American sounds and turns of phrase in my speech now, so this "from America" may have been added to make me feel responsible for the coming mayhem. Hurricane Katia was turning on Scotland in her death throes. The news delivered, he said a brisk farewell, jumped spryly onto the ATV, and took off like The Wild One. And I took off like Grandpa Walton, and walked laboriously and thirstily over two bridges to the Kinlochewe Hotel. "Cold lager, drinking lager ... " Propping up my poles and pack against the wall outside, I went into the hotel's empty bar to announce myself. A lanky young man with an early-Beatles haircut was behind the counter. I sat on the edge of a barstool.

"My name's McWilliams. I have a reservation for the bunkhouse."

"Right ho. Wait just a minute and I'll take you over." He had a soft voice, full of detached humor.

"Hmm, since I'm here, could you do me a pint of ... diet coke?" Looking forward is so much more delicious than satisfying.

The barman's name was Scott. After I gulped down my coke, he led me to the bunkhouse right next door. I was to come across other country hotels in Scotland with a bunkhouse attached, and I think they're a brilliant idea. You stay in accommodation befitting a hiker, and spend the money you save in the hotel's bar and restaurant. This bunkhouse, it should be said, had a kitchen that Charissa would enjoy cooking Thanksgiving dinner in, so self-catering was an option too. It had everything else I needed as well—a drying room, a fridge for my remaining perishables, and of course a hot shower. I grabbed a coveted bottom bunk by spreading my sleeping bag on it. There were three men already settled in. Peter and his sons, Mark and Paul, were Londoners. Peter made a joke of their saintly names, assuring me there was no Andrew or James yet to appear. Peter now lived near Glasgow with his "Scots lass". I assumed the "boys" were from a previous marriage. They were on a regular get-together break, bagging munros. I asked Peter how he liked Glasgow. "Close to the hills," he said.

After cleaning up, I went to see Scott for the postponed cold lager. The food in the bar was excellent too. In fact, I was so pleased with the Kinlochewe Hotel that I asked the owner if I could stay another night if I wished. I could, she said, and I promised to confirm my plans in the morning. On top of concern about the weather *from America*, there was the question of my ribs. There was a definite pain accompanying certain actions—getting up from a chair, clearing my throat—but not nearly as bad as I knew it could be. Sleep would be the test.

# 7

## 9/11 in Kinlochewe

On Sunday morning I took stock. The weather forecast was lousy. "Gales and heavy rain for most of the day," said the MWIS. Monday looked no better. I had only a rough idea of my route south, and it involved camping. I had slept well enough, but changing sides was painful. It seemed smart to rest the injury for a day. It was my middle daughter's birthday too, and I wanted to be sure of being near a telephone. So I went next door to confirm the extra night, and then returned to the bunkhouse kitchen. Peter and sons were frying bacon. I sat at a corner of the heavy table, out of their way, and set about studying maps. Peter offered to share their breakfast.

"Thanks, I'm good. Anyway, you'll need the calories for Slioch," I said, naming their munro of the day. My intention after Kinlochewe had been to reach the Inverness to Kyle of Lochalsh railway at Achnashellach, ten miles to the south, and then cross very remote country to the SYHA hostel in Glen Affric. This was a farther 18 miles as the Osprey flies, and a great deal more taking into account the hills to skirt, the rivers to ford, and the bealachs to cross. The plan had been to put down my tent wherever I happened to be when night fell. As Katia approached to soak already sodden land and flood already swollen burns, none of this seemed a bright idea any more. I decided now to stay nearer to the coast, where there would be paths and probably accommodation.

I went across the road to the café in the Kinlochewe Stores and post office. I was on my second cup of instant coffee, bacon roll half eaten, when the newspapers came in. The *Sunday Herald* was full of 9/11 10th anniversary coverage. I skipped it for now, but later in the morning I took the paper to the hotel lounge, and settled into a deep chair. People in Scotland had already asked, when I said I lived near New York, if I was there on the day. I was in Midtown, away from Ground Zero, but like so many others, I have sharp-focus memories of the day's events. I walked out of Grand Central Station just after 8 a.m. and recall the sunshine and deliciously cool air when I crossed Madison Avenue. It was bliss after the summer's humidity. After just minutes in the Reuters office on Times Square, I saw my colleagues lining the tall windows of our high floor. I assumed there had been a car wreck on the street below. Then we pieced together the unfolding events as people wandered the office keen to share what they knew. We could see the smoking towers three miles down 7th Avenue too. But mostly I looked at my Reuters screen, at the red news alerts scrolling in, typed by journalists on adjacent floors. The alerts shouted that first one tower, then the other, had fallen. When I went back to the crowd at the window it was almost a surprise to see the words on the screen proven in the real world. I went out at lunchtime, but there were no crowds to fight on Times Square, no naked cowboy making the tourists giggle, and just a handful of silent diners in Teriyaki Boy. Later in the afternoon, they said that trains would begin to run again, and I met a friend at Grand

Central to ride, jam-packed into the cars, back to Connecticut. We were the Midtowners, shoes as shiny as the moment we left home. The Downtowners, our fellow passengers, were covered in dust from head to toe. We stopped at every station along the route, paramedics calling in to ask if anyone needed help. My family was lucky. We did not know anybody who died or lost loved ones. But a man on our neighboring street did not return from work, and the unclaimed cars at the stations were sad memorials for days to come. Weeks later, crossing the Whitestone Bridge to JFK Airport, I looked out over Queens and the East River. The Manhattan skyline was still magnificent, but for a second it was like smiling into the mirror having forgotten your front teeth had been pulled. Some people changed their lives after 9/11. It did not occur to me that I could. I had a young family and a new mortgage. I took from the day—like a day four years before, when a young cousin had died the day after we saw her very much alive at my mother's funeral—that the end can come out of the blue, and we can't count on abundant tomorrows to redress our shuffling through today.

From my comfortable chair I got talking with the owners of the hotel. He was a Scot and she, from her accent, a Kiwi. They seemed business-like at first, but proved friendly and helpful. He gave me a pamphlet listing independent hostels in Scotland, and I found places in it that might help on my way through the storm. By lunchtime my plans were firming up. Tomorrow I'd walk to Strathcarron. It had a station on the Inverness to Kyle line, and I could take a train to a hostel in one of the villages in the direction of Kyle. On Tuesday I'd ride back to Strathcarron and walk over the hills to a hamlet called Camusluinie. There was a bunkhouse there, the pamphlet said. I would then climb over more hills to the SYHA hostel at Ratagan on the coast at Loch Duich. At the call box opposite the hotel, I booked the stays at Camusluinie and Ratagan easily, but could not get through to anyone at the places on the railway. I decided to try again after settling scores with my wooly assailants of yesterday, and headed to the bar for a lunch of lamb stew.

Kinlochewe is a tiny place. It sits at the junction of a quiet east-west route with an even smaller road heading southwest to remote villages on the shore. I have mentioned its hotel and store. As I ambled about this afternoon, I saw a gas station, a rapidly emptying caravan site, and two churches. I took shelter from a downpour in the door of the Free Church of Scotland. At the call box, I found a shabby man having an agitated call. He seemed half-drunk. Rather than wait, I strolled down Slioch Terrace, and found cottages and a war memorial. The list of the dead, as always in Britain, was far longer for the First World War than the Second—11 men even for this place. Back at the phone, the man was still pleading and whining, holding the door ajar to let out his cigarette smoke, and his noise. So I crossed to the bunkhouse and, at a loose end, *foutered* with my gear. Now there's a good Scots word my parents used. In this case it means to fiddle with. For some reason I remember Scots words for things I ought not to do or be. I was told not to *fouter* with this or that, and also not to be a *thrawn willy*—a stubborn lad. I should not *skiddle* in the sink. Skiddling is watery foutering, as when you feign to wash the dishes but are really just goofing around.

It was impossible to be in Scotland and not think of my mom and dad much more than I do at home. In spite of everything, their presence in my thoughts gave me more pleasure than sorrow. I knew the course of their lives, but not really what made them tick, then stop ticking. They had hard-up, depression-then-war childhoods in Glasgow, or just outside in my mom's case. There was post-war national service away from home for both. By the early 1950s, they were back home, dad a reporter on the *Scottish Daily Express*, mom a pharmacy dispensing assistant. They met at the dances. In their wedding pictures, they are beautiful and radiant, and surely confident of their bright future. Mom's first pregnancy ended with a stillborn baby girl, and mother herself at risk. Against doctors' advice, pregnancies followed that yielded Jackie and I by Caesarian section. I think my parents were happy while we kids were small. Why wouldn't they be? My dad was doing well at his job too, and Britain was anyway becoming more prosperous. They bought a semi-detached house in a middle-class area of Glasgow, and then successively posher homes down in England. But then things started to go wrong. I date it to when I was 11 and Jackie 13. We were not always a happy family before then, nor forever miserable thereafter, but I can feel to this day the silent, moody tension that increasingly filled our home. The unhappiness had no single, obvious cause; nothing as simple as an affair or gambling debts. I suspect my mother was bored and isolated, and my father could not bring himself to see that he, two teenage kids, cooking, and pruning the roses might reasonably not be enough for her. If there were shouting matches, I remember only a few. It was a cold war, interspersed with periods of détente. Drink became their refuge. I found my escape on long country walks with our dog. Here, perhaps, mom and dad inadvertently sowed a seed of my journey now, as they sowed others in happier ways.

I went back to the phone, and this time it was occupied only by the smell of stale tobacco. I called the hostels along the railway line, and still got only recorded messages. Then I remembered from a trip with my youngest this past summer that there was a hotel right next to Strathcarron station. They found the number for me at the Kinlochewe Hotel, and I called straightaway. I explained that I was hiking and would be a mess when I arrived. "Nae bother," said the friendly woman at the other end of the line. So I booked, having no idea just how much of a mess I would be.

The new MWIS forecast was available in the bar. Huddled like generals over a battle plan, a group of us studied the sheets spread out on the counter. I took comfort that the worst of Katia was destined for farther south, and decided to set out on the 17 miles to Strathcarron in the morning. It turned into a cheery evening in the bar. There was the handsome young couple hiking to Cape Wrath. They had come from where I was going and vice versa. We traded information. There was the couple in temporary charge of the caravan site who had abandoned ship and taken a room in the hotel as Katia advanced. But mostly I remember the retired trawler captain from Grimsby on the North Sea coast of England. He came in already tipsy, but jovial and ready to be the butt of his own humor or any that was going around. In retirement, he had turned to amateur photography, and this was the cause of the celebration. A candidate for the most coveted prizes of the Grimsby Photographic Society, he thought that today he had finally taken the picture that would silence the competition and win over the hard-nosed judges. It sounded cutthroat down there. Behind the bar was Scott, and behind him a shelf of malt whiskys. I don't usually drink whisky, but the captain wanted to buy a round. It would have been rude to refuse, and rude not to buy one in return, would it not? Scott, a cool and funny MC, kept the party going. But he told me he lived in Shieldaig, a drive as many miles along a single-track road as my hike over the hills to Strathcarron tomorrow. I decided it would be rude too to keep him late, and foolish of me not to get a long sleep. Back at the bunkhouse, it was now just Peter, his sons, and I. They were heading south tomorrow too, first to Glasgow, and then a flight to London for Mark and Paul. "I don't envy you your walk tomorrow," said Peter.

# 8

## *Limping to Strathcarron*

My map showed a footpath hugging the A' Ghairbhe river for
about a mile before rising into the hills. It became obvious
almost immediately that the map was the only place it existed. I
left the bunkhouse in drizzle, went a short way along the main
road, and turned down a track beside the Church of Scotland. The
track went through a metal gate into a field of tall, wet grass—and
disappeared. I had feared something like this might happen, but
was exasperated that it happened so soon and completely. Keeping
the river close on my right, I pushed on apprehensively, and was
soon blocked by a wire mesh fence. Next I was on my knees, pulling myself up a wooded bank by roots and heather. The only good
news was that carrying the pack again was not troubling my ribs.
From the top of the bank there was a way forward for a while,
above the river; but then I was blocked again. This time it was a
good-sized burn with wooded banks, just beyond the overgrown
ruin of a building. I should have taken my boots off and paddled

through the stream. Instead I stretched from stone to stone and leaped the last channel. Then there were more obstacles—a steep edging-down to a smaller burn; the struggle, squeezed between undergrowth and deer fence, to scale its far bank; fallen limbs to clamber over or around. Somewhere in all this I slipped. As I flailed about trying to stay upright I stamped on one of my poles, and gave it a kink for the rest of the journey.

All of a sudden, a spanking new kissing gate stood before me, and pristine signs marked the way ahead. I was thankful, and my gratitude lasted as far as the next kissing gate. This one stood beside a conventional farm gate. You pass kissing gates by stepping into a wee enclosure and bringing the gate around so that you can exit on the other side. Humans can do this but livestock cannot. I backed, pack-first, into the enclosure, and pulled on the gate. It came nowhere near to clearing my body. I placed my pack alone in the enclosure. The gate stuck on it. The farm gate was chained and the fences high, so I had no alternative to this contraption. Finally I shoved my pack roughly to flatten it up and jerked the gate around it. "Damn stupid gate," I spat.

I took out a new Ordnance Survey map—the "Glen Carron & Glen Affric" sheet. It showed a steady climb through planted conifers to open moor 1,000 feet above Kinlochewe. But the trees had been felled, and I walked through a wasteland of stumps. On the moor, the wind blew strong, and thick gray cloud flew across Ben Eighe on the other side of the A' Ghairbhe valley. Still, it had been much windier and wetter, without a hurricane, on the Marble Road. Two and a half hours after leaving it, Kinlochewe was still visible below, its buildings and trees in dispiritingly sharp focus. The path became an intermittent, foot-wide puddle through green-brown grass and heather. On the highest part of the moor I became aware of pain along the inside of my right thigh. It was sharpest when walking downhill or stepping down onto my right leg. One or other contortion of the morning's struggle must have done some damage. On the 600-foot descent to Torran-cuilinn, I realized it might be serious damage.

The path entered planted forest, and turned steep and slimy. It would have been slow going anyway, but now I went at a snail's pace, seeking firm footing and painless steps. When I hobbled out of the trees I saw that Torran-cuilinn was a name attached to a single house and outbuildings. There was smoke from a chimney, but no other sign of life. It was raining hard. I went beyond the buildings to rest in the imperfect shelter of a big Scots pine, and studied the map as drips thwacked off the paper. The next mile would be flat, and then there would be a steady climb to the Coulin Pass. I figured this would not cause me much difficulty, and pressed on. From a bridge over the Coulin River, I looked at the scene. No amount of worry or weather could diminish its beauty. There were two clusters of buildings, wee Torran-cuilinn behind and a bigger cluster of white cottages at Coulin ahead. All around the bridge lay flat pasture, where cattle grazed on either side of the river that flowed into Loch Coulin just downstream. Beyond the loch was the massive gray silhouette of Beinn Eighe cut off by low cloud. Dotted here and there were stands of Scots pine, and deciduous trees showing signs of coming autumn. Even the monotonous conifers planted in rows on the surrounding slopes looked mysterious in the dripping air. I wondered where the inhabitants were this Monday morning. One, for sure, was warm beside a fire in Torran-cuilinn. Were others helping hunters to bag a stag in the corries? Or had they all taken a Land Rover to the shops in Kyle?

I walked away from Coulin on a track lined with long piles of lumber. To the extent that I had a plan, it was just to get to the station at Achnashellach, "the field of the willows". I really did not have any other choice. After a mile the track crossed the River Coulin again, this time on a squat arch of black stone. It was another pretty place, even in soaking rain. Farther up the glen

I sat on a rock for lunch. In spite of Katia's approach there was no wind here, and midges soon moved me on. There is just no rest sometimes. The scattered trees in the glen below were Scots pine, remnants of the great Caledonian forest that was felled in the course of millennia to feed husbandry, industry, and war. The Coulin Pass was announced by more dense conifer plantation. The pass was 750 feet above Glen Carron, where the railway and road ran. The descent was going to test my leg, but I took comfort that it would be on good Forestry Commission track, and drawn out over a mile and a half. Then, less than halfway down, there was a notice. It said the track was closed for "harvesting". Walkers should use the "old pony path" instead. It's right here, see, down to the left. I did not like the sound of it. The "lame old codgers' path" would have suited me better. I took a look down, and it reminded me of the South Kaibab Trail into the Grand Canyon, except that this one was muddy and dotted with long ponds of water. "That's all I bloody need, a bloody old pony path," I groused to the assembled trees. But again I had no choice, and began to inch down. After one very bad step, when a sharp pain shot from thigh to inside of knee, I heard the 3:08 to Kyle of Lochalsh rattle past below. With it went one of my options for rescue. The next train was at 7:30. It was a low moment, but not rock bottom yet. The old pony path finally came out at more Forestry Commission track, and the incline eased. I passed a deafening torrent pouring off the hills, the color of strong tea and foaming like bitter beer. Then I emerged onto the A890, just east of Achnashellach.

Edging down the old pony path I had started to confront the real possibility that my adventure was over. There was no question now of hiking on to Camusluinie tomorrow. I would probably not go straight home, I told myself. I could explore on public transport until my leg might carry me again. But that would not add up to walking the length of Scotland, would it? I stopped brooding when I reached the road, and thought instead about what to do right now. My leg did not feel so bad on the level asphalt. I walked to the lane that led to Achnashellach station, and stopped to weigh my options. It was all a bit different from the triumphant departure to Inverness for a day off that I had imagined for this place before Irene set me back. Now the comfort promised by the Strathcarron Hotel became my big incentive. I did not want to wait three hours for the next train. I'd miss dinner if I did. I could have walked to the station to see if there was a phone number for a taxi, but my map showed a climb, and I did not relish the painful walk back down in the event of failure. So I decided to set off on the six and a half miles to Strathcarron. Someone might offer me a ride, though I had to admit that I would not pull over for me—a soaked, mud-speckled, grumpy, middle-aged man.

I had been offered rides without asking for them several times on this trip already, and did not bother to stick out a thumb now. The few cars and lumber trucks on the road mostly whizzed by, but there were places they had to slow down. Here, I tried to look nice, stepping off the road with a smile to let them by. But it was no good. My last fling was an exaggerated limp when I heard a car coming slowly up behind. It sped up, and I resigned myself to walking all the way. I did fine for the first few miles, along the shore of Loch Dùghaill and over the railway crossing at Balnacra. I was fading by the cottages at Coulags, where a shabby old man came out and tipped a bucket of filthy water onto his yard. "Gulags," I thought. Then, where the road passed through forest in a premature dusk, and Katia's rain came on full pelt, I hit rock bottom. I was drained, aching, and wet, and I did not want to be for one moment longer. As I slogged on, hood up and head down, I cursed my sore feet and my aching leg, cursed the rain and the drivers that did not stop, and most of all cursed the whole daft idea of hiking across Scotland.

There was something deliberate about this angry self-pity, as if I knew it was therapy, theater to get me through pain, fatigue, and isolation. I didn't enjoy it, but I suspect it took the place of something worse, of facing up to my inability to do anything at all about this situation except continue to walk joylessly through this bleak evening until I had walked far enough. And, sure enough, when I knew the ordeal was nearly over, the gloom lifted from me as quickly as it was falling on the strath. I walked with the strange sensation that the road ahead was climbing gradually into the distance, although I knew from my map that it was going gently down. On an illusory rise ahead, I saw, at last, the junction to the hotel. I turned left, and walked toward a bridge over the River Carron. Just short of the bridge a camper van came from behind and pulled up beside me. It was left-hand drive. A passenger rolled down her window.

"Hello. Do you want a lift?" she asked with a German accent. I nearly laughed. How welcome this would have been six miles back!

"Thank you, but I am staying at the hotel just over the bridge." I must have looked done in, because the kind frau persevered.

"Let us take you there, please." I had now walked 120 miles from Cape Wrath, the last six only because luck failed to deliver a ride. I wasn't going to throw away that kind of bad luck now and spoil my unblemished walking record.

"Thank you. I'm fine, really." I watched their "D" sticker disappear into the gloom. Then, rounding a bend, the Strathcarron Hotel appeared, a big red Tennent's "T" lit up on its wall. Cold lager, drinking lager. A wilderness bothy could not have looked more welcoming.

I showered quickly and rushed downstairs for dinner as fast as my legs would take me, which is to say sluggishly. There was a fire in the bar, and a couple warming themselves a discreet distance from it. There were diners and drinkers at the tables, and two men playing darts and conversing in a strange tongue. I ordered steak and ale pie, and spoke with the couple at the fire while I waited for it. Paul and Wanda were youthful empty-nesters from upstate New York, cycling the Highlands on a collapsible tandem they brought over on the plane. They were stoic in the face of Scottish weather. Katia was battering the south of Scotland and north of England. There were 80 mph winds down there. In the Highlands she had brought rain, but the Met Office was warning of strong winds in her wake. Paul and Wanda were planning to ride into the teeth of them tomorrow.

I finished my pie and chips. Getting up from the table, I put weight on my bad leg, and winced and staggered. "Have you hurt yourself?" asked a couple sitting nearby. They introduced themselves as Joe and Brid, from Ayrshire, and I told them about my walk from Kinlochewe, leaving out the embarrassing bits. At that point I did not have a plan other than to see how I felt in the morning, and take a train to Inverness or Kyle of Lochalsh if I thought I needed a doctor. Brid said that the staff in the Kyle pharmacy were very helpful, and at once that became my plan. It cheered me up no end that there might be a magic potion from the shelves to sort me out.

The darts players were at breakfast in the morning, still talking in that strange tongue. I had heard enough Gaelic over the years on radio and teach-yourself CDs to know it was not that. But the men seemed native, at home with darts and warm beer. Then they spoke to the owner in English, and I heard their Welsh accents. The railway station was just across the car park from the hotel, and I went over in good time for the morning train. Brid came into the waiting room. She and Joe looked about retirement age, but he was up here on an electrical engineering job. Brid was off to the shops. We spoke about the Welshmen. Brid said that she was originally from Donegal and could understand Gaelic, but not Welsh, from her Donegal Irish. The ride to Kyle took 40 minutes. The train was brightly lit and spotlessly clean, busy with locals and tourists alike. It felt good to be moving without effort for the first time in ten days. I sat at a window and looked at scenes that changed much faster than on my hike. It was like watching a movie on fast forward. We followed the shore of Loch Carron to Plockton, and then ran beside open sea as we neared Kyle. It was a relaxing journey. Nobody yelled into a cellphone. A calm, recorded female voice announced the stops—Attadale, Stromeferry, Duncraig, Plockton, Duirinish. Outside, lambs scattered from the rattling train and cows sauntered on the beach.

Kyle station sits on a pier that sticks out into Kyle Akin, the narrow strait between the mainland and the Isle of Skye. I wasted no time getting to the pharmacy. I didn't know where to look but Kyle is small enough that I ran across it in no time. At the prescriptions counter I explained my predicament. The pharmacist was due to bring forth a new Highlander quite soon. She was briskly helpful, and I walked out with a tube of ibuprofen gel and a thigh support of the sort I associate with rugby. I went immediately to the public toilets to rub the gel in. Then, just in case it worked, I used the call box directly outside to rebook my Camusluinie and Ratagan accommodation for a day later. I had no inclination for tourism today, and limited the rest of my day out to going to the bank, sending e-mail from the post office, and finding lunch. Charissa and I spent a night in Kyle 18 years ago when we were expecting Katie. Our room looked out on the car ferry that shuttled back and forth to Skye. The slipway is redundant now, pink-slipped by the sleek bridge that opened in 1995. Another memory of that visit was being served Chicken Kiev that was cold and raw within, and for some perverse reason I went back to that place for lunch. As I ate, I heard an unfamiliar language again at a nearby table. Kyle is the last mainland village on the only road to Skye. Skye, and indeed the mainland around Kyle, is home to some of

Scotland's larger clusters of Gaelic speakers. This is where you would most expect to hear the language outside its Hebridean strongholds. So I wondered, to explain the unfamiliarity, if Gaelic here might be rather different from the BBC version. Then, as happened at breakfast, an English speaker came to the table, and the tongue was revealed again as Welsh. Is this what it has come to, that in the Highlands (the *Gàidhealtachd*, gaeldom) you are more likely to hear Welsh than Gaelic?

If you had visited the territory of modern Scotland 1,000 years ago, you would have found a Gaelic-speaking world in almost all of it. Only in the far northeast and extreme southeast were other languages dominant. In Shetland and Orkney, and on the northeast tip of the adjacent mainland, Norse reigned. And next door to English Northumbria lay "the land of the English in the Kingdom of the Scots", where Old English was spoken. In the rest of the territory, Gaelic was in the ascendant—from king, lords, and bishops to the humblest in the land. Even in the Hebrides, then ruled by Norse kings, Gaelic was an important tongue, and on the verge of putting Norse into terminal decline. Pictish and British (the ancestor of Welsh) were dead or dying by 1000. Latin was used only by religious and scholarly elites. Gaelic may even have been widely known as a second language in the Old English-speaking southeast.

Gaelic's advance from the western shores facing Ireland in the centuries before 1000 owed much to the prestige of its association with the church and court of Alba, as the Gaels call Scotland. We are told that Malcolm Canmore (King of Scots, 1058-93) translated at court for his English wife, implying that he was a Gaelic-speaker with some command of Old English. The speed and degree with which Malcolm's successors turned their backs on Gaelic is unclear. But in the centuries following his reign, Scotland's kings and ecclesiastics looked increasingly to Europe for inspiration at the expense of the Celtic west. The tide of language turned accordingly in favor of Norman French and English. French arrived in England with the Norman conquest of 1066, and in Scotland with the planting of aristocratic Norman colonists from south of the border by King David I (1124-53). The waning of Gaelic as the language of power would have been gradual and fitful, but the direction was clear. It is likely that Scotland's greatest king, Robert the Bruce, born in Ayrshire in 1274, knew French, English, and Gaelic. William Wallace, the other great patriot of the Wars of Independence, may well have known little Gaelic. As a minor Lowland noble of the late 1200s, he probably spoke English and French.

In *Butcher's Broom*, a novel set in Sutherland in the early 1800s, Neil M. Gunn introduces the language spoken by Dark Mairi, the old healer at the center of his story:

> *"In truth, it is an immensely old tongue, and a thousand years before Mairi it was richer in its knowledge, wider in its range, and was given to metaphysics and affairs of state. The thousand years have slowly pushed it back, have shut it up in the glens ..."*

The next milestone in Gaelic's retreat was this shutting up in the glens, its reduction to a mainly Highland language. To Lowlanders it became no longer *Scottis*, but Erse, Irish, a foreign tongue. The title of *Scottis* was, by the 1500s, reserved for the tongue that had grown out of Old English. I will use "Scots" from now on for the language that took over the Lowlands and confined Gaelic to the remote glens.

We can assume that Lowlanders, over many generations, took up Germanic Scots and gave up Celtic Gaelic because they found Scots the more useful tool. It was more useful because the people and places of power and wealth increasingly used it. The ascent of Scots probably had two main motors, both rooted in the royal preference for European over Celtic influences. David I's practice of installing Anglo-Normans as feudal lords was continued by his heirs, and extended into Gaelic-speaking regions. This happened first in the south of Scotland, and then in areas now centered around towns like Perth, Aberdeen, and Elgin. The "alien friends of the kings" were now increasingly Scots, rather than French, in speech and their use of the language would have hastened its adoption by the wider upper classes, and finally by the common people.

Perhaps more important for the retreat of Gaelic than alien overlords was the growth, with royal encouragement, of burghs— towns with laws and privileges designed to promote trade. None were large but, from Berwick on the English border to Dingwall in the north, they were never Gaelic-speaking. Their merchants and tradesmen were drawn in the 1100s from the Germanic world— Scandinavia, Flanders, England, and those parts of Scotland where Scots was developing. Their citizens would have become users and forgers of the Scots tongue. According to historian T.C. Smout:

> "[T]hese little groups of Teutonic aliens up and down the country ... must have involved the common people in their unfamiliar language for so many of the ordinary economic transactions of life."

It is impossible to put a date on when "involving" common Lowlanders in Scots ended with their total adoption of it. There would have been centuries of bilingualism before Gaelic died out as a Lowland tongue, and Scotland was divided into two language camps. But by 1521 the philosopher John Mair could write that Gaelic was used "by the Wild Scots and the island Scots" but not by the "civilised Scots".

That Gaelic was confined to the Highlands, and the Gael the object of Lowland suspicion and contempt, did not, of course, diminish its importance to the sizeable part of the population that still spoke it, and it alone. As late as the 1700s, a fifth or more of Scots were Gaelic-speaking Highlanders. Even so, their language was already a shrinking asset in the centuries before the Highland catastrophes of the later 1700s; and not just with reference to Scots, but in terms of what Gaelic had once been. The organic development of the language meant it was no longer an easy step from spoken to Classical Gaelic, and therefore to the rich culture shared with Ireland. The absence of a written form of everyday speech fostered illiteracy among Gaels. And as their clan chiefs mastered Scots and later English, they had less interest in supporting Gaelic scholarship anyway. Gaelic was becoming a vernacular of field and hearth.

The Highland catastrophes were the repression after the defeat of the clans at Culloden in 1746, and the Clearances that began roughly 30 years later. The first unleashed the fury of the British state against the Highland way of life. The second hastened economic changes that increasingly sent Gaels to Scots- and English-speaking places, either seasonally or for good. The catastrophes were parts of a single process that saw the Highlands bound more tightly to the rest of Britain, and the end of isolation was inherently bad for Gaelic. Clan chiefs embraced the new order, sending their sons south for an English education. But the Gaels were not always passive victims. The repression after 1746 was undoubtedly brutal and the Clearances often so. And there was a stigma to Gaelic as a root of backwardness, revolt, and unsound religion. But many Gaels grasped the opportunities to migrate, and to learn the language of progress even if they stayed at home. It was often the Gaels themselves who insisted their children be taught in English. The 1901 census counted 230,806 Gaelic-speakers, still half or more of Highlanders. But only 28,106 spoke Gaelic only. English had become an essential tool, and Gaelic was on the verge of becoming exotic even in its own glens.

In the area around Kyle, according to the 2001 census, 20% of the people could speak Gaelic. This was the highest of any area I walked through, but I heard not a snatch. Why would I? One fifth of the population was just a few hundred people scattered over a lot of country. I guessed that even here, the place of its last stand on the mainland, Gaelic must be heard only in private and, as has been said of the Scots language, spoken: "as an underground activity practiced by consenting adults". The public funds that Gaelic has received for 40 years have not reversed its decline. In 2001 there were 58,700 real speakers of Gaelic in all of Scotland. And of those barely more than a quarter lived in communities that were majority Gaelic-speaking. So until, one day, I cross the sea to the Outer Hebrides or take the long road to northwestern Skye, I will have to get by with Radio Nan Gaidheal for a Gaelic fix. Or I might try Wales.

I took the afternoon train back to Strathcarron. Sitting at the window on the other side of the aisle was Mrs. Doubtfire's twin sister. We both dozed, chin on chest. Back in my room I took a shower and ran steaming water over my thigh as long as it lasted. I applied more gel, and waited for it to soak in. Then I put on the support and went downstairs feeling rather rugged. It was a much more comfortable descent than even a few hours before. I trotted through a downpour to the post office-cum-store next to the hotel, mailed home more used-up maps and, with optimism growing, bought what little the store had by way of trail food. I went to the bar again that night. Paul and Wanda were at the fire. They had started to pedal to Applecross but the headwind had been just too strong, and they ended up on a minibus tour instead. Tomorrow, they said, the weather would be better and they would cycle to Skye. I admired Paul and Wanda. I got into a longer chat than last night's with Joe and Brid. Our talk drifted, but was anchored in our travels. They had visited and lived in an amazing number of places. It might have been when I was giving my reasons for this walk that we wandered into family history. Many of my forebears, I said, came to Scotland from Ireland.

"Where in Ireland?" asked Joe, interested.

"County Cavan and ..."

"Ohhh! Stubborn, pig-headed people!" Joe laughed when he said that, as if I had revealed a surprising, even incriminating, secret. The Cavan countryside is where one set of my mother's grandparents lived, before they settled in the Lanarkshire coalfields in the very early 1900s. I knew that Cavan people were considered tight-fisted. Maybe stubbornness is a related virtue.

Joe and Brid made me think of mom and dad again. They were a little younger than my parents had been when they died more than a decade ago. And Joe and Brid lived in Ayrshire, near where mom and dad retired. It was not hard either to imagine my parents—my mother more enthusiastically—befriending a walker in a country hotel. If things really did start to fall apart when I was 11, mom and dad stuck together for 26 more years, resolving nothing, going downhill, till death them did part (mom first, dad a year after). When I thought about my connection to Scotland on the descent to Kylesku a week ago, it occurred to me that there were two parts to it—a connection that my parents gave me, and a later one that I made myself. I would not have been interested in the second if the first had not been rewarding. My parents made it so. As Jackie and I grew up down south, mom and dad neither rammed their homeland down our throats, nor let it altogether vanish. On vacation, they took us with them to the top of a ben or two, or to paddle a loch or fish a firth. We stayed in island cottages, went to the towns where our relatives lived, toured a battlefield, played in a castle. We could make of this what we wanted. For me the planted seeds sprouted. If I try, I can imagine how my life might have been better if my parents had been happier; but the tragedy was theirs much more than mine, and they never made me feel a cause of it, or inconsequential beside it. So when events on this journey made me think of them, it was a peaceful meeting. I liked what first they had helped me to see, and felt sure they would have understood what I was doing here now.

# 9

# *Willie's Nubble*

My leg was feeling better, and I decided to test it on the 11-mile walk to Camusluinie. At breakfast, the sun peeped through the clouds outside. "What's that?" someone asked, pointing at the alien glow. I put on my waterproof pants but, in hopeful mood, left my rain jacket off. The hills north of Loch Carron were lit by sun, but in the east, rain blew across the strath. The day might turn either way. I crossed the railway, and set off along the A890 toward Attadale, a name on my map where a half-dozen buildings were shown scattered on flat land where a river came down to the loch. The road—two lanes, scant traffic—hugged the railway and the strath floor for a mile, then went sharply up and down. My leg accomplished the descent without pain, and my hope grew. It helped, too, that my pack was sitting more comfortably on my back. It was a new purchase for this journey, and in the hotel I had found previously unnoticed straps to adjust.

Inevitably, a shower caught up with me. It did so at the entrance to a driveway signposted to Attadale Gardens. I stopped to cover my pack and put my jacket on. It was, anyway, where I needed to leave the road. But I lingered. Although I wanted very much to keep going, to see how far my leg would take me, I was also reluctant to cut myself off from the warmth and encouragement I'd found at the hotel. I hoped now to see Paul and Wanda pedal past on their way to Skye, and dallied in the hope of a wave. But when they did not show, I turned onto the driveway. My track into the hills began somewhere behind the gardens, but I could not see where. The Japanese garden, the conservatory, and other points of horticultural interest were well signposted, but not the track. I saw a man playing with his child outside a cottage.

"Excuse me! Do you know where the path up the river starts from?"

"No. Sorry pal. I'm from Edinburgh."

So I was left to work it out for myself, which wasn't too hard in the end. I found a broad, flat track that followed the edge of the floodplain of the River Attadale. I stopped a few minutes along it and looked over the rough fields of the little plain, and across two miles of Loch Carron to the village on its far shore. Rough hills rose behind the village and, yet farther behind, massive, dark bens barely showed through mist and rain. I swung over the river and climbed gradually into the lower hills before me. Somewhere on the climb, on the edge of a forest and flush with optimism, I stood my pack in the middle of the track, placed my camera on it, and took the first of a very few self-portraits on this journey. There I am in my black waterproof pants and blue Gore-Tex jacket. My watch is visible at the end of a sleeve. By then a permanent ring of moisture lay beneath its glass. On my head—damp from sweat and showers—is the faded blue baseball cap that I wore every walking day. My optimism came from my functioning leg, but also from a steady waning of my fear of defeat since my first days out.

The going *had* become tough. At those times of greatest discomfort, I knew my family and home were a snap decision and an easy journey away. But I had never seriously considered jacking it in, and my optimism now came from greater sureness of my resolve as well as my physical recuperation.

The track veered into a misty, eerie forest and came to a junction with a weathered sign. The sign pointed to Killilan, the next hamlet on my route. But there was also a track to Loch an Iasaich, and I had read that this loch was beautiful. I could have lunch there, I thought. It would mean a short climb and—importantly—a descent on the way back. I hesitated. I did not want to take my leg for granted, but in the end could not resist the lure of a loch high in the hills. It was worth the gamble. The conifers that wrapped half its shore gave the scene a Great North Woods feel; but the south side was pure Scotland—bare, green, craggy. I left my pack and walked over sodden, hummocky ground among spindly pines to the water's edge, and felt twinges in my leg as I did so. They did not feel ominous. I was back at my pack and rummaging for lunch when I was surprised by voices. They belonged to a retired couple. "Every day is a Saturday!" he said. I told them I was going to the bunkhouse in Camusluinie. "That must be Willie Nicolson's place," she answered, adding they were not going that way themselves today because the path would be very wet. I became anxious about the task ahead.

The path to Killilan was indeed wet, and narrow and rutted also. The rain was more on than off. On the descent into Glen Ling a herd of deer took flight below me, the same color as the hillside and moving over it seemingly without effort. The showers created an ever-changing scene, as hills were revealed and covered up again, lit then plunged into gloom. There were power lines in the glen. They detracted from the view but, shut them out, and the valley of the powerful River Ling was very beautiful. Every pore of the land was leaching water. The waterfalls, in particular, were spectacular, pouring off Ben Killilan on the far side of the glen. They were unsung too; no well-marked trail leading up to them, no fenced-in viewing decks, no names on my map.

I followed the drive of Nonach Lodge down to a single-track road. Patches of brilliant blue appeared in the otherwise turbulent sky. At the road, a woman and dog were returning to their car. We said hello, the woman and I. As I started up the road toward Glen Elchaig and Camusluinie, she called after me as if she had just remembered a very important message; "Tomorrow the weather will be good!" Soon the road crossed the River Ling on a metal bridge, and turned sharp right for Camusluinie. But my map showed a public phone among the buildings of Killilan, straight ahead. I wanted to call home and say my leg had done well. It would mean a detour, but there was no cell coverage, and I doubted there would be in Camusluinie either. At the start of the road to Killilan there was a bench set on an immaculate bed of gravel. In fact, everything here was immaculate—the white wooden fence, the low stone wall around the pebbled parking spaces, the maroon sign that said all this was the Inverinate Estate. I left my pack unguarded at the bench and walked the half-mile to Killilan. The idea of theft here was absurd. The phone worked, of course. The place was deserted.

The road into Glen Elchaig was lined with straggly trees, which yielded briefly to reveal a band of rain closing like a lace curtain across a mountain called Carnan Cruithneachd. A few twists of the lane later, and I came to Camusluinie; or Camas-Luinie as the roadside sign preferred. As to pronunciation, I had been saying Camus-LOONEY to myself until the retired couple at the loch corrected me. It was, they said, Camus-LINEY, although their outsiders' accents cast doubt on their authority. The name means "ship bay", intriguingly for a place two full miles from the end of a five-mile sea loch. The briny must have retreated over the centuries. A handmade sign—"Enquiries for Bunkhouse"—pointed to the first house. On the porch, I found a beautiful collie, and another handwritten sign: "Bunkhouse 200m at end of road. Back 6pm".

At the bunkhouse, there was yet another message. It told me to enter and get comfortable. The main building was a solid cottage of whitewashed stone, but there was a jerry-built extension between the cottage and a big adjoining shed. The extension contained a fridge and clotheslines, and was roofed with clear, corrugated plastic. Rain drummed on the plastic, creating a soothing place to hang out. In the cottage, on the ground floor, were a bedroom, living room, bathroom, and kitchen. At the foot of rickety steps up to the loft, there was an iron stove. I climbed to the low-ceilinged loft, lay on a bed in my sleeping bag, and tried not to doze. I'd had company now every evening since Shenavall, and was hoping to have this place to myself. I was back under the plastic roof when Willie came by, collie at his side. Willie was stocky, energetic, and open, about my age. I liked him immediately. He told me I would be alone. A hiking group had booked, but had run into floods a few days south.

Willie then helped me with my onward route. I was weighing three options to get to Ratagan tomorrow. A big circle via the Falls of Glomach would likely be the most scenic, but I was worried that the climb shown on the map beside the falls would be precarious after rain and injury. I had more or less ruled out this route already. Option two was to walk toward the falls but cross the River Elchaig before reaching them, and then go over the hills on a gentler-looking path. This was my favored option. The map showed a footpath crossing the river, but Willie pointed something out that I had not considered—there was no bridge! The river would be in flood, and very likely this option would have turned into a seven-mile wild goose chase. The third option was to climb into the hills right here behind Camusluinie, and Willie agreed that this was the easiest of the paths to Loch Duich and Ratagan. He suggested we go outside so he could point the way.

"Do you see that nubble up there in the saddle?" he asked. I squinted and did, just. It was a tiny pimple on a long ridgeline.

"Aim for that. Just make sure you stay to the right of the burn. Oh, and the path is not good."

"You don't say," I thought. With "Willie's Nubble" now named ineradicably in my mental atlas, we went back inside to light the stove. Before he stooped down with his matches, Willie delved into his pocket and, like a magician, produced a white egg which he held in front of me.

"I brought this for your breakfast."

"That's very kind, Willie, but I'm afraid I don't eat eggs," I said, feeling real regret.

"Never mind, but tell you what, I'll just put it here while I light the stove. Don't want to crack it in my pocket now, do I?", and he placed it gently on the kitchen counter.

I spent an evening of complete contentment on a straight-backed chair by the stove, feeding it logs from time to time. There was a lattice screen around the stove, and I tied my boots to it by their laces, and hung my socks, gloves, and cap to dry too. The cottage was soon so warm that I even took out my tent for the first time since Inchnadamph, and hung it to make sure it was bone dry. I had a supper of Old El Paso tortillas with Shippam's crab spread. I had carried the little jar of spread all the way from Inverness. For some reason, when meals were chosen, it was always left behind. It was surprisingly good. I made tea from bags left in the kitchen, and drank it black. Willie came in briefly to feed the stove some more, bringing the sound of outside with him. It sounded like pouring rain.

Reveling in my solitude, I wondered why being alone felt so natural and comfortable. For 12 days now I had been apart from people far more than with them, and each morning when I started out it never occurred to me to be bothered that I might have only the most fleeting company all day—or none. I had fallen into the company of strangers, of course. This had been no "into the wild" journey. I was seldom more than a half-day's march from somewhere where somebody would shoot the breeze with me. Nonetheless, it had been a lot of time alone that did not turn into loneliness. I tried to think what loneliness was. I knew it was not the same as solitariness. I remembered times in my life when I might have said I was lonely, and there had always been people about, but they were people I had never got to know, or people I knew but did not feel close to at that moment. Loneliness, I decided now, was wanting to connect with people—wanting their understanding—but being unable to do so. It can happen in the wild or in the hubbub of a home; it can last a lifetime, or half an hour. I wasn't lonely when I was alone on this walk because I did not want to connect or because I was never truly disconnected. The next pub had never felt too far off, and strangely enough neither had my loved ones. I knew where they were, what they would be doing, and that we were firm. You carry your relationships with you on a solo trek as surely as you tote your pack. But the relationships become less intense and urgent, and there are benefits to that. Being around loved ones is comforting and mostly rewarding. But it is also demanding—sensing needs, decoding words, remembering promises, being heard, coordinating action. Solitude is a holiday from all that.

It was an unambiguously fine morning that I saw framed in the skylight when I opened my eyes, the first such encouragement for 11 days. Briskly, I rubbed gel into my thigh and loaded my pack. I put on my dry cap and footwear at the cold stove, and set off up the track through the cottages of Camusluinie in search of the path to Willie's Nubble. I walked right past the start of it, and only noticed the homemade "Footpath to Dornie" sign when I came back scratching my head. It soon became clear that Willie was dead right, and this was another path that really existed only as a dashed line on the map. At most there was the faintest trace of a line now and then in the wet bracken, heather, and coarse grass. I adopted the tactics I had honed beneath Bealach na Croise, setting my sights on Willie's Nubble while choosing intermediate features to target—a heathery mound, a stunted birch, a patch of ferns. It was steep, arduous going, and I stopped often to look down into Glen Elchaig. Its slopes were dark still, but trees on the glen floor cast shadows onto bright green fields. A sunlit layer of mist hovered above the fields, slowly rising. I was above this mist already, after climbing a few hundred feet. The moon was out, faint in the blue sky. On the southern slopes of the glen, across the burn that Willie had told me to cross at my peril, tumbled Eas Ban, the "white falls". I reached the Nubble about 9:00. It turned out to be a ruined, heather-clad wall at a crossroads of footpaths. It was 650 feet above the glen floor, and I could now see the layer of mist stretching as far as a bend in the glen where both mist and glen vanished behind a dark mountainside. The air was calm at the Nubble, and a few midges were out, but I refused to be moved on until I was ready.

I turned south toward a 1,700-foot bealach, by some margin the highest point yet on my walk. On the ascent, on a moor without cover, I needed—and I will try to be delicate—to do a number two; unseemly to mention, but it is a part of hiking as unavoidable and recurring as using a compass. I found a secluded spot, well away from surface water. I had not seen anyone all morning, and did not much fear for my privacy. My business done, I buried it with the plastic trowel I carried, and washed my hands in a rock puddle. As far as the bealach, the scene—appreciated from a walking or squatting stance—was finest to the north. The mist rising out of Glen Elchaig was dissipating on the tawny moor, and far-off peaks rose behind this flimsiest of veils. The peaks were, for once, sharply defined. I could not be sure which mountains they were, but thought I was looking at least as far as Beinn Eighe, 20 miles back. At the bealach, views to the south opened up, and I saw the toothy peaks and ridges of bens Sgritheall and na h-Eaglaise beyond the hidden trench of Loch Duich, in which lay Ratagan.

The descent from the bealach was very steep at first, 700 feet in under a mile. It ended at an overgrown ruin, a shepherd's hut most likely. I rested there, and then followed the path along another piece of unsung nature. This afternoon it was an *allt*, a stream, full of rapids, chasms, and waterfalls, and lined with 1,000-foot cliffs. The day was now so bright and warm that I thought of rummaging in my pack for sunscreen. The change of weather brought to mind Davie and Alan in *Kidnapped*, roasting on a rock as they hid from the redcoats:

*"... and it ran in my mind how strange it was, that in the same climate and at only a few days' distance, I should have suffered so cruelly, first from cold upon my island and now from heat upon this rock".*

Aye, Davie lad, I know what you mean.

The path was crossed now by burn after burn, all small enough to cross shod. At one I sat on a rock and washed and chilled my feet anyway. I had seen nobody since Willie. But then I saw Loch Duich far below, as blue as the Mediterranean, and knew I'd soon return to a busier world. It is a sea loch, best known for the picture postcard castle of Eilean Donan at its entrance. I would walk some way around Loch Duich on a bigger road than any I had tramped so far. The descent had been hard on my leg. It would have been hard on an old pony, but I still felt in much better shape than back at Achnashellach.

# 10

## *Shore Leave*

M y map showed a string of buildings called Inverinate along the loch. It was lunchtime, and I hoped the village would sell me a sandwich and ice-cold drink. I was walking now on the A87, stepping off it now and then to get out of the way of the big buses speeding to Eilean Donan, Kyle, and Skye. The map also showed a lane leading off the main road to follow the loch-side through the village. So I passed up the shop in the gas station in the hope of finding something nicer later on. I didn't. In fact, I didn't even find Inverinate. The lane did not show itself, and I continued to plod along the A87. It was, mercifully, shady. Glimpses of ben and loch hinted at majestic scenery behind the screening trees. Buses aside, the traffic was about as heavy as on a Connecticut country road. At the head of the loch there was a causeway and bridge. Here the shade vanished and the scenery appeared. I looked over to Ratagan on the far shore, a tiny hamlet against the hills. My feet were sore after the miles on tarmac, and

I thought only how far-off it looked. At Shiel Bridge, I came to the turn for Ratagan. As much as I wanted only to get my boots and pack off, this final stretch proved enjoyable, a quiet lane between stone walls beside the Loch Duich foreshore. It was, said Ordnance Survey, an "Old Military Road".

I turned off the old military road to follow the lochside into Ratagan, but the road continues to the village of Glenelg on the strait between the mainland and the Isle of Skye. The road was built in the 1750s to connect the government garrison at Fort Augustus to barracks at Glenelg. Its construction was not an isolated project. In 1715, and again in 1719, the Jacobite clans[32] had risen up in support of the exiled House of Stuart. The 1719 revolt was extinguished at the Battle of Glenshiel, just inland from here. Unsurprisingly, the London government came to view the Highlands as barbarous and dangerous, a grave threat to the young Kingdom of Great Britain; and from the 1720s it built roads, bridges, and barracks to watch and cow the clans. The infrastructure did not prevent the uprising of 1745. Indeed, Charles Edward Stuart (the romantic "Bonnie Prince Charlie") used the roads to speed the southern advance of his Highland army. The military road to Glenelg was built only after Charlie's defeat at Culloden. Nobody knew at the time that the battle had marked the end of the armed Jacobite cause.

At my English secondary school in the 1970s, we were taught English history. The history of Britain's "Celtic fringe" came up only when it impolitely invaded the grand narrative. Even for history after the creation of the United Kingdom, our texts for the doings of the UK government had titles like "England, 1870-1914" and "English History". Since the Irish, by the 19th and 20th centuries anyway, were better at forcing themselves into English history than the by-then-accommodated Scots, I learned far more about Ireland than Scotland. We were taught American and European history too. I am not complaining, I liked any history. But the separateness of the English and Scottish education systems, even back in the 1970s when the UK had only one parliament and government, meant that I stayed almost totally ignorant of the story of my own birthland. When I left Oxford with a history degree, I knew more about events in Constantinople and Concord than anything that had ever happened in Scotland. The point here is to preface my explanation of why this narrative gets sidetracked with stories like that of the Old Military Road to Glenelg. When I began to explore Scotland for myself in my 30s, my interests meant that I set about its history as well as its landscapes and cities. At the end of vacations, I bought history books in Glasgow and read them in faraway places. I had picked up scraps of Scottish history, of course, more from my mom and dad than my teachers—Robert the Bruce was inspired to fight on by a spider[33]; Mary Queen of Scots lost her head; Campbells massacred MacDonalds at a place called Glencoe; and the Bonnie Prince fled to Skye dressed as an Irish maid. It was like owning a handful of intriguing jigsaw puzzle pieces. Then, as I read my books, I saw how big and colorful the puzzle of Scottish history was, and all the more compelling for being a part of my heritage that, like photographs of ancestors discovered in an attic, had remained hidden for so long. So now, as I stumbled upon history as I hiked—an emptied landscape, an enigmatic place-name, an old military road—I felt for the first time that I could put these pieces in their right places.

The Ratagan hostel boasted a lovely setting, which I took in as I changed my boots and socks in the lochside garden, waiting for the door to open at 5:00. The midges enjoying the evening calm made it a fidgety wait. But they couldn't stop me ogling the Five Sisters of Kintail, across a corner of Loch Duich. The shapely sisters are peaks on a spiky ridge that winds inland from the head of the loch. I could see the Kintail Lodge Hotel across the water too. I liked the idea of something with chips and beer very much, but I decided that the four-mile roundtrip would outweigh any reward. So I bought a frozen pizza at the hostel reception and headed for the kitchen. There, and in the dining room, I discovered that my fellow-hostellers were a dull lot. I tried to chat, but the groups had circled the wagons, and the singles replied monosyllabically without making eye contact. One guy seemed so irritated by my presence that I wondered if by mistake I had walked into his home, showered in his bathroom, and was now cooking in his kitchen. An early night was an easy decision.

Before I went to bed, I thought over my next steps. I would head out again on Saturday, having paid for two nights here before my involuntary day off in Strathcarron. I could have pressed on tomorrow anyway, but decided another day off might be good for my leg. It was, of course, a lame excuse. Fort William was now 30 miles southeast as the hooded crow flies, but it was not obvious how to get there on foot. My "right to roam" meant there were plenty of options. The constraints were my safety and capacity for hardship. Willie had told me about the party that ran into flood trouble in this area. The weather forecast was neither good nor awful, but I had to assume that fords would be swollen. Most topography in this part of the Highlands runs east-west, the mountain ranges and elongated lochs making for awkward north-south routes. The glens are east-west too, and many have single-track roads along them. Finally, I did not know of any lodging at all in the country between the A87 (running east from here) and the A830 parallel to it 20 miles south. My inclination now was to reach better trails along the Great Glen[34] by going east, rather than go south into the remotest country. I did not reach a conclusion before bed.

Bed demonstrated some of the inconveniences of hostelling. As in Inverness on my first night in Scotland, the dormitory filled up after I turned in, and there were lights going on and off, murmurings, and shufflings of gear as I tried to sleep. Then the room grew clammy, and full of the snorts and wheezes of a dozen men sleeping fitfully. I woke early and wanted only to get out into fresh air. So I went to the loch to gaze upon the awakening Sisters. Broken gray cloud, tinged pink underneath by the sun rising behind the peaks, was reflected in the gray, rippled surface of the loch. Maybe this inspired me, because within minutes I had everything sorted out. From Achnashellach I had been going to walk south to Glen Affric but, under threat from Katia, took a westerly line. Now I would hike into Glen Affric from the west, and stay at the SYHA's remotest hostel on the final weekend of its season. I would then hike south to the Cluanie Inn on the A87. This would put me within a day's road-walk of marked and maintained trails in the Great Glen if it came to that. Now I wanted to see an otter.

There was a whiteboard in the hostel where people had noted their sightings of wildlife. Otters figured prominently. But there was another reason to think they might be here. Not far around the coast was Sandaig Bay. There, in 1959, naturalist Gavin Maxwell wrote *Ring of Bright Water*. I saw the movie of his book when I was about ten. The story was simple. Graham buys an otter in a London pet shop, names him Mij, and takes him to Camusfeàrna (as Maxwell calls Sandaig in the book). There, Mij plays, wanders, and meets wild otters. Graham meets the village doctor, played by Virginia McKenna. Like everyone who has seen the movie, I remember its sad, sad end. The stories in the book are different and richer. I find it hard not to envy Maxwell; not his friendships with animals; nor, of course, his depression, secret homosexuality, and premature death. What I envy is his time at Sandaig, and the naturalist's knowledge and poet's eye he brought to its wonders. For me, the best chapters of *Ring of Bright Water* are the first, before he brings Mijbil back to Britain from a journey to Iraq (the pet shop was an invention of the movie). He writes about arriving at "Camusfeàrna" for the first time, at a "landscape and seascape of such beauty that I had no room for it all at once".

He was, happily, to have ten years to find room for it before *Ring of Bright Water* was published. All around him were various and beautiful worlds, ever-changing by season and weather. They were to be found in and beside his burn; around the rocky bay; on rough islands with white-sand beaches; in the immense sea, sky, and hills. I envy Maxwell his ability to observe and describe the micro-worlds that most of us, even walkers, overlook as we hurry to our next destination. I envy his "long familiarity [with Sandaig] in which every lichen-covered rock and rowan tree show known and reassuring faces."

I did not see an otter, so I went inside and booked the Glen Affric hostel at reception, and called the Cluanie Inn to book there too. Then I came out again to wait by the road for the bus to Kyle of Lochalsh. It turned out to be a minibus, arriving from Glenelg (or, if anybody had called for it ahead of time, from even farther around the coast, beyond "Camusfeàrna"). It was full of old ladies with shopping bags, and one sick-looking old man. It seemed to be the shopping and health center run, returning to the villages after two hours in Kyle. It was the only bus of the day. The journey took 30 minutes, with swings off the main road here and there to pick up more old dears in villages along the way. On Tuesday I rode the train 18 miles to Kyle from the northeast. Today we arrived on Station Road after the same distance from the southeast. The ill-looking man and his wife went directly into the health center. I saw them later around the shops, smiling hand-in-hand. Good news, I hoped.

I had a late breakfast at a café called Hector's Bothy. It was next door to Hector's Plaice (fish & chips), and a stone's throw from Hector's 2 Go (more take-out). Then I went down to the water, stared across the half-mile strait to Skye, and began to kill time. To the west, the shore was dominated by the flattened hump of the Skye Bridge and, closer in, the elegant white bulk of the Lochalsh Hotel. East, the prominent buildings were the lifeboat station and health center. The sign on the wall of the latter said "Lochalsh Healthcare Centre—Ionad Cùram-slàinte Loch Aills". "Slàinte" is a rare Gaelic word widely known by non-speakers. "Slàinte mhath!" means "Cheers!"; or more exactly, "good health". Outside the lifeboat post there were little palm trees, evidence that winter here on the coast is not as frosty as you would expect of a place on the latitude of the Alaska Panhandle.

Kyle gets tourists but has a workaday feel. There is a prominent gasholder, and railway tracks, containers, warehouses. I liked this about it. Tourists and yachties are just one part of the scene. I went to the library after lunch to use a computer. At first, the assistant was standoffish, but after I read my mail, I offered a modest contribution in return for the free service. She positively melted but said there was absolutely nowhere they could put my money. So I whirled around the Co-op with extra coins in my pocket. I bought food for the trails ahead, and a cottage pie to heat up tonight. I went back to the pharmacy for more gel. By now, the minibus back to Ratagan was long gone, and I would need to catch a Glasgow bus and get off at Shiel Bridge. But first I needed a pee. No sketch of Kyle would be complete without mentioning its public convenience. It is, quite simply, the best I have ever used. There is an attendant to give you change, the 20 pence it costs for the privilege of entering. And the facilities are more than just spotless fixtures. The place is filled with so much stuff, both useful and merely decorative, that it should count as an information center, library, art gallery, and greenhouse too. If the whisky bottles contained anything, it would be a pub as well. I do hope the Ladies is just as interesting.

The big, shiny intercity bus seemed to reach Shiel Bridge in no time. Yesterday it took me hours to walk a quarter of the same route. The bus stopped only at Eilean Donan castle, where a young American couple climbed on board, self-consciously goofy in Andean-style woolen hats—all flaps, tassels, and color. When the bus put me down at Shiel Bridge and roared off, my world went suddenly quiet, and remained so on the walk between the stone walls and beside the loch. At the hostel, everything was much nicer than last night. Prickly characters had moved on, and the new arrivals were sociable. I had met two of them in the morning. They'd arrived in the middle of the night, slept in their car, and were just then checking in. They were munro-baggers from the north of England, 50-somethings. When one was out of earshot, the other turned to me:

"Great bloke, but completely scatterbrained. Left his camera up in the hills yesterday. I waited while he went back to look for it. Then I heard him shout. He was waist deep in mud when I got to him. Said he'd seen a footprint on it so thought it was OK. I said to him, 'Doesn't matter. Always use your poles'. Barmy." It was funny, because up near the bealach yesterday I had thought about quicksand, provoked by some very soupy mud beside the trail. The barmy bagger must have walked into something similar. I made a mental note to watch my step when I hiked on. The lighter atmosphere in the hostel tonight allowed me to enjoy doing my laundry, and hanging out in the kitchen while my cottage pie—or random bits of it—heated in the microwave. Then I took a glass of wine and my maps into the lounge, and sat in one of the few unoccupied chairs. I was soon in conversation with a Dutchwoman and a Scotsman. I shall call the Scot Ben. It is not his real name.

It was not long before the Dutchwoman dropped out of the conversation, nor much longer before I, as an equal participant, did so too. Ben was a talker more than a conversationalist. At one level, he was good company, and he knew his Scottish outdoors. But there was a hard edge to his talk that hinted at violence beneath the surface. He was in early middle age, lean, and muscled; and he liked to tell stories with a Braveheart theme. I said something to him about the Letterewe Estate and Paul van Vlissingen. Ben said he once had a run in with him, and told me a story that ended in stirring dialog:

"This is my land," said Ben's van Vlissingen.

"Aye, but it's my country!" said Ben. Ben's next story was his best. A couple were out enjoying the Falls of Glomach. The husband took a risk to get a good picture, and fell into the ravine. His wife called 999 on her cell. When emergency vehicles came onto the Inverinate Estate, the track to the falls was blocked by a locked gate and an estate official. The police told the official to open the gate, but he refused. The landowner, he said, had instructed him to keep it locked at all times. The landowner was an Arab sheikh. The official was arrested, and the emergency services broke through the gate and rescued the injured man. Then the sheikh decided that his official would be defended in court by a top English lawyer. When the case came up, the Scottish magistrate refused to recognize the English lawyer's credentials to work in his court. The official was fined, and sternly warned that next time he would go to prison. It was rousing stuff again, egalitarian and nationalist. The only problem is that I can find no evidence that it ever happened. It is true that the Inverinate Estate is owned by the ruler of Dubai. Also true is that Scotland's legal system is different from England's, but a top English lawyer might be expected to know that, and not waltz willy-nilly into a Scottish court.

I went into the kitchen to refill my glass. Ben came with me and poured brandy into his coffee mug. We went back to the lounge, to more stories of confrontation. This time Ben parked his car and started to walk onto an estate. A gamekeeper stopped him, saying that the estate was closed off. Ben said he was going anyway.

"Is that your car?" asked the gamekeeper. Ben took this as a threat.

"Aye. Is that your house?" Ben replied.

"Are you threatening me?" said the gamekeeper.

"What I'm saying to you is, if anything happens to my car, I'll burn down your wee house." Ben relished these last words so much that he carefully repeated them.

"I'll burn down your wee house with you in it!" He had gone too far for me now. No longer amused, I was uncomfortable with his intensity, and the growing violence of his speech. He was not drunk, but more brandy was only going to fuel the fantasies. So we said good night amicably, and I went up to my dormitory, relieved that Ben was sleeping in another.

# 11

# Glen Affric

I had to retrace three miles of Thursday's steps, back to the causeway on the A87 at the eastern end of Loch Duich. I didn't mind. It was a bright Saturday morning with no sign of the forecast showers. Where the Old Military Road neared Shiel Bridge, I startled a group of horses in a quagmire of a field behind a low stone wall, and they splashed in knee-deep muddy water to escape me. I reached the causeway at the Jac-o-bite restaurant. Had the Jac-o-bite been open, I would have gone in for a bacon roll, but also on account of its droll name. The next mile and a half followed a single-track road, first beside foreshore, then on the flat bottom of Strath Croe. I rested my pack on a bridge parapet among the cottages of Allt a' chruinn and started breakfast with an apple. When the tarmac ended against the hills, I added a pork pie beside the River Croe. Then I crossed the river on a wooden bridge and searched for my trail. It shared a trailhead with the southern route to the popular Falls of Glomach, but there was no sign or information board, just planks laid across a ditch beside a child's swing dangling from a tree. I was left with a nagging doubt that this was the right way until, farther on, landscape unequivocally matched map.

The path was narrow, but distinct; gravelly wet, not muddy. I felt strong, and the unfolding landscape invigorated me farther. The path climbed a short distance, and I stopped to look around. Back, the way I had come, stood Ratagan, tiny across Loch Duich, itself now just a sliver of mirror-flat water under furrowed mountains. Ahead stood A' Ghlas-bheinn, to no great surprise "the gray-green mountain". Massive rocky gashes ran down its side. My route to Bealach an Sgàirne, and Glen Affric beyond, was still hidden by the base of a close-up hill. But as I worked around this spur, Gleann Choinneachain, thrown in shadow by the 3,000-foot bens surrounding it, began to show itself. The path wound up the glen's south side, keeping a good height on a steep slope above the burn coursing below. Here I stepped off the path to allow three fast-moving climbers to pass. They were heading for the summit of A' Ghlas-bheinn, and soon were distant figures at the top of the glen, dwarfed by the bulk of a "lumpish hill".

Soon, looking across to the north side of the glen, I saw a tight green gorge rising between crags. I thought how wild it looked and, simultaneously, that Bealach an Sgàirne too must soon show itself ahead of me. I came to a burn pouring off high, rocky peaks, but still did not see the bealach where I expected it to be. I studied my map and realized to my delight that the tight green gorge was the entrance to the pass. Under harassing fire from midges, I found a place where a combination of stepping-stones and leaps got me over the burn, landing on a green slope beneath Meall a' Bhealaich, the lump that had dwarfed the climbers. It was a half-hour's ascent from there to the top of the pass, counting stops to gape and take in a breath. Bealach an Sgàirne was more dramatic than the pass after Willie's Nubble, though both stand at 1,700 feet. Here, the trail rose between slopes of grass and scree that encroached ever closer. I half expected to be ambushed by desperados. The summit was marvelously atmospheric, another frontier; to the west, the craggy gorge; to the east, a loch and softer glens.

Two weeks ago I was trying to follow the cliffs south from Cape Wrath, opposed by burns and geos. I had walked 150 miles since, in ten walking days. The journey so far had fulfilled my hopes, mainly by taking on the flavor of an adventure, unpredictable and tricky. The weather had been the great disrupter, throwing me off routes and out of my tent. I had not expected endless sunshine, of course; but the sheer persistence of storm and murk had surprised me. It was not of no consequence, a trifle overcome with the right gear and attitude. At times, sunshine and a dry wind would have made all the difference. But I still felt amply rewarded by what I had seen and felt, and fine weather is not always pure gain. Would I still have had Shenavall to myself? Would I have seen curtains of rain closing over the hills? My injuries too had thrown up challenge and uncertainty, but I seemed to have come through them too. Feeling stronger than ever, I made ready to push on. A lone hiker came up from Glen Affric. Richard was a young Slovakian, crossing Scotland too, though east-west. He warned me that the path into Glen Affric was wet and muddy, *very wet and very muddy*. He had gone in up to his waist! I delivered the better news about his onward trail. But that made two warnings now about ending up in goo. It wasn't going to happen to me!

I acquired, quite recently, a certain fascination with Glen Affric. Up until then it had not been on my mental map of Scotland at all. Strictly, I would barely touch it on this journey, reaching the River Affric just a little before tonight's accommodation, and leaving the glen again in the morning when I hiked south. But that is just a nicety of labeling. The glen and *allt* I would follow this afternoon both descend to join Glen Affric, forming part of a single tree of glens stretching from Bealach an Sgàirne to the village of Cannich 22 miles east. My fascination was in part about the glen's remoteness. It is little known outside Scottish outdoor circles, an overlooked tract away from the main travel routes. The glen is also substantially tarmac-free. I would walk today on road-less moor for 8.5 miles from the trailhead to the hostel. If I were not turning south tomorrow, I would walk the same distance east just to meet the single-track road that leads ten miles into the glen from Cannich. Another part of my infatuation was Glen Affric's beauty. I had seen its eastern half this past summer with my youngest daughter—green, watery wilds, bare but for one wood of Scots pine. Despite the beauty of the many glens I had hiked since Cape Wrath, none had sapped my wish to see this one again.

On the foot-wide path down from the bealach, the attributes of the scenery ahead were indeed greenness and utter treelessness. The green was pale where the sun reached, dark where shadow was cast. The descent was shorter than the climb up, and the path leveled out still 1,300 feet above sea level. Here, at an imperceptible divide between glens heading north and east, was Loch a' Bhealaich—black, gray, silver, or blue depending on the whim of the light. I will guess that its name means "loch of the pass", as Meall a' Bhealaich, throwing its darkness over the loch's surface, is the "lump of the pass". The walk around the loch was squelchy, and I tried not to follow in Richard's visible and treacherous footsteps. Indeed, that whole afternoon's walk was slowed by an elusive trail and waterlogged ground. I had thought Richard's warning overdone. I changed my tune when I slipped, staying upright only with an outlandish song and dance routine that would have looked very comical to an observer—all flailing limbs and poles, and shouts of alarm. But there were no onlookers, not even a sheep in this nature reserve. This was the wilder, mountain end of the glen, shut

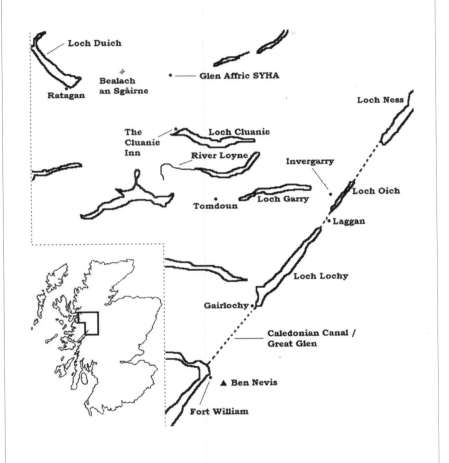

Map 3: Ratagan to Fort William

in by *sgurr*, ben, and *stob*, and I was happy to go slow. The weather was fair, sunny even. A solitary shower hovered down the glen, so slender that it looked to be in pursuit of a single victim to soak.

As I walked, I tried to imagine what this land looked like in centuries past. One thing was certain, it had not looked forever as it did now. Today's "wild" landscape owes much to human activity. There is evidence of human settlement in Glen Affric going back 4,000 years at least. I imagined the great Caledonian Forest going far up the slopes of the bens, and wondered if farmers millennia ago had made clearings in the Scots pines to plant oats and barley. Or was the climate here always too wet and the soil too poor for even those hardy grains? By the 1400s the glen was occupied by Clan Chisholm. Did they clear more forest to graze the cattle that were the center of the Highland economy? How many homes dotted this now deserted glen? We know more about what happened next. The Chisholms themselves began to sell the pines for timber and charcoal. Then, by the mid-1800s, the clan and their cattle had made way for 30,000 sheep. These sheep, and the sport deer that followed them, made sure the pinewoods did not return. It is tempting to roam the Highlands today and fancy them a wilderness, but we walk among ghosts, and are lucky that what they have bequeathed us is still beautiful.

I could see the widening out of the glen from some way off, the flat place where the River Affric is made from the burns of three branch glens, and Glen Affric proper begins. Then, at last, I saw the red and orange roofs of the SYHA huts too, insignificant at the fold between floodplain and steep slope. My path dropped down to the river, became a good track, and at 5:00 I pushed open the porch door of the hostel's main hut. I was met by a young chap in slippers, who said he was Colin, the warden. I was taking my boots off.

"Before you do that, you might want to take your stuff up to the bunkhouse. The men's side is on the right. Then come back here for a cup of tea," said Colin. So I went the few yards to the bunkhouse, passing a pair of struggling trees, the only timber for miles. Then I realized I'd forgotten which side of the bunkhouse was which. I gingerly opened the right-side door and entered. There was no one there; but the gear piled up on tables, dangling from hooks, and strewn on bunks was reassuringly masculine. I claimed a bottom bunk. Hostels usually provide a duvet and sheet, plus pillow and pillowcase, but Glen Affric's isolation meant sleeping bags were *de rigueur*. I was actually pleased, as getting the sheet over the duvet was always a bloody fouter. I went to the kitchen for the cup of tea. As the kettle boiled, Colin gave me a tour of the "eco-hostel" (the SYHA's designation, not his). Electricity came from a windmill and batteries, and Colin asked that unneeded lights be switched off and showers kept short. He sounded like I do at home. He pointed out the official warning about the burn-sourced water, but added that he'd been drinking it since April with no ill effects. Everything else consumed here that was not carried in by guests was hauled along the track from Cannich, mostly by Colin on his "quad bike". This included coal and propane. The bunkhouse was spartan and cold, but the main hut was kept cozy with a fire in the kitchen. The hostel had a satellite phone for emergencies, and no cell coverage. It was six miles to the nearest road. If that does not sound impressive, consider that in all the Lower 48 you can get no farther than 30 miles from tarmac, and you must go to Yellowstone to do so. For most of us, six road-less miles in every direction is quite a novelty.

Colin and I nattered over cups of his strong tea. The other guests had not yet arrived, or were still coming down from the munros. Colin was from the English Midlands, but had been visiting this area since he was a boy. He clearly loved the Scottish hills. This affinity made it all the more surprising to me that he made no concessions at all to local place-name pronunciation. A bealach was a "bee-luck". He said "Cannick", and I thought he meant Cannock near his Midlands home, not Cannich at the end of the glen with its aspirated Scottish "ch". I do not mean this as criticism. I just didn't have a ready explanation. I am certain it was not ignorance or disdain. For Colin, it may have been about authenticity, a discomfort at adopting the local costume. Anyway, I took his advice and, before the others arrived, showered as briskly as possible. I had low expectations for flow and warmth, but both were better than some hotels I could mention. When I returned to the kitchen, Colin was dutifully brewing up tea and conversations with arriving parties of climbers. I grated cheese from my trail rations to make a quesadilla, which I supplemented with nuts. Then, feeling under the feet of more ambitious cooks, I took an apple to the site of a notorious midge attack.

As I have said, in July my youngest and I walked into Glen Affric from the east. It was, we knew, the height of midge season and prime midge weather. A few miles into the glen, we stopped at a bridge over a burn to take a picture, and were set upon by a swarm that rose from the wet vegetation like a million scrambled Spitfires. We might have chickened out of camping that night if I had brought enough money into the glen for the hostel, but we had no choice, and pitched our tent by the river. (Colin told me today that many a desperate camper flees to the hostel of a summer's evening, ready to sell their grannie to sleep indoors.) It all went well enough for us until I pushed tent pegs into the ground. Then we were assailed by the densest cloud of bug I have ever seen. I zipped Marjorie into the tent, and dove in myself soon after. Given stories of bloodied faces and insufferable itching, we got off lightly, more bothered than bitten. We lay inside waiting for the short night to descend, and I wondered out loud if the Scottish midge could be wiped from the face of the earth without side effects. Marjorie insisted that it could, but I have since done some research.

My research took the form of a short book called *Midges in Scotland* by Dr. George Hendry. I picked it up at Glasgow Airport on my way home, and highly recommend it for education and entertainment. The Highland Midge is not a variety of mosquito, as I had assumed, but a fly. It is tiny, boasting a wingspan of less than one 16th of an inch. All biting is done by the pregnant female, in need of blood to feed her eggs. She finds her victims by their breath and sweat odors. She chemically alerts other midges to the presence of a meal. ("Hey, girls, here come sweaty hikers in shorts!") The good news is that midges are not by any means all-weather predators. You won't be much bothered if you are out in the sun or enjoying even a slight wind. They are gone three seasons of the year, and a dry spell (ha ha!) at the right time cuts down summer numbers. Dr. Hendry writes that the great majority of us, local and visitor alike, react in much the same way to midge bites. A few unfortunates have severe reactions, and a few happy locals suffer reduced effects. Research suggests that some of us emit stuff in our breath and sweat that makes it difficult for midges to find us. For the rest of us, it's about sensing "midgy" moments, and either changing our plans or breaking out the DEET. I do think fleeing is key. I also noticed that two incidents happened after I disturbed vegetation. At Loch Stack two weeks ago, I drove my poles into the ground. With Marjorie, I pushed in tent pegs. Midges hang out in ground vegetation when they are not up and about looking for blood or a partner, so I probably provoked my own misfortune. And what about eradication? We know now that chemical warfare on bugs causes knock-on poisoning. Midges are bird and bat food too. We would put something out of kilter. But Dr. Hendry makes the best point, and it goes back to fleeing. Biting insects everywhere keep big animals like ourselves on the move, and "should be recognized as an important element in limiting human activities". In other words, midges keep the Highlands empty and unspoiled. I'll drink to that, inside the pub.

It was a sign that the midge season was approaching its end that I was able to linger by the river at dusk to eat my apple. I even stomped on the grassy spot where Marjorie and I had pitched our tent, but it summoned up no swarms. Back at the hostel, I left the kitchen to the tight clans of climbers, and took my maps and notes to the wee common room. There I met a middle-aged couple who had hiked in this evening on the trail I would take out in the morning. It was, they said, *very wet and very muddy*. We found common ground in the beauty of maps, OS maps particularly. At least, he and I did. When I said how much I liked to pore over them, she nodded toward her husband and said in a confidential tone "he's the same" as if we had stumbled upon shared membership of a secret society. When they left to make supper, I spread out my maps, theoretically to plot my route after the Cluanie Inn. But they were so wonderfully detailed that I got carried away in the "landscape" I saw right here. Wouldn't it be great to sit beside that lochan surrounded by cliffs and scree, the one wrapped in the 700-meter contour? Or what about scrambling over the ridge to that glen, the one that runs back from the big loch and, over five miles, tapers to nothing at the 3,800-foot peak?

In the morning I said thank you to Colin as he readied his quad-bike for another run to "Cannick", and goodbye to my fellow map-lover and his wife as they set off, GPS prepped, for the peak called Sgurr nan Ceathreamhnan. Then I started out myself on the seven-mile trek to the comforts of the Cluanie Inn, leaving for my imagination alone the walks I took on the map last night. I also turned my back on the eastern end of Glen Affric, and with it the remote chance of spying a wildcat. These beasts fed my imagination as a boy. In nature books they were always shown snarling defensively, and my dad said they were untamable. It did not matter to me that they bore more than a passing resemblance to our neighbors' tabbies; or that the only one I ever saw, caged in a zoo near Glasgow, looked as savage as a rabbit. When, ten years old and alone, I fished a little loch behind our hotel on the edge of the Cairngorm Mountains, I looked expectantly up to the wooded crags around it as much as at my line in the water. I had not read *Ring of Bright Water* then. If I had, my imagination would have been in even greater ferment. Maxwell wrote of the cats he saw around Camusfeàrna that "They bear as much relation to the domestic cat as does a wolf to a terrier." They fed, he continued, on rabbits, spring lambs, and red deer calves. Today the Scottish wildcat is rare, and interbreeding with domestic cats is one reason. Maxwell knew this happened but said that half-breed kittens seldom survived, often killed by their wild fathers. He gave an account of this:

> *"In the dark background he heard a savage sound of worrying and snarling, and flashing his torch towards the byre he saw the wild tom in the act of killing a kitten. There was a green ember-glow of eyes, the flash of a big bottle-brush tail, and then the torch lit up nothing more but a pathetic trail of mangled new-born kittens."*

There are about 400 pure-breeds left. Glen Affric is not a stronghold, but they are seen sometimes in and around the regenerating pine wood. For me, they would have to remain beasts of the imagination.

My day's navigation got off to an inauspicious start when, yards from the hostel, I took a wrong turn on my way to a bridge I could very plainly see. I had thought there would surely be a well-trodden path to it, and set off along the main east-west trail in search of one. But, in the end, I had to squelch on a faint line through high, rough grass to the River Affric, and bounce across to its south bank on a rickety structure. Then the path, such as it was, followed the river for a half-mile, and began to climb gently into a straight, steep-sided glen. Perhaps the past weeks had changed forever my definition of "very wet" because boggy as this trail was, it was, as I later wrote in my notes, "only averagely so". I turned to look behind me often in this glen, hoping for a clear view of Sgurr nan Ceathreamhnan. The peak is a byword for impossible Gaelic, sometimes dubbed Chrysanthemum Hill in parody of its baffling letters. For the record, it sounds something like *skoor nan ker-uh-van*, and means "the peak of the quarters". The quarters refer to old divisions of land, and indeed the peak did seem on my beautiful map to fall away into four main corries and glens. Late in the morning I was rewarded with a view of wispy cloud drifting across its top, its slopes painted in the distinct greens of sun and shadow. Then, near the watershed between glens Affric and Shiel, a helicopter flew overhead toward the west. I wondered if someone had taken a tumble wooing the Five Sisters. The watershed—another imperceptible one—was 1,300 feet up, but I'd started the day already at 900. I picked up a breeze after this gentle summit, and soon—double-blessing—the puddled and broken path gave way to a broad track and a steady descent to Loch Cluanie. Here the helicopter went back whence it came.

Back in Ratagan, when I told a fellow hosteller—an Aussie touring Britain by car—about my walk, he said "Christ mate, what the devil do you think about?". It wasn't really a question. What he meant was "I can't imagine what goes through your head with all that time to yourself". He wasn't the first to wonder, and the question sometimes seemed to say "I bet you're thinking big thoughts". On the descent to Loch Cluanie, the Aussie's words came back to me, and I gave some thought to what *the devil* I had thought about for two weeks. It was not by chance that I was doing it here. I was on a good path, my route to dinner and bed was straightforward, the weather was fair, and I was not worn out or uncomfortable. If any of these circumstances had not applied, I probably would not have thought of anything as abstract as what had occupied my mind. Since Cape Wrath, these circumstances had rarely coincided, and so my brain had whirred with humble stuff—where to place my feet, how tough that hill ahead would be, where the goddamn path had gone. Discomfort is an enemy of big thoughts too. If your pack straps are digging into your shoulders and rain is dripping from your nose like snot, a better man than I might ponder the correct philosophical stance in the face of life's insignificance against time and cosmos.

But my thoughts had not all concerned navigation, aches, effort, and greasy food. Solitude had, in fact, made space for new lines of thought, just not lines I had anticipated. Before leaving home, I had imagined sorting myself out on the walk in preparation for the new direction that would follow it. I would cast into the Scottish wind old ways of thinking, keeping only attitudes that would be useful to build a consulting business. Into the gale would fly bad habits like self-doubt and easy discouragement. But the walk had sparked no such introspection. Instead, when the practical stuff made way and the scenery ceased to captivate for a while, my mind had turned to story-telling. I made an audience of a conjured-up friend or family member, though the stories were definitely for me. Sometimes they resembled the history essays I had to write at Oxford, but now on Scottish subjects ("'Early Scotland was a fusion of five peoples.' Discuss.") Sometimes I related, usually to a daughter, what I thought we knew about our ancestors ("Now, your gran had a gran who was born Jane Docherty in an Ayrshire industrial village at about the time of the Battle of Gettysburg"). But mostly I told stories about what had happened to me on the walk—places, conversations, mishaps, storms. I think I spun these stories for the same reasons anyone does. They helped make sense of things; they let me "share" exciting events, sometimes troubling ones; they distracted me when all else failed. It was not until I was nearing the end of the walk that I realized I'd started to write a book in my head.

The Cluanie Inn was positively jumping. Lunchers filled the tables outside and in, cars and buses abounded. Even before I reached the door, I was warmly greeted by a party of beer-drinking Japanese, and by a friendly American who, pointing to the summits, asked if that was where I had been. His face fell a little when I confessed that it was not. On the other side of the road, on a neat platform of lawn, a man and dog were camping beside the flagpoles. I was going to like it here! But when I emerged from my room all scrubbed up, the Cluanie had turned back into a country hotel on a Sunday afternoon, as quiet as a library. The landlord said the earlier buzz was caused by an accident that blocked the A87. It was open again now, and everyone had moved on. The helicopter I had seen was an air ambulance. So I went back to my room and spent what was left of the afternoon washing my shirts and boxers, making cups of coffee, and getting over the disappointment of hearing on TV that Celtic had lost the first "Old Firm" game of the season. These are the games with cross-city rivals Rangers, and infinitely more bitter to lose than a mere Yankees-Red Sox tussle. Mostly, though, I worked on a plan for tomorrow.

I was fed up with sogginess underfoot, and looking forward to the maintained trail that I knew there would be in the Great Glen. I was low on food again too. I did not rule out taking a bus the 22 miles to Invergarry. It would be a one-off, pardonable blemish on my boast of walking all of Scotland, would it not? But, back at Ratagan, I'd seen a hotel online located southwest of the Cluanie. The Tomdoun had looked fancy and pricey, but perhaps I could camp outside and eat inside. Now the landlady of the Cluanie called the Tomdoun for me, and reported back that they'd said: "send him to us, and we'll look after him". She added that the Cluanie could make me a packed lunch for tomorrow. So that took care of food, but what about my route? The map showed tracks and footpaths through the hills that would lead to Tomdoun in 11 miles, but I would need to wade the River Loyne, and it looked substantial. We had enjoyed four mainly dry days, but it had rained plenty up until then. By evening I'd decided there was nothing to lose. If the Loyne was too high, I could be back at the Cluanie in time for the afternoon bus. And with that, I went to the bar.

The bar at the Cluanie Inn was a subdued place compared to its exuberant peers in Kylesku and Kinlochewe. There did not appear to be many other hotel guests, and diners only dribbled in from the road. The Cluanie's owners were soft-spoken, even shy. I took a stool at the little counter, and studied my maps over dark ale from Skye. My dinner began with Cullen Skink, a milky soup of smoked haddock and potatoes. Gradually, the owners and I chipped away at our reserve. Their baby helped, chuckling away as dad played with him on the counter before bedtime. The ice cracked farther the more I stroked their old, limping dog. A teenage girl was helping around the bar, Scottish beside their English voices. They treated her like family, which made me wonder if she was their daughter and they had moved up here when she was little. There would have been the same contrast in reverse between my parents' accents and mine. But I was probably getting the wrong end of this stick.

# 12

## *River of No Return*

I walked 300 yards beside the A87, then turned down a track where a sign, pointed at craggy hills, said "Tomdoun 9m". At a bridge over the River Cluanie, I looked back at the white, gray-roofed inn, so conspicuous against the green-brown land. East, stacked above Loch Cluanie, the morning sky was in chaos. There were patches of brilliant blue, edged in dazzling white. But underneath lay huge gray slates and—bottom of the stack—puffy cumulus sat on distant hills. Rainbows proclaimed the confusion. Then, passing signs telling me to stay out of the mountain corries because there was a "DEER CULL IN PROGRESS", I began to climb gradually on a broad track. It reached fine views of Loch Cluanie, stretching like a sheet of steel between dark slopes toward the Great Glen. It looked like a timeless landscape. Then I saw the loch's ruler-straight end, and the line of bare rock where its level rose and fell. Loch Cluanie, as it looked now, was barely older than me. In the 1950s, hydro dams swelled several lochs in this area beyond their natural size, bringing power to a region where homes had been lit with paraffin lamps and the tatties boiled on Primus stoves.

I swung away from the loch into the hills, up to a handsome stone bridge. Time had turned it almost into a natural feature. Lichen and mosses grew on its parapet as thickly as on nearby rocks, and the track was as grass-edged on the bridge as it was everywhere else. Then the day darkened, and soon it was raining. I had to be on the lookout for the path over to the River Loyne. If I missed it, I'd end up at a watery dead-end. Before the hydro schemes, this track was the A87. Gavin Maxwell recalled being stuck in April snow drifts right here as he drove to Camusfeàrna in the 1950s. Today the track disappears under Loch Loyne three miles ahead of where I was walking. In the end, the path was obvious enough, and I turned southwest onto its wet and narrow line, twisting up to a plateau beneath peaks skulking in the mist. Here—1,600 feet up—I briefly entered the clouds. Then, as the path began to drop and the mist to thin, a wide glen appeared below, empty of any sign of human life. Snaking through it was the River Loyne. I had come to think of it as, hopefully, my river of no return. Wade across, and my journey would continue unbroken. Failure would mean an ignominious retreat to the Cluanie and a bus.

On the map, there was a footpath crossing the floor of the glen, fording the river, and heading confidently into the hills over to Glen Garry and Tomdoun. If it exists, I never saw it. So I picked my way to the river over rough ground, and walked its rutted banks looking for a place to wade. Here the water ran too fast and deep in a tight channel. There the banks, or the boulders in the flow, were too steep and high. Elsewhere, pools sank into darkness. Finally, I chose a place that looked as safe as any. Confident of my solitude, I took off my pants, boots, and socks, and waded across without difficulty. On a boulder on the far bank I dallied over drying and dressing, delaying what I knew would be a tedious and anxious search for the onward path. I could have been anywhere on a half-mile stretch of river, upstream or downstream of the elusive path. There was no going back now, but no obvious way forward either.

I moved downstream on sodden, lumpy ground, eyes peeled for any hint of a path heading back from the river. I scanned the other bank too, knowing that picking out the trail there would point to its continuation on this side. I found nothing. This was one of the few times on my walk when a GPS might have been useful (or, alternatively, the most detailed OS map, showing the smallest burns, and every twist and islet in the river[35]). But now, trying to contain rising anxiety, I worked with the map I had and a compass, trying to match landscape to paper from a pebbly bend in the river beneath a 1,000-foot crag. It was, my plight notwithstanding, a beautiful place to study topography. I noticed how the map-path hugged a map-stream south for 200 yards, and started to follow a likely looking real stream. After a few minutes, there was a feeble flattening of grass heading in the right direction. My hopes soared. I followed it doggedly, uneasy when it vanished, elated when it reappeared. Then it began to climb and became an unmistakable, slender corridor of wet earth through the heather. When all doubt was gone, I stopped to unpack my Cluanie lunch on a rock high above the glen. It was not hard to see how glaciers had carved its flattened U, to imagine it filled to the crags with ice. Its slopes were so bare that the ice might have finished its scouring just yesterday, and the scene so wild that I half-expected to see grizzlies cropping the riverbank.

I heaved on my pack without calling it names, and headed up the hill. Soon I was done with, not one OS map, but two. From Ratagan I had been switching between the overlapping "Glen Carron & Glen Affric" and "Loch Alsh, Glen Shiel & Loch Hourn" sheets. Now I put them away and unfolded "Fort Augustus", noting with pleasure that it would take me to within five miles of Fort William. I climbed again to 1,600 feet at a pass called Màm na Seilg. On the way up, there was a dwarf of a tree wearing fine autumn colors, sheltering all alone in a gully. At the pass, the path vanished into bog. Tomdoun lay southeast, and I might have marched off that way but for the memory of my wrong turn after Bealach na Croise. Wiser, I paused, took out my map, and set a more southerly course. The path came back after the briefest of bog-hops. Simultaneously, a palpably new land appeared before me, with a new name—Lochaber. I scoured it for Ben Nevis. Scotland's highest mountain was 20 miles away as the sea eagle flies, but I could not see its distinctive bulk. Then I descended over 1,000 feet into Glen Garry in little more than a mile, arriving at a single-track road at about 4:00.

Glen Garry was pretty, but not a patch on much of what I'd seen, its charm tempered by transmission lines and abundant planted conifers. Still, the road was peaceful, as empty as the hills where I hadn't met a soul all day. I occupied myself by speculating how much I'd be willing to pay for a bed at the Tomdoun Hotel. It was a showery evening, with midges dancing here and there, but there was no reason not to camp. This desire for comfort made me feel soft. After a mile of moor and another of pine forest, a red phone box beside the road heralded some version of civilization. I tested the phone, thinking of a call home tonight. Like so many rural phone boxes in Scotland, it was broken. Everyone has a cell, and the phone company doesn't keep these isolated services going. I had a cell too, but it was expensive for transatlantic chats. I walked a few yards farther, and saw the red-ivy walls of the Tomdoun Hotel. There was a red motorcycle parked outside.

Of twilight on his first day of travel in the Cévennes—a disastrous day when his load slipped repeatedly from Modestine's back; when he guiltily beat the obstinate donkey; when he was laughed at by the local peasants, and lost his way to the lake of Bouchet—Robert Louis Stevenson wrote:

> *"My shoulder was cut, so that it hurt sharply; my arm ached like toothache from perpetual beating; I gave up the lake and my design to camp, and asked for the auberge".*

Without suffering equal trials, I gave up my own design to camp, and passed through the *auberge* door. Inside the Tomdoun, there were muted voices coming from a back room, but only Labradors in reception. I called toward the voices, and a man in his 40s with the slightest of foreign accents came out. This was Zoltan, I learned later.

"Do you have a single room for tonight? I'm walking." Zoltan looked in a big book.

"Yes. It has a shared bathroom. We can do it for 40 pounds." I got the impression the price didn't come from a list, but was an on-the-spot assessment of what a middle-aged walker with a tent in his pack might be willing to pay on a dry-ish Monday evening. And it was a decent one, although I might have gone just a little higher. While Zoltan was sizing me up, a man with some resemblance to John Cleese in height, moustache, and general aspect joined us. He led me upstairs to my room, and pointed to the bathroom at the end of the landing.

"Someone has just had a bath. Better wait half an hour for the water to warm up."

For the first hour of my stay I didn't know quite what to make of the Tomdoun Hotel. It was elegant and hushed. The welcome was cordial but more reserved than I had become used to. And there was a definite "Tales of the Unexpected" feel to the place, a mood that not everything might be as it appeared. I wondered about the "someone" who had just bathed. "John" (as I shall call

him, because I never learned his name) had made the person a
mystery. There had been a hesitancy in the way he said the word,
as if he chose ambiguity at the last minute. He could have said
"another guest", "the chef", or "Mr. Cameron from the fish farm".
Was there a mad aunt living behind one of the closed doors, let
out every Monday evening for a soak, and locked up again before
she scratched the guests? I did not want to be an only guest either.
What I wanted was a few pints and a good laugh. After a bath in
tepid, peat-stained water, I went apprehensively downstairs, and
quickly saw what a load of tosh my first impressions had been.

   In the lounge, embers were glowing in the fireplace, and a middle-aged couple was reading in their warmth. In refined Scottish
accents, Ken and Hester introduced themselves. I said how glad
I was to see them. "There is another guest too," said Hester, "and
Mike, the owner, pretty much insists everyone gets together in the
bar." Things were looking up. In the bar, I found Zoltan tending
another fire. I grabbed yesterday's *Sunday Telegraph*, fetched my
wet boots, and slowly stuffed them with the absorbent newspaper
as I finished each section. I had reached the sports pages when
a young woman came in. Her name was Ellen, and she owned
the red motorcycle outside. Judging from her freshly bathed fra-
grance, she was the "someone" too; in which case, John should just
have said, "a nice, smart Dutch woman has just had a bath". Ellen
was on holiday in search of remoteness. She had chanced upon
the Tomdoun and was bowled over by the scenery around it; "We
don't have anything like it in the Netherlands. There is nobody".
But Ellen had a dilemma. Her boyfriend was not a biker, and
had stayed home. She was missing him, and might return early. I
wanted to talk her out of this, not from a lack of sympathy exactly,
but because it seemed daft to come so far only to turn around on
the threshold of the very best Scottish scenery. If she was bowled
over by Glen Garry, what would she make of Wester Ross and
Sutherland? I thought, but did not say, "The boyfriend will wait,

for God's sake!" I took out my maps, and talked up the bizarre mountains of Assynt, the Inchnadamph Hotel, Kylesku's snorting seals, and even a scenic road to Applecross that I'd never seen. By now John and Mike had joined us. They wanted to help Ellen too. She dealt with us well, using quiet confidence and graciousness that said our thoughts would be considered. Then we learned a bit about John. He was a friend of Mike's who helped out at the Tomdoun now and then. He was born in Scotland, but had spent many years in South Africa, whose accent he spoke with. "But, please, don't call me South African," he said.

Zoltan had set two tables for dinner, one for Ellen and I, and one for Ken and Hester. When Ken and Hester came in, we moved all the silverware and glasses to one. Dinner was very nice—mushrooms from the Glen Garry woods, and a casserole of game that had grown up locally too. Our talk wandered—Dutch politics; Ken and Hester's years in Malawi; the scarcity of Scottish-owned tourist businesses in the Highlands. But one conversation stood out. Hester was the first person on my journey to declare herself a nationalist, that is, a supporter of full independence for Scotland. Admittedly, politics had rarely come up until tonight. Hester thought that the election for the Scottish Parliament that had taken place in May would prove a milestone on the road to independence. From the Treaty of Union with England in 1707 until the restoration of the Scottish Parliament in 1999, Scottish laws were made in London. Since 1999, the "devolved" Scottish Government has been, in its own words, "responsible for most of the issues of day-to-day concern to the people of Scotland". From 1999 until 2007, this Scottish Government was a coalition of parties fundamentally in favor of Scotland's remaining a devolved part of the UK. From 2007 until May's election, the government in Edinburgh was a Scottish National Party (SNP) administration, but without anywhere near an absolute majority of seats. In May, the SNP won a stunning victory, achieving an absolute majority in the Scottish Parliament and 45% of the popular vote. I said I thought Alex Salmond, the SNP's leader, was a wily operator. Hester had once thought him "a wee bit of an oily slug", but his acumen was winning her over. The election of his pro-independence party to govern Scotland without partners did not amount to a demand for "independence now". It was probably, for many voters, a protest at hard times. But they had dealt Mr. Salmond a strong hand, and we wondered now where his luck and canniness might take Scotland next.

The Tomdoun's veranda was furnished with a rough table and plain chairs. It was a good place for my pre-hike checks. Were my map, camera, and glasses at hand? Was my grub at the top of my pack? Did the tube from my reservoir stick out conveniently? It was a bright morning, and I considered stowing my waterproofs, but a sharp shower killed the idea. My friends of last night were coming out to sniff the air, and set about their days. John was arranging something with the hotel's *ghillie*, but broke off to tell me about a route to the Great Glen on open moor. I listened, but knew already that I would not use it. Ken was sorting stuff in his car for a munro-bagging expedition. Ellen was readying her bike. I went inside to check out, and Mike said: "Send us a postcard from Portpatrick". There is no cookie-cutter for a Highland hotel, but the Tomdoun had been especially idiosyncratic; and they looked after me as they said they would.

I set off through pine and birch, my poles click-clicking on the single-track road 200 feet above Loch Garry. Despite the squall as I packed, it was a lovely autumn morning. The road was empty of traffic, except for people I now knew. First the *ghillie* overtook me with a wave. Then, near the cottages at Inchlaggan, I heard a deep throbbing from behind and knew it must be Ellen. At breakfast,

I learned more about her. She had worked in a clinic, but ended up disliking the antisocial hours. Now she was a secretary at a software firm, a job she liked well. Best of all, I learned that she was riding north this morning. Now, through her helmet, she said goodbye. Minutes later, so did Ken, honking on his way to the munros.

John's route to the Great Glen, under the unmistakable cone of Ben Tee, would get me to Fort William in the fewest miles. But its trails looked likely to be uncertain and wet. I'd had enough of that for now; and, besides, I'd nearly run out of food. I wanted to meet the Great Glen Way, the marked and maintained trail that runs the 70 miles from Inverness to Fort William. It promised solid ground, easy navigation, and a grocery store. So I pushed on along the six miles of single-track that lay between Tomdoun and my old friend, the A87. I passed a salmon farm near Ardochy House, and then rested on a slipway sticking out into the loch—sticking out into the sun, a breeze, and views to humpy hills I could not name, but that ended in the jagged mountains of Knoydart. At the start of this journey I felt trepidation about what I had taken on; the absence from home, the certainty of discomfort, the risk of failure. As I inched south, this apprehension had faded, but here by Loch Garry I knew that it was gone for good. I could finally agree with Neil that, barring an unforeseeable calamity, I would make it.

# 13

## The Great Glen

At Invergarry, where coal smoke seasoned the still air, I arrived in the Great Glen. After lunch, I wondered where I might spend the night. Fort William was 25 miles away. I wanted to get far enough toward it today to reach it tomorrow. I pulled out the hostel guide they'd given me in Kinlochewe, and found a place in South Laggan, three miles away and on my route. I called immediately, and soon had a bed booked through an efficient lady with a Down Under accent. Also in Invergarry, I swapped the A87 for the A82, the Inverness to Glasgow road. It was still but a two-lane highway, but by far the busiest I had used. The Great Glen Way—the Inverness to Fort William trail—was unreachable here on the far side of Loch Oich. So, stepping off the tarmac when a bus or truck threatened, I set out for the Well of the Heads. I knew about the Well only from the photograph on the cover of my current OS map. It showed an unremarkable obelisk—unremarkable but for a hand clutching a bunch of severed heads.

Where the road came down to touch the loch, the monument appeared, unremarkable still. It would have been easy enough to overlook it, even the seven heads and dagger-bearing hand atop it. The Well itself—a spring—was hidden somewhere beneath the monument. The story is this:

In 1663, two young members of the MacDonalds of Keppoch—the clan chief Alexander and his brother Ranald—were murdered. The killers were also MacDonalds, another Alexander and his six sons of Inverlair. The murders took place 12 miles over the hills from the Well, and were probably caused by an argument over land. There was no swift justice. One Iain Lom (Gaelic for "Bald Iain"), a kinsman of the victims and Bard of Keppoch, waged a one-man campaign for vengeance (as a bard, I suppose he would have called it poetic justice). Two years after the killings, the Privy Council in Edinburgh issued "Letters of Fire and Sword" against the murderers. Thus armed, Iain Lom led a band of 60 to Inverlair where Alexander and his sons were killed and beheaded. Iain wrapped their heads in plaid, and took them to the powerful MacDonald chief at Invergarry Castle, stopping at the Well to wash them before the presentation. Since then the place has been known as *Tobar nan Ceann*, the Well of the Heads. As if to make amends for having done nothing for years, the authorities ordered the heads "affixit to the gallowes standing on the Gallowlie between Edinburgh and Leith".

The monument was erected by Clan Donald in 1812, but before I could read the inscription to learn the sympathies of its sponsors, the clouds burst wide open, and this Robert Lom legged it to the store on the other side of the road. I had planned to resupply there anyway. At the checkout, I asked the shopkeeper about places to eat in Laggan. She answered, almost inevitably, in a north of England accent:

"There's the barge down in Laggan Locks. It's a floating pub. But it's Tuesday, and he might not open. There's always the water park."

I sheltered under the store's meager awning, and set off again when the cloudburst dwindled to mere rain. The road stuck to Loch Oich now, the least of three lochs that fill the Great Glen, dwarfed by Ness and Lochy to north and south. At Loch Oich's south end the road met the Caledonian Canal. Here Laggan Swing Bridge moves the A82 out of the way of craft on the canal. Today, dry in his glass cage, the operator read a newspaper. On the east bank of the canal, at the entrance to Great Glen Water Park, I asked a young couple if they knew where the hostel was. They were foreign, park workers maybe, and they told me with smiles that I had a half-mile to go. I reached the Great Glen Hostel—a fine old house—just as little children were coming home from school in a minivan, and the owner (mom, I assumed) was lifting the shutter in reception.

After I got my key, I asked the owner the same question I had asked the shopkeeper and was given the same eating options. But the barge began to tantalize, sounding more like a fickle person than a business.

"You can never be sure he's going to open. I went by earlier and he was shut. Better to give him a call. You need to pre-order anyway," she said in her Australian or New Zealand voice. I did call, and got an old recorded message. But the Eagle Barge was certainly more tempting than a water park café on a wet evening, and I decided to walk to it later.

The hostel—independent of the SYHA—was as fine inside as out. It was spotless and recently renovated. My dormitory was airy, and empty but for me. I showered in the immaculate bathroom, put on the togs I tried to keep decent for evening use, and went downstairs to work on my route and notes. My route tomorrow was uncomplicated, 22 miles of Great Glen Way. The weather was not. The MWIS headline said "Stormy and wet before improvement to afternoon showers", but the detail described atmospheric mayhem—hail, strong gusts, lightning. On the mile walk to Laggan Locks, the sky menaced, as if the mayhem promised for tomorrow could break out ahead of time. Dark gray clouds were coming over the big hills to the southwest, and tumbling and churning above the glen. At the head of Loch Lochy I came to a stand of pines, and took the track that ran through them to the cluster of buildings at the locks. Beyond the top lock, there was a big sign that said PUB. I walked toward it and soon passed a group of exuberantly inebriated men coming from its direction. They were carrying half-full beer glasses. "He" must be open.

The woman behind the bar in the bowels of the barge was a Londoner, a touch stony-faced. I asked about dinner, and she said she would ask him. In all of Laggan (no mighty realm, it must be said) "he" and "him" clearly required no further explanation. Presently she came back and said I could have seafood pie or lamb shank, but I would have to wait. I asked for lamb shank, and sat at the little bar to wait patiently. He came in and out of the galley with food for those smart enough to have pre-ordered. He bantered with a hard-edged humor. He was not a man to be messed with. The lady behind the bar was Jan, and she turned out to be anything but unfriendly. "He" was her husband, and at last had a name. On a break from the galley, Jan said to him:

"This man's walked all the way from Cape Wrath!"

Paul looked at me and said, "You bloody idiot!" And then Paul spoke to Willy, who sat on the corner bar stool, a grin of the most angelic good nature permanently set beneath his wooly hat. Willy had come in with a new pump, required to keep the water running at the Eagle Barge. It was unclear from Paul's inspection of the pump if it would cut the mustard, but Willy grinned anyway as if he had saved the Titanic.

Paul's lamb was excellent, the meat juicy and falling off the bone. He loosened up when the meals were all served, and I stayed to natter. Paul was once a London policeman. One day he was called to a disturbance at a wedding. The bride's mother had not been invited, but turned up anyway. When Paul intervened, she slashed him around the eye with a Coke can ring. It sounds farcical, but wasn't for Paul. He retired, without compensation for the injury. Mom was only fined. The cooking, Paul said now, was therapy, and hinted that the therapy might be for something worse than the injury too. He solved the mystery of his erratic opening hours. He and Jan worked just the right amount for their takings not to pass the limit for Value Added Tax registration. Tonight there was a group of couples, Scots mostly, who seemed intent on drinking the Eagle Barge well over the threshold. They were walking the Great Glen Way. Paul addressed them: "I know I'll never be Scottish, but I like the way you are up here. You can get behind your little flag, and cheer your country. If you do that in England now, they say you're excluding someone." Then he drew their attention to the soft Celtic music playing in the barge. "I'm even playing your music."

"Actually, most people here like the *heidbanger* stuff better," piped up one of the walkers.

Paul offered me a ride back to the hostel. But, on my way in, I had tested the call box at the stand of pines, and it worked. I wanted to call home on my walk back. When I climbed out of the barge, there was still no storm, but I was taken aback that it was dark. It was like coming out of a movie theater after two hours of windowless enthrallment. I had not brought my headlight. Near the locks a little light was thrown by buildings, but when I reached the track I realized it was the blackest of nights—no moon, no sky glow, no house lights or street lamps. I could not see my feet, never mind the track ahead or a telephone keypad. I moved as if on stepping-stones, making sure each step landed on tarmac and not in a ditch. Back on the main road, a few cars came by to light the way briefly before darkness reclaimed the glen.

I did not have great expectations of Wednesday September 21st; not for splendid solitude, nor breathtaking scenery or haunting atmosphere. I had a job to do, that was all; and it was to get through the gale to Fort William. I walked back to Laggan Locks, heavy rain on and off, and there surprised a man in mid-pee outside his camouflage bivy tent pitched in the lee of a dumpster.

"Did you stay dry then?" I asked.

"Aye, more or less," he replied cheerfully, as unabashed as if I'd caught him pruning the roses. I took off my cap to cross the canal on the lock gates, or it would surely have flown into the water. Then I walked along the very top of Loch Lochy. The loch possesses no greater lochiness than any other lake or sea arm in Scotland; its name means "loch of the dark river". It is more than nine miles long, and I would walk every one of them, and more to get around its bays and braes. It is Scotland's fourth deepest loch (540 feet, barely half the depth of Loch Morar, 25 miles west). To my knowledge, no Nessie or Morag cruises its peaty depths. I climbed above this mass of water on another single-track, past woods, rough field, farm, and moor, until the road became a dirt track at the planted forest. I saw occasional cabin cruisers down on the loch, and vehicles driving the main road along the distant east shore. On the wide forest track I went flat out—or tried to. I was curiously short of energy. Inclines that should not have troubled me tired me out. I was hungry. It was pouring. Fort William seemed a tall order.

Hikers came from the south now and then, and we exchanged sardonic words about the weather. Once I thought that a huge raven was walking toward me, its wings partly unfolded. But it was a tiny Frenchwoman, dressed head to toe in black, with ruffling wings of poncho. I took short rests in the imperfect shelter of conifers, or when the deluge fleetingly ceased. On one such breather I had a breakfast of crumbly Cheshire cheese and a pork pie. At mid-morning the wind turned from strong to ferocious. Even the track puddles developed whitecaps, and I began to fear that trees would topple and branches fly. I stopped to put on an extra shirt, and spied a shelter overlooking the deepest part of the loch. The water's surface was a boiling gray and white, rain and spray whipping over it at incredible speed. When I reached the shelter, I saw it was a flimsy thing with gaps in its side planks. The planks broke the wind to a degree, but the roof was so leaky that more water was channeled onto my pack than outside; so I heaved it on and stepped back into the storm.

I emerged from the forest at the hamlet of Clunes, eight miles and three hours from the hostel. As much as I would have liked a coffee shop, it contained only a few Forestry Commission homes and one upscale residence. I walked on, now on single-track road. The wind had dropped, but heavy rain was still more on than off. There were stately conifers beside this road—Scots pines and transplanted sequoias, the latter on nothing like the scale of their ancient Californian cousins. I rested by a jagged stump in the dark shelter of a thick tree. When I started walking again, hikers came up from the other direction. "It's going to be better this afternoon!" one of them announced. For a self-described lover of walking in the rain, my hopes were mightily raised.

Beyond Bunarkaig, the Great Glen Way left the road to hug the loch. The rain paused, and so did I. Loch Lochy was placid now, though thick gray cloud sat just above it, chopping off the nearest hilltop with a sharp line. The rain resumed. Approaching the end of the loch, the path went into pinewoods as dense and dark as in a fairy tale, and came to a swollen burn over which I was relieved to find a footbridge. I climbed, weary now, back to

the single-track. There, a Great Glen Way marker (a post stamped
with a stylized thistle) told me to go still farther uphill on a wooded
path. I cursed the effort, but complied. I could easily have worked
out that the flat road was going to exactly the same place. Oh,
how obedient we can be! Sure enough, I soon returned to the road
and walked downhill to a bridge across the Caledonian Canal at
Gairlochy locks. The bridge marked the end of my lochside walk,
but also a place more or less 200 miles from Cape Wrath by my
route. I opened a new map too; Sheet 41, "Ben Nevis".

It was still ten miles to Fort William, but the towpath meant
they would be level miles. I left the locks in a squall, but before
I had walked far, the sun appeared shyly in a thinning patch of
cloud. The towpath here was on a spit of land, the static canal to
my right, the fast-flowing River Lochy on my left. I heard shouts
from the river and saw kayaks riding its swollen current. At a
swing bridge taking a farm track across the canal, the sun shone
with greater sureness in a sky showing patches of blue. I broke for
lunch at a picnic table. A Saltire[36] fluttered beside the bridge. The
canal, blue-gray, rippled between cropped-grass banks.

The Caledonian Canal was opened in 1822, after 19 years
of construction. It runs from Inverness to Fort William along
the Great Glen. Canal proper covers only one-third of this distance, the rest of the waterway consisting of lochs Lochy, Oich,
and Ness. The canal has its share of engineering marvels—swing
bridges, locks, aqueducts. But for all the cleverness, it was essentially a white elephant. The canals in Scotland's Central Belt,
mostly built decades earlier, took coal from mine to factory, and so
sustained Scotland's industrial revolution. The Caledonian Canal
achieved no such grand historical purpose. The idea was to create
a safe route for sailing ships that otherwise would have rounded
Cape Wrath—or tried to. But, by the time the canal was finished,
sail was giving way to steam and wooden hulls to iron. The new
vessels neither needed nor fitted the waterway. Perhaps the canal
was more successful in its social purpose, which was to employ

distressed Highlanders, and so help staunch the tide of emigration to the Lowland cities and the colonies. The Highland landowners wanted the Gaels off the useful land, but not out of the Highlands altogether. Labor was still needed, dammit. It might have been crofters from places like Assynt, or men who had once farmed the strath at Shenavall, who boosted their meager incomes on this big dig. By some accounts they were not the most reliable laborers, returning home most unreasonably when it was time to bring in the potatoes and cut the peats.

It turned into an afternoon of meteorological theater. I walked against a stiff southwest wind, and it was as if the gods of weather were dueling overhead. The benevolent deities to the west promised sunshine and a drying breeze. They appeared, just about, to be prevailing over the storm gods lashing out from the Nevis range. A consequence of the struggle was rainbows. Near the Torcastle Aqueduct that takes a track and burn beneath the canal, a beauty arched over the water, a pot of gold in the land of storm, another in the sunlit hills. On the last of the towpath I looked often to my left in the hope of glimpsing Ben Nevis; but the path was tree-lined, and the churning cloud over the mountain made a view unlikely anyway. Finally, near the end of the canal, there was a break in the trees and I could see toward "The Ben". It was a blurred view even of its lower slopes and crags, and the summit was hidden in impenetrable cloud. I was joined by a stout and shabbily dressed old man out with his dog.

"Were ye out in that big hail?" he asked.

"No. No hail," I said, adding that I'd come in from Gairlochy.

"Oof!" His high-pitched exhalation emphasized just how bad the hail had been. "It'll all have fallen as snow up there," he went on, nodding at The Ben. "And it will lie at the top until spring. Now, if yer looking for walks, there are some good ones over there."

"I've just walked from Cape Wrath, so I'm not really looking for more," I said in what I hoped was a humorous, self-deprecating tone.

"Och yer a glutton for punishment!" I laughed, and he turned my information over in his mind again for a few seconds.

"Cape Wrath! Yer a glutton for punishment alright." Then he said it was going to hail again, and he didn't want to be out in it, so he led his dog hurriedly away. But it did not hail, the bright weather hanging on as I toiled along the last yards of the towpath to reach the outskirts of Fort William at the bottom of a flight of eight locks called Neptune's Staircase.

*14*

# The Garrison

A t the foot of Neptune's Staircase I omitted to look out for
Great Glen Way markers to guide me to Fort William town
center, and ended up relying instead on Ordnance Survey—inad-
equate for town streets—and a bare-bones mental map from previous visits. I made a long loop through the houses of Caol, nodding to youths drifting home in anarchic school uniforms. Then
there was a long footbridge over the River Lochy, and after that a
road beside railway tracks and playing fields that led to a housing
estate in the suburb of Inverlochy. Fort William is not a big town,
but it felt like one. Even with just 10,000 inhabitants, it was by
far the biggest place I had visited in three weeks. It isn't quaint
either. It has sprawl, industrial estates, an aluminum smelter, and
housing monitored with CCTV cameras. It has traffic jams and
double-decker buses. All these features of a working town produced an unexpected sensation in me, that of arriving in Scotland.
The physical world from Cape Wrath had been unambiguously

Scottish of course, but people were few and far between, and many of the few were visitors or incomers. Fort William is still the Highlands, but also more like the kind of place that most Scots live in. The accents and conversations I overheard now made me think of Glasgow more than Kyle. Perhaps Highlanders feel the Highlands in the town, but I felt the urban Lowlands, my first Scotland, the scene of visits to grans and granddad, uncles and aunts who lived in houses not unlike these in Caol and Inverlochy.

These evocative suburbs seemed nonetheless unending to my burning feet and sore ankles. They did end, eventually, at a familiar supermarket next to the railway station. Then I walked up the High Street. Before leaving home, I had imagined walking up the High Street into Fort William. It would be my midpoint; and I'd be fit, elated, and deserving of a nice hotel and a long soak in a deep tub. The reality now was more humdrum. I did not feel mightily fitter than when I set out for Sandwood Bay (proof, I decided, of having been in good nick from the outset). I was delighted to have accomplished half the journey, but my high now was no higher than so many others along the way. As for comforts, the bad weather had paradoxically provided more, as my tent stayed unpitched, and evenings had mostly brought a shower and hot meal. But my plan was still to spend two full days in Fort William, less now in triumph than just to get ready for a week on the West Highland Way.

I ignored Fort William's nice hotels and went up the hill behind the High Street to a hostel. It was a clean and friendly place, but in the room there was space for little else but the bunk frames. Lolling on one bunk were two young guys with long hair and a stack of beer cans. One was English, the other Dutch. The English lad was nice and considerate. He even offered me a beer, which I declined only from distaste for warm lager. The Dutchman I soon disliked, not because he commented on the stink when I took off my socks, but because he exuded an even stinkier air of too-cool-for-my-backpack. As fast as I could, I hung my wet kit in the drying room, took a shower, and headed for the High Street. On my way out, I ran into the Dutchman, and he struck up a conversation. He said, among other things, that everyone he knew who had undertaken a walk like mine had been "looking for something". He meant something big, like meaning, salvation, oneself. What about me? No, I replied, I was not looking for anything more than a little adventure in a place that inspired me. As I walked down to the High Street, I did a U-turn about this Dutchman and decided he was a smart, polite fellow. I also questioned the completeness of the answer I gave him. But any budding Big Thoughts were lost in the animal pleasures of a curry at Cafe Mango, followed by beer and endless bags of chips in the Crofter Bar. I felt like a glutton, but not for punishment.

Back in Strathcarron, Joe and Brid had told me there were services on the West Highland Way that collected your backpack every morning and delivered it to your next overnight stop. It highlighted that the WHW would be a different kettle of fish from the walk so far. The country would still be rough and remote in places, but I was south of the Great Glen now, in a somewhat more settled and visited part of the Highlands. What's more, the WHW, like the Great Glen Way, is a marked route, described in abundant specialized maps and guides. About 30,000 people a year walk the entire 95-mile route, nearly all of them in the Glasgow to Fort William direction. When Joe and Brid mentioned baggage transfer, I listened politely but did not think it was for me. I would need to know where I was going to stay each night for a week ahead, and back then I still had illusions of making camp wherever the day waned. But the vagaries of this autumn's weather and the lure of shedding my pack changed my mind, and on Thursday morning I phoned an accommodation booking service. If you are not wild camping, the range of stops on the WHW is limited, and so also your choice of daily marches. I chose to take seven days, fitting nicely with the 14 miles per hiking day I had averaged since Cape Wrath. I told the booking service the places I wanted to stop and, for a very reasonable fee, they reserved six nights of bunkhouse, hotel, and SYHA lodging. They did not do baggage transfer for awkward north-southers like me, but gave me the number of someone who did. And booking the transfer with Bill of AMS was unnervingly easy. He seemed to note my overnight stops way too fast. Then he said:

"Just leave £50 with your pack on Saturday morning, and we're all set."

My next job proved trickier. I now needed a day-pack. At Mountain Warehouse in the High Street there were lots of small packs, but most appeared designed for school not Highland trails. I could not see myself on the Devil's Staircase in a bright pink, Ipod-compatible mini-pack with reflective piping. Most of them, like my backpack, had an "H2O" badge, but they were missing the accompanying slit for a reservoir tube. I asked the sales girl about this.

"H2O means they're waterproof. They don't have an opening for a bladder," she said. I doubted this information very much, but at least I had learned that "bladder" was British for reservoir; and I thought how very like them (how very like *us*) to choose a word associated almost exclusively with urination when a name conjuring up a clean and abundant water supply was freely available. Anyway, in the end I bought a "bike bag". It had the requisite slit by its H20 badge, and its fabric looked reasonably waterproof. I fretted it might be too small, but at least it was iPod-compatible with reflective piping.

Normally, presented with two days in a place, I would try to find something interesting to do. In Fort William, that might mean the scenic train to the coast at Mallaig or, if the weather was right, hiking the Mountain Track to the summit of Ben Nevis. But I had tasks to do, and the weather wasn't right, and my legs were

tired even if it had been. So in Fort William I worked languidly
through a to-do list, breaking off for meals and walks along the
High Street. At the post office, I sent maps home. I used the inter-
net at the library. I did my laundry at the hostel, and caught up on
my notes over cups of coffee in the Sugar & Spice Cafe. I haunted
the phone boxes at the edge of the old parade ground at one end
of the High Street. It was there I booked my WHW accommodation and backpack transfer, called home and UConn, and told
my relatives that I hoped to arrive in Glasgow next Friday. My
surviving aunt, still living in the town where my mother was born,
as usual, made me feel that my call was quite the best thing that
could have happened to her today. It was six years since I'd seen
the cousin I called, but speaking with her was no less heartening.
We agreed to meet on the Saturday and—something I had hoped
for—to visit her dad, the last of my father's siblings. I couldn't
have felt better if I'd climbed to a clear view from The Ben.

In 1654, Oliver Cromwell's occupying English troops built
a fort at the mouth of the River Lochy to stifle any attempt at
royalist rebellion. Thirty-six years later, long after this republican
army was gone and the English and Scottish monarchies restored,
Fort Inverlochy was strengthened and renamed Fort William. It
was, to say the least, a politically charged name, for the William
so honored was William of Orange. At the instigation of English
parliamentarians, William had chased King James into exile in
1688. James was Catholic, and in June that year his wife had produced a Catholic heir. Since the Regal Union of 1603, Scotland
and England had shared the same monarch, and this heir would
be James VIII of Scotland and III of England. But both kingdoms
also shared established Protestantism, although of different fla-
vors, and the prospect of a Catholic dynasty was unwelcome to
many. On April 11th 1689, the same day William and his wife
Mary were crowned in England, the Scottish parliament dis-
missed James VII, and offered the throne of Scotland to William

and Mary. However, support for the new regime in the country at large was not universal, and within days of James' ouster the standard of Jacobite rebellion was raised for the first time. The Lochaber region around Fort William, and the Highlands as a whole, were rich in Jacobites, and it was during the defeat of this first rising that Fort Inverlochy became Fort William. For some years after, the town surrounding the fort went under different names than the stronghold itself, but finally it too became Fort William. To rub salt deep into Jacobite wounds, this time the honored party was William, Duke of Cumberland. I remember that my father—a man mostly immune to Scottish historical grievance—put much emphasis on this duke's sobriquet of "Butcher Cumberland", earned for his "pacification" of the Highlands after the last of the Jacobite rebellions in 1745-6. In Lochaber, pacification took the form of a year of murder, destruction, and robbery by redcoats instructed by Butcher to teach the clans a lesson they would not forget. The Gaelic name for Fort William is An Gearasdan, the garrison, and it suggests mere sullen acceptance of the fact of alien conquest. Unloved by the local people at birth, it has stayed unloved and unlovely since. It is derided for its 1970s developments—including a by-pass that cuts the town off from its Loch Linnhe shore—and for its overall failure to be a charming little Highland town. Personally, I had already found it pleasingly workaday. Now I had time for a closer look.

Many times over two days, under uniformly *dreich* skies, I walked up or down Fort William High Street. Everything I needed was on it somewhere. It was the temporary extent of my world. The High Street ran a half-mile from a roundabout at one end of town almost to the railway station at the other. Once or twice I ventured a little beyond the station—to Morrisons supermarket, or McDonald's for breakfast—but never much farther. From the roundabout end, the High Street went first to Station Square. The gaily painted Sugar & Spice Cafe was on this stretch. At Station

Square, there was neither station nor square, just an intersection on which there was a barber shop that I should have patronized. Right next door was Gordon Square, more square-like, and today the official end of the West Highland Way. Sitting on a bench in Gordon Square, outside the boarded-up Grand Hotel, was a sculpture of a seated man. He seems to be rubbing a sore ankle, so he must be a hiker. He can see Loch Linnhe across six lanes of road.

The next section of the High Street, going almost to the phone boxes at Parade Gardens, was pedestrianized and less shabby. The town's status as an outdoor sports center was announced by gear shops, and the influx of tourists by the souvenir emporia. The latter were a study in themselves. Some, like The Edinburgh Woollen Mill (of which the High Street boasted two), clearly wished to be upmarket, but still found it necessary to stock Saltire light switch covers; "InstaKilt" towels with integrated sporrans; exploding golf balls; and sporran coasters. A creative assortment of this kind of tat was sold at other shops with names like "Traditions of Scotland" or "House of Scotland". And of course there were mountains of tartan-packaged shortbread, and stacks of CDs of the kind of music that Paul would play at the Eagle Barge while his Scottish customers pined for *heidbanger* tunes.

Somewhere between the two Edinburgh Woollen Mills was Cameron Square, a true square with handsome buildings. One of them housed the eclectic collection of the West Highland Museum. I recall a stuffed golden eagle, and the gun that was the likely murder weapon for the real killing that Robert Louis Stevenson made the cause of Davie Balfour's fictional flight into the heather. But the most eye-catching exhibit was an anamorphic portrait of Bonnie Prince Charlie. I knew of the Jacobite subterfuge of passing one's glass of wine over a glass of water when the time came for "ladies and gentlemen, The King". The toast thus became to "the King over the water", in other words the Stuart king in exile across the sea. The portrait was in this vein. It was painted on a tray as a formless blur, but when a special cylinder, or even a shiny goblet, was placed on it, a likeness of the Prince was produced on the cylinder. The Jacobites could toast Charlie, and hide him away quickly if disturbed.

At the very end of the High Street were the lawns and monuments of Parade Gardens, presided over by the stately Alexandra Hotel and the Church of Scotland. One of the monuments was a hefty bronze statue of Donald Cameron of Lochiel, magnificently turned out in full Highland dress. "Lochiel" is the customary title of the chief of Clan Cameron, and Lochaber is Cameron territory. This bronze Donald was the 24th Lochiel, and his life and that of his predecessors reflected the changing fortunes of the Highland chiefs. The 19th Lochiel, another Donald and bronze Donald's great-great-grandfather, was wounded charging the government army at the Battle of Culloden in 1746. Seven years later, his brother was executed for high treason in London, the last Jacobite to suffer the fate. But how times change! Bronze Donald's father, the 23rd Lochiel, fought for king and country—the Hanoverian king of the United Kingdom, not a Stuart king of Scotland—at the Battle of Waterloo. Bronze Donald himself, born in 1835, attended the exclusive English "public" school of Harrow. He joined the diplomatic service and several London clubs, and became a Conservative Member of Parliament.

# 15

# Ben Nevis and the Lairig

I moved into a B&B, another Ben View, for my last night in Fort William. I wanted a room to myself to organize my gear, divide it between day-pack and backpack. Into my new day-pack I put my reservoir and enough trail food for a day. In case it got cold on higher ground, I added gloves, wooly hat, and fleece. I put small stuff—compass, lamp, phone, extra packets of nuts—into the pack's small pockets; and flat stuff—notebook, valuables pouch, map—into its flat front pocket. I found space for my camera. Finally, I slipped in my trowel and toilet paper. When I was done, the pack was so stuffed that I had to drain some water from the reservoir to close the zipper. There was no room for my rain jacket. If I ever got to take it off, it would just have to hang from a strap.

It felt odd to leave my pack at the front desk of the Ben View and trust that it would reappear in Kinlochleven this evening. And walking out of Fort William carrying just my day-pack induced a kind of separation anxiety, so used was I to hiking with the Big Bastard. But, with a new lightness to my gait, I came in a quarter of an hour to a roundabout at the edge of town. There was a sign marking "the original end of the West Highland Way". For me it marked the beginning, and I began my 95-mile walk to Glasgow with a sidewalk stroll along a leafy lane up Glen Nevis. Everyone on the lane this dry Saturday morning was up to something sporty. Numbered cyclists raced downhill; cars carried kayaks on their roofs; two Indian-Englishmen asked me where the path up Ben Nevis began; and I bumped into a hiker who I had bumped into before. He was one of the middle-aged northern Englishmen who abound in the hills and hostels. He had moved in to share my dormitory in Laggan when I was out at the Eagle Barge, and the next day overtook me on the canal towpath. We chatted then about walks and weather. Today he was coming down from the SYHA hostel in Glen Nevis, to catch the scenic train to Mallaig, he said. Only later did I wonder about him. He was reserved in a way that could have meant either serenity or sadness. Was his life as solitary as his wandering, or filled with family and friends, from whom Scotland was just a brief absence?

Complacent that the Way would be superbly marked, I missed the place where it left the lane, and added to my day's march by going a half-mile farther up Glen Nevis than necessary. I doubled back, and this time saw the inconspicuous marker pointing down a track across a rough field. The track led into a stand of pines, where two Germans were packing up their camping gear, and then joined a broader track that began to climb the side of the glen. This track rose straight and steady until, 600 feet above the glen floor, it made a hairpin turn. Here the summit of Ben Nevis lay three miles east and three-quarters of a mile up. I wanted to see if the old man, he who accused me of gluttony for punishment, had been right that lasting snow had fallen on the peak. Across the glen I could see The Ben's massive west-facing slope, slashed

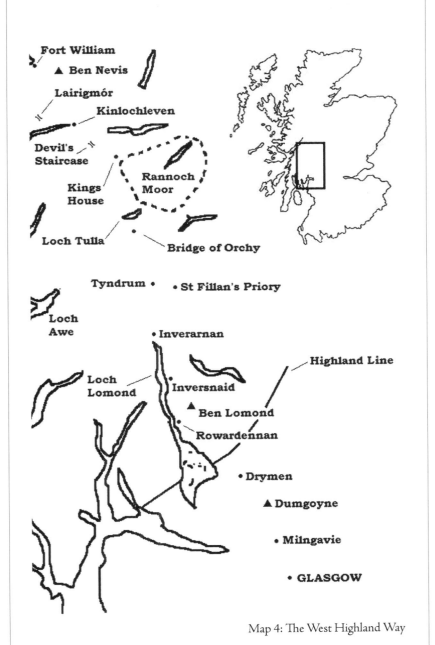

Map 4: The West Highland Way

by ravines; but the mountain's topmost 1,000 feet were hidden in gray cloud, as indeed they usually are. The view north, down Glen Nevis, I would have thought beautiful at almost any other time, but it paled beside the empty glens of the northwest—the valley of the River Loyne; glens Affric and Elchaig; Strath na Sealga. On the map of Scotland, the ruler-straight line of the Great Glen, and the firths at either end of it, look like a tear that could be used to rip the northwest of the country off, like the detachable part of an invoice. And the Great Glen does follow a geological fault; its long, deep lochs making the northwest an almost-island, the utmost and least populated part of the land. A few days ago I looked forward to easier walking. Now, looking down Glen Nevis to the Great Glen and beyond, I felt a sense of loss for the empty, faraway lands.

I rounded the hairpin and made my second error of the morning. It was a broad Forestry Commission track now, and I followed it blindly into an area where the forest had been felled. The track grew worse and worse, covered with bits of broken tree and rutted by the tires of heavy equipment. The ruts had filled with rain. It was like hiking a World War One battlefield. After half a mile or so, even the semblance of a track disappeared among the shell holes of torn-up roots and the barbed wire of conifer debris. There was no way forward, and I had to retrace my steps, composing a sarcastic letter in my head to whoever manages the WHW. Then I spied a small, but quite distinct, path leaving the forest track for another field of stumps, and the equally visible marker where it did so. I had simply failed to notice either on my way in. Perhaps my eyes had been lifted in the hope that the mist had blown off a snowy ben. I resolved not to expect signs of highway dimensions on the WHW, and went down the smaller path. It was not a pretty walk through the stumps, and not much more beautiful farther on where the planted forest still stood. Even when the path came out onto open hillside, the notes I took later said: "Out of woods to new views, but nothing spectacular". Eventually, near a footbridge over a burn lined with spindly birch, I saw The Ben again. It was shrouded at the same elevation as before, but the cloud was whiter, and blue sky had made an appearance nearby. My southerly progress had revealed the gullies on The Ben's southwest flank and—clear of mist—the 3,350-foot subsidiary summit of Carn Dearg.

The morning had been solitary since the lane along Glen Nevis, but now I hit a surge of hikers coming north. Because everyone leaves the WHW's limited accommodation stops after breakfast, they hike in bunches, and this week I was to meet most of my company all at once, usually about lunchtime. Today, inflated with weekenders, they arrived about 1:00, as I came down into more rows of white stumps. From Cape Wrath to the Great Glen I had come across few hikers, and those I did encounter were a seasoned lot. The walkers in the surge were a different breed. They were in bigger groups; they were finding the going tough; and their looks, and words, said: "it seemed like a good idea at the time". A young man and two young women went by. The first two managed a feeble greeting, but looked morose. The girl coming up the rear kept her eyes down, and seemed on the very edge of a tantrum. There were exceptions. I met a father and daughter sitting on rocks by a burn, eating lunch. They looked healthy and happy.

"Nice day now," I said.

"Beautiful." They were Canadian, on the final day of a rainy hike from Glasgow.

"Pity about the scenery," I went on, gesturing at the mangled forest, and the power lines running over a nearby hill. They looked at me with incomprehension, as if I had sniffed at the sight of Shangri-La.

"Hey! At least it's not raining!" he said. The trail widened, as once again I joined an Old Military Road. It took me through the stragglers of the surge toward a wall of hill. I sat on a rock for my

own lunch, and chewed as well on the fact that it was three weeks
and 220 miles since I left Cape Wrath.

The wall was a hill called Mam na Gualainn. As soon as an east-
erly turn of the track put its slopes to my right, the imperfect landscape of the morning gave way to a magnificent glen. It would
take me nearly to Kinlochleven, but the map gave it no name. The
track came down to the glen floor and the vestiges of a shieling
and sheep pens. Coarse grass grew as high as the mossy remnants
of stone walls. Sheep cropped among tumbled stones. Behind
the ruins was an *allt*, and beyond it the bare slopes of the *mam*.
The map called this place Lairigmòr, "big pass"[37]. The glen was
hemmed in by steep hills; the high Mamores range to the north,
mere 2,600-footers to the south. Among the hills there was a *beinn* or two of course, but there were tops too that the map labeled
*stob, sgurr, tom, mam, binnein, meall*, or *mullach*. There seems to be
agreement only on the translation of some of these labels. A *sgurr*
is a peak and a *mullach* is a summit. *Binnein* is also usually given as
peak, especially of the pointed variety. A *tom* is a hill, particularly
one that is rounded or knoll-like. A *meall* is similar—a lumpish
hill. *Mam* caused me some confusion. My place-names book gave
it as "gap", but other sources as a breast or rounded hill. The most
prominent peak in the glen was Stob Ban, its west face as smooth
and pointed as a clothing iron. The place-names book translated
*stob* as "stump"; but "peak", even "pointed peak", seems to be a more
common rendering. Stob Ban did not look stumpy any more than
it looked fair ("ban"). Finally, to confuse me further, there was a
peak of fully 3,000 feet above this glen for which my map had no
name at all.

You would expect the Gaels to have had a rich vocabulary
for hills, and to have used it without strict definitions or rules.

But how were those living names transferred to the "paper landscape" of Ordnance Survey? The OS maps are now the authority for Highland topographical names, and in most of Scotland there must be very few Gaelic-speakers, if any at all, with enough knowledge of their local landscape to challenge any old mapmaking errors ("That summit is not Stob Ban. We locals have always called it Mullach Dubh."). We have almost certainly accepted as authentic names that were published in error 150 years ago. The OS mapped Scotland to six inches to the mile in the 1800s (the standard OS map today has a scale of "only" 1.25 inches to the mile). It was a huge achievement, but it must have been inherently error-prone. In theory, surveyors arrived in a glen like this and asked the "best authorities within their reach" for the "correct orthography" for the name of each "object". So, if possible, someone with the status of an estate factor or schoolmaster would tell surveyors that yonder peak was S-t-o-b B-a-n, and that corrie up in the swirling mist was C-o-i-r-e R-i-a-b-h-a-c-h. The names and the authority for them were duly noted in "Original Object Name Books". In some cases spelling was amended by interpreters and educated Gaelic-speakers. But for the big task of giving the right name to the right feature, the process was very reliant on the accuracy of information from a small number of individuals. The OS liked to use residents "of some position", but compromised this principle in the Highlands where owners, professionals, and *gentlemen* were thin on the boggy ground. The pool of expertise must have been further drained by the upheavals in Gaelic society, not least a tenantry evicted from once-familiar landscapes. One wonders who was at the disposal of the surveyors in this part of Lochaber in the 1860s and 1870s to name the landscape. As for missing names, we know that OS discarded some names to reduce production costs. Maybe my 3,000-footer was among them. It is a wonderful thing that the Highland landscape is still named primarily as its ancient occupiers referred to it, and that the end of gaeldom did not bring with it the Anglicization of its world. But I suspect that what looks to us like a wealth of Gaelic natural feature actually records but a part of the Highlander's points of reference in his world, and that what we have is less surely correct than we assume.

A mile beyond Lairigmòr, there was another ruin, less wholly dilapidated. Its walls, chimneys, and gables were intact, but the roof had collapsed and the doors and windows were gone. This was Tigh-na-sleubhaich (house of the something or other), and soon after it the track reached the height of the pass at a modest 1,100 feet. I suppose the pass separates two glens, but the transition from one to the other went almost unnoticed. On the other side, the track was the same, the scenery familiar, and the sky ran the same gamut from black to blue. Apart from an *allt* now flowing east to Loch Leven instead of west to Loch Linnhe, the only change was that now I had company.

First I heard the putt-putt of small engines far behind. The noise faded, and I thought no more of it until it started up again and began to close on me. When it became too close to ignore, I turned and saw two flabby guys coming very slowly down the track, standing on motorbikes. They farted past me at perhaps twice my speed, filling the air with fumes. I was annoyed that they were here, bringing the noise and smell of the urban world into this superb glen. Up ahead they left the track repeatedly as they tried to ride up the course of burns or straight up the sides of the glen. Whenever this exercise took a bit of time, I overtook them, but soon they were thumping up behind me again. I refused to step off the track to give them more space, and resolved that if one of them fell under his bloody bike in a burn, I bloody well wouldn't help to pull it off him. It went on like this for a mile or so, until they stopped as they passed me for the last time. They were an Englishman and a Scot.

"We found these on the path back there. They're not yours, are they?" asked the Englishman, holding out a pair of sunglasses.

"No, not mine," I replied, curtly.

"It's not a bad day for walking, is it? Except you've got us ruining it for you," he went on. I was mollified that at least they knew that their fun was spoiling mine. It was half an apology.

"So what are you doing?" I asked, less curt now.

"These are trials bikes. We were trying to find some runs, but no luck." I pointed to the sheer face of Stob Ban. "What about that?" They laughed, and thudded back whence they came. I set off for Kinlochleven a little more at peace with humanity.

The close walls of the glen's south side began to fall away, opening up ever more extravagant views. They were dominated by the conical peak of the Pap of Glencoe. I had seen the Pap many times before, but from its other side, where it announces the infamous Pass of Glencoe on the A82. The clouds over the hills were black and rowdy, but above the Pap there was a break, and a shaft of vaporous sunlight pointed down toward Loch Leven, still invisible behind a foreground ridge. A few minutes later, the sunbeam was gone, and a stripe of rain was moving in front of the Pap. In the brighter, seaward distance, I could now see a patch of Loch Leven, six miles away and 800 feet down. Beyond this silver splinter of a sea loch rose the mountains of Appin. Alan Breck, Davie Balfour's rescuer and friend in *Kidnapped*, is a man of Appin, coastal country that runs southeast from Loch Leven. Davie's judgment on first seeing it for himself was harsh: "*It seemed a hard country, this of Appin, for people to care as much about as Alan did.*" I could see just a few Appin mountains. They looked tall and rugged, easy to care about.

A woman in her 60s came up the path from Kinlochleven, still fresh despite the obvious climb behind her. She was doing her daily circuit to the Mamore Lodge and back, she said; and I thought how a four-mile stroll before tea, beginning with an 800-foot climb, would keep body and soul together. I set off down the path she had climbed, and had to take short steps and lean backward to stay upright on the steepest bits. The path emerged from birches onto a quiet lochside road just where the road arrived in Kinlochleven. There was a sign pointing to where I'd come from: "PUBLIC FOOTPATH TO FORT WILLIAM BY THE LAIRIG". So that was it. The glen was "The Lairig". I followed the sidewalk and lampposts into the village. It was a working place, a smaller version of the suburbs of Fort William. Across the bridge over a swift River Leven stood a building that looked like a refurbished warehouse, as big as a cathedral. Huge pipes ran down the hillside behind it. I went to the Co-op to buy a soda, and read the directions to my hostel as I drank outside. I had walked 15 miles, not counting wrong turns, and did not feel tired. It's amazing what losing 40lb can do for you.

The Blackwater Hostel occupied refurbished industrial premises too, though far smaller. I found Callum working in a shed next door. "I'll put you in with Pete," he said. "He's a nice older gentleman, Dutch." But Callum was worried about Pete. He'd gone up onto the munros, and should have been back by now. "Too bad he went out wearing dark clothing," added Callum. "At least if you're bright, mountain rescue will see you." My backpack—hallelujah!—was waiting for me inside, and I took it into the room I would share with Pete—if he made it. It was cramped and dimly lit. Pete had arranged his stuff neatly. There was a small, old-fashioned suitcase on the floor, and on top of it an old-fashioned shaving kit of badger hair brush, soap mug, and safety razor. There was also a framed black and white photograph of a young woman taken a long time ago. I felt as if I was intruding in a stranger's bedroom. I made up the top bunk, showered, and made a quick dash to the village to use a call box, every bit of its glass lying crushed at my feet like hail. Back at the hostel, Pete had still not shown, and there was no sign of him either when I went out again to look for supper.

The Tailrace pub reflected Kinlochleven's contrasting personalities—a locals' place with a smattering of walkers. Families were out for Saturday evening, the bar full of banter, laughter, and crying babies. Among the walkers, I recall a European huffily handing back his mac and cheese ("It is not what I expected"). The barmaid, graciously I thought, gave him another shot at the menu. With help from the locals, I pieced together what I'd seen. A hundred years ago, an aluminum smelter was built here, powered by a hydroelectric plant driven by water channeled from a vast reservoir in the hills. This explained the pipes on the hillside. The smelter closed in 2000, and most of its installations were pulled down. The "Ice Factor"—the world's biggest indoor ice climbing facility—occupies a refurbished part of them, the cathedral-dimensioned warehouse I'd seen. Tonight I would sleep in the smelter's old laboratory. The hydroelectric plant is still going, connected now to the UK National Grid. At its height the smelter employed 800 workers. Its closure was devastating for Kinlochleven, the village it spawned in 1907. Jobs were scarce, a barmaid told me, and many locals drove the 22 miles to Fort William for work. It would, she added, be much worse without the spending of walkers. I bought another beer.

Pete had returned. Our room was unlocked. He wasn't in it, but his bunk had been sat upon, and clothing lay where it had not been before. I went to the lounge. There, an old man was bantering in a foreign accent with a group of boisterous Scotsmen. They treated him like an act, and he appeared happy in the limelight. He said "hamster" when he meant "hamper", and this caused immense mirth. Pete was small, and looked too frail to be climbing mountains. He was in his late seventies at least, his skin translucent and covered in liver spots. I went over to talk when he was done with the Scots. He was garrulous. He said he got to know "the Brits" in Rhodesia, where he lived for a while until 1974. By then the writing was on the wall for the white regime, and he did not want to deal with uppity Africans. I mentioned the photograph on his suitcase. The woman was his wife. She died ten years ago. She had smoked. Pete knew the Highlands well and had learnt the Gaelic place-names, like his compatriot van Vlissingen. He let me know that he knew some of the landowners personally. Now, he said, he wanted to watch *Match of the Day* on the lounge TV. He said also that Callum had told him that a group had moved on, and I could have my own room if I wished. I left to move my gear. When I returned, *Match of the Day* was in full flow, highlights from to-day's English football, not the Scottish games. Pete kept up his own commentary, especially when Dutch players got the ball. I left halfway through, and went to my spacious new digs with Pete still chirruping away at the TV.

# 16

## *Crossing Paths with Davie*

Today's hike would be my shortest on the West Highland Way, but its eight miles would take in the top of the Devil's Staircase, at 1,800 feet the highest point of my walk so far. My incentive was the Kings House Hotel on the edge of Rannoch Moor, and maybe in time for lunch. From the hostel porch I looked out at the day. A lady-hiker was doing likewise. It was gray but dry.

"Leave off the raingear, do you think?" I asked.

"You could try it." I didn't, and felt sweet vindication when a heavy shower swept through the instant I set out. I rejoined the WHW at the bridge opposite the Ice Factor, and followed it, by way of a circuitous loop, to the Old Military Road. The road crossed the huge pipes where they neared the end of their downhill run, little jets of water spurting from holes in their tubes.

The Old Military Road—a perfectly graveled track here— climbed steadily, screened from the pipes and any views by slender birch. At 500 feet above Kinlochleven, the track passed a dam and waterfall, wheeled sharply north, and became steeper and exposed to the strong southerly wind. There were views to yesterday's Lairig and, behind me, the dark ridge of Aonach Eagach. At 1,000 feet, the track reached the top of the pipes, fed here by a conduit bringing water from the reservoir in the hills. The trees gave way to bleak moor, and the track became a thin path into the heather. Greater elevation, and reduced effort as the path leveled out for a while, chilled me, but I didn't want to mess about in the rain to put on a fleece. I worried too whether my new pack was keeping the rain out. At 11:00, a solitary girl came from the south wrapped in a clear plastic poncho. She looked too young and delicate to be out alone. Then more of today's surge of hikers came along, earlier than yesterday since they had only to cover the scant miles from the Kings House.

The path came to a wooden bridge across a burn, and began to climb again. I stopped to look back. The gorge of the River Leven, only its rims visible, cut across the land. Beyond it, everything was treeless, just massive slopes beneath and around the corries of the Mamores. Heavy clouds brushed the very top of the range, drifting over the conspicuous notch between the peaks of Sgòr Eilde Beag and Sgùrr Eilde Mòr. At 1,600 feet, I rounded a *sron*—a nose—sticking out from Aonach Eagach, and immediately the country to the east came into view. It was hilly and bare still but, in contrast to the steep, tight hills around me, rolling and open. At its center lay the Blackwater Reservoir, the latent power for all the smelting and generating. When its dam was completed in the early 1900s, nine miles of moor, river, and lochan were put underwater, along with a onetime drovers' inn. But now that there is nobody left alive to miss fishing in vanished Lochan Inbhir, let alone to remember resting with the black cattle at the inn, the drowned land may be considered truly gone, erased from both landscape and memory. The path now crossed a corrie where the storm gained strength. I was amazed to see two hikers, otherwise apparently sane, coming down into its bowl with battered city umbrellas raised hopelessly against the elements.

What I found at the top of the Devil's Staircase was just as astonishing. The southerly gale came head-on with untrammeled force. It set my clothes flapping; it chilled and deafened me; it sent me behind a cairn for cover. But I had to brave the wind to take in the scene that the pass commanded. Its dark drama seemed in some way emblematic of my journey. A thousand feet below snaked the leaden River Coupall. Ahead, nearer above than the river was beneath, was a huge cloud, among the blackest I have ever seen. It seemed to form part of the mountain called Buachaille Etive Mòr, as dark as its slopes, obliterating its higher reaches. Between the cloud and the river, to the east of the curved face of the mountain, lay space that was at once the brightest part of the scene, yet filled with rain. The picture changed subtly a little way down the Staircase. The black cloud had lifted a few hundred feet up the mountain, and below I could see a small pinewood, adding its dark green to the palette of this most brooding mood of a brooding landscape. More light came in now through a newborn patch of white in the midst of the black clouds. It made wet rock glint, and increased the transparency of the far-off rain to reveal the faint silhouette of yet farther-off hills.

The Devil's Staircase is the path that ascends 900 feet from Glen Coe to the cairn where I sheltered, zigzagging as it nears the top. It did not seem diabolical to me, not after the slimy slope above Crofton and the old pony path at Achnashellach. But I wasn't slogging up it, and I certainly wasn't building it. It was apparently the soldiers who labored on its construction around 1752 who gave it the name. Today there were walkers laboring on it, most of them for some reason very willing to stop and talk with me as I drifted down. There was a cheerful Englishman and his dog walking for charity from Land's End to John o' Groats, and behind him two Scots women who had walked from Glasgow.

"So what's it been like?" I asked.

"Well, the weather's not been good at all. And along Loch Lomond there were tree roots all over the path! Then a few days ago—where was it, Ailie?—that burn came right over our boots!" I felt like saying "So what did you expect?" but settled for "I'll look forward to that."

As well as these "thru-hikers", there were those who had parked at the foot of the Staircase to have a crack at the climb. Some were woefully unprepared. Not far from the bottom, a weedy man stopped in front of me and announced, "I'm suffering already!" I looked at him from toe to top—flimsy sneakers that were called plimsolls when I was at school; gray dress socks halfway up his white shins; tennis shorts; a track top over a t-shirt. No hat or raingear were visible. Maybe they were stored in the gaudy mini-pack that he must have bought at Mountain Warehouse in Fort William. "I'm suffering!", he repeated, and I thought "Not nearly as much as you're going to."

Barely better equipped than this man, Robert Louis Stevenson's Davie Balfour and Alan Breck crossed the line of my walk today on their fictional flight. In the wood of Lettermore, 12 miles west of the Devil's Staircase, Davie witnesses the murder of the "Red Fox"—Colin Campbell, King's factor on the confiscated lands of the Jacobite Stewarts of Appin. A loyal subject of King George, Davie runs up the hill above the wood to pursue the gunman— and runs right into Alan. Neither is complicit in the murder, but Alan knows the redcoats and Campbells won't see it that way, and their flight to the Lowlands begins. They go to the house of Alan's kinsman, James of the Glen, at Aucharn. Like Lettermore, it is a real place, mapped today as Acharn, a few miles southwest of the scene of the murder[38]. From Aucharn they walk and run to Glen Coe, but to a place six or seven miles down the glen from the Staircase. It was here they roasted on a rock among the searching soldiers. They escape from the rock and take refuge in a mountain cleft that Stevenson calls "the Heugh of Corrynakiegh". It is none other than Coire na Ciche, high on the Pap of Glencoe. For Davie, it is an enchanting place:

> *"From the mouth of the cleft we looked down upon a part of Mamore, and on the sea-loch that divides that country from Appin; and this from so great a height as made it my continual wonder and pleasure to sit and behold them."*

Where, exactly, Davie and Alan go next is unclear. After leaving the heugh they attempt to flee east across a moor. Stevenson does not say that it is Rannoch Moor but, defining it broadly to take in the wilds around today's Blackwater Reservoir, it must be. To reach the moor, they travel through the night "to the end of a range of mountains". These mountains can only be those that run east from the Pap, in all probability Aonach Eagach. The place where Davie and Alan saw the moor ("a piece of low, broken, desert land, which we must now cross") was perhaps not a precise, actual location for Stevenson. But they would have had to cross the line of the WHW somewhere between the top of the water pipes and the top of the Staircase. I conjured up a satisfying picture of the ragged duo slinking off into the open country I looked on from the nose of Aonach Eagach.

The Devil's Staircase ended at the main road by the dark green pinewood I had seen from higher up. The Way now hugged the A82 for half a mile, and then veered away to climb a few hundred feet up the slope of Beinn a' Chrulaiste. From there I looked back to Glen Coe. It is a majestic glen, perhaps in its way as beautiful as Glen Affric. It is just that the A82 runs its length, filled in the summer months with cars and tour buses. It is of course the site of an infamous massacre. When I was a boy, I learned a story of simple clan feud, conveniently requiring no further explanation. Campbells and MacDonalds fought as naturally as cowboys and Indians. That was it. In fact, the event was triggered by Scottish and British politicking. As part of negotiations to end the first Jacobite revolt (the one that saw Fort Inverlochy become Fort William), Jacobite clan chiefs were required to sign an oath of loyalty to King William by January 1st 1692. The chief of the MacDonalds of Glencoe, Alasdair MacIain, did not sign until January 5th, making his clan the perfect target for those in the Scottish government who wanted to make an example of one disloyal clan or another. William gave instructions *"to act against these Highland rebels who have not taken the benefite of our indemnity, by fire and sword, and all manner of hostilities; to burn their houses, seize or destroy their goods, catell, plenishing or cloaths, and to cut off the men."* A Campbell regiment of the King's army came into Glencoe on February 1st, and lodged with those they would afterward slay. Early on the morning of the 13th they fell on their hosts, killing MacIain and about 40 of his kinsmen. The same number of women and children died of exposure after fleeing into the frozen hills. Terrible as it was, it could have been worse. The orders given to the officer on the spot, one Captain Robert Campbell, were to "put all to the sword under 70". If the late arrival of supporting troops had not allowed many MacDonalds to escape, many more men would have been "cut off", and goodness knows how many more women and children would have perished for want of houses, *cloaths* and *catell*.

I was alone again on an empty trail. The gale had died, although this gentle slope of Beinn a' Chrulaiste was still 1,000 feet up. Ahead of me, the country opened up as it had not since the far northwest—the mountains more distant, the folds of the land gentler, the sky bigger. I could see the Kings House Hotel on the edge of this country from some way off, white-walled and gray-roofed like the Cluanie Inn, screened from the brown moor by clumps of planted spruce. It was an isolated spot. The nearest village was 12 miles away[39]. There was little obvious mark

of civilization, bar the hotel itself and the line of the A82, both
dwarfed by the scale of their setting. The Way came down to a
paved track, and somewhere along it the rain lashed down again.
By the time I reached the hotel, via a stone footbridge over the
River Etive, my waterproofs were glistening and dripping from the
downpour. There was a sign at the main entrance directing guests
one way for the "Climbers' Bar" and another for the "Cocktail Bar".
A friendly looking chap was standing in the porch peering at the
weather with distaste. I looked carefully at the sign, then at my
*droukit*[40] self, and finally at him:

"Cocktail Bar for me, right?" In the Climbers' Bar, the barman
sent me to reception to check in, but I'd seen enough of his place
of work to know I wanted to go back. Once I'd checked in, un-
packed the few—and dry!—contents of my day-pack, and hung
my raingear in the drying room, there was nothing more to do.
My big pack would not arrive until later, and without it I could
not shower or change my clothes.

If there had been a trapdoor in the floor of my room, I could
have dropped straight into the bar. As it was, I had to wander a
labyrinth of corridors and, since the bar had no inside entrance,
dash through the still-pouring rain. Once there, I could think of
no better place to be on a wet Highland Sunday afternoon. While
deer cropped the riverbank outside, I ate a sandwich, sipped beer,
and caught up on my notes. The bar showed Scotland at its best.
It was the September Weekend holiday in Glasgow, and a steady
procession of happy, droukit walkers came through. There was a
group of boy scouts, without adults, who hung up their waterproofs and settled down to fizzy drinks and chips. Dogs wandered
and slept among the table and chair legs, one of them clearly quite
stimulated by his dreams. Then there was the group at the big
table, all men, plus a lad of 11 or 12 who everyone treated as a son.
They were eating and drinking unhurriedly after a morning's exer-
tion. They were fit; they were happy; their chatter was lively and

seemingly without contest or friction. As their numbers dwindled
to go home to watch a recorded Rugby World Cup game, I talked
with the last designated driver. They were from Bannockburn,
the village near the site of Robert the Bruce's famous victory
in the Wars of Independence[41]. That morning, they had scaled
Buachaille Etive Mòr, the storm-wrapped mountain I saw from
the Staircase. He called it "the Beuckle". When I was about to leave
the bar to check if my pack had arrived, he called out to his mates:

"This guy's walked from Cape Wrath." And I left to a thumbs-
up from this crew of amiable strangers.

In the evening, I went to the Cocktail Bar for dinner. It was
a grand name for a basic pub lounge, but it was, I suppose, a cut
above the dirty boots and dripping macs of the Climbers' Bar. For
me, it wasn't as convivial, at least not to begin with. Everyone was
in self-sufficient groups around tables, except for a young couple
at the bar. But they went upstairs in the nick of time, before their
mounting affection treated us all to impromptu adult entertainment. I was about to hit the sack too when Jim McDonald
walked in. Jim stood out from the other guests. It wasn't that he
was dressed scruffily, or because he was in his mid-50s or older.
There was nothing unique in that here. It was that he was alone,
and came into the bar without the hesitancy of the first-time visitors. He made his way directly to the counter, took a stool, and
ordered a pint of soda water. We exchanged a nod and civilities,
and gradually fell into a rambling conversation. Jim and his friends
stayed regularly in a nearby hut, thanks to a "friendly arrange-
ment" with its owner. They used it as a base for walking and, by
Jim's admission, a fair amount of boozing afterward. I won't say
that Jim and I had a lot in common, for our lives were very different, but there were shared points of reference to keep our blether
going. I explained what I was up to that had me sitting here alone
with maps, and Jim said that he once took part in a march all the
way to London. It was a protest, an unsuccessful effort to save

a Lanarkshire steel works from the harsh industrial restructuring of the Thatcher years. My mom's father and grandfather were Lanarkshire steelworkers, though at different works, and years before Jim's march. This was the branch of my family that came to Scotland from County Cavan. And Ireland and family led naturally to Jim's story of a dying wish.

I do not remember with certainty whose dying wish it was. It could have been Jim's mother's or his grandmother's. Whosoever it was, she wanted to know where the grave of her brother or her son lay. This man was also a James McDonald, and Jim's uncle. The family knew only that he was in the Royal Air Force during World War Two and that a ship carrying him had been torpedoed after leaving a British port. Jim's research led him to Ballycastle, County Mayo, in the Republic of Ireland. He was given short shrift by the local priest—"There are no Brits buried here!" Dismayed and leaving town, Jim got talking to the bus driver. There was another Ballycastle, the driver said, in County Antrim, in Northern Ireland. Jim found the local minister there very helpful. He drove Jim to a ruined friary where he knew of graves that might fit the bill. Jim poked around the grounds and, parting undergrowth, uncovered a stone bearing his uncle's name. Presumably James drowned after the U-boat sank his ship, washed up on this Ulster shore, and was identified from his tag. Jim said he now goes to Ballycastle every Armistice Day to remember the uncle he never knew. I liked his story for many reasons—as a reminder that past generations bore loss more routinely than we do; for the blinkered priest who had no interest in the fate of one of his flock, and the minister who was his opposite; but mostly for the affirmation that knowing our ancestors is a deep human need. It is said that Highlanders waiting to charge the enemy lines at the Battle of Culloden recited their lineage going back 20 generations. Perhaps our digital tools will give us, too, a measure of that perspective and sense of continuity.

# 17

## *Rannoch Moor*

O utside the hotel, where yesterday I arrived dripping, the world was transformed. There was abundant blue in the sky, the summits were mostly clear, and sunshine had brought out the greens in the moorland carpet. This fine weather was particularly welcome, as I thought the dozen miles to Bridge of Orchy today might be the best of the West Highland Way. Fortified with a Full Scottish Breakfast, I headed southeast on a paved track. As if to remind me to take nothing for granted, a few drops of sunny rain fell, but never looked like a serious attempt at a shower. The Beuckle was visible from top to base, but thrown in shadow by gray cloud amassing over its south slope. The summit seemed to dissolve the cloud, keeping everything to the north bright and blue. I crossed the A82, took a graveled track, and began to round a last shoulder of the big hills before they gave way to Rannoch Moor.

The moor stretched out east, a 50-square-mile plateau of bog and lochan. About 10,000 years ago, it was the center of an ice-dome, Scotland's last big glacier. The dome formed when "the cold snap" unkindly ended a warmer interlude. During this interlude, first grassland and then trees had advanced north into the post-glacial tundra, followed by wildlife and perhaps the first humans ever to inhabit Scotland. The cold snap put an abrupt end to all this busy colonizing, and for a millennium the Highlands were again deep-frozen. When the dome melted, Rannoch Moor was next gradually covered in dense forest. Then the restless climate wrought another revolution, creating—still thousands of years ago—the peat bogs of today's landscape. The peat is the erstwhile forest decomposing. Now, from the shoulder where I stood, I saw lochans and low, gentle hills out on the moor. There were no trees at all. On the moor's far edge there were big hills again, on a north-east-to-southwest line. Straight east of my position, they were 12 miles away, but they closed rapidly as I walked south this morning. The adjectives used for Rannoch Moor are usually variations on wild, bleak, sodden, inaccessible. I had no reason to doubt them; but from this edge on a sunny day, the place looked quite benign.

Not everyone has felt the same way. In the hit 1996 film *Trainspotting*, the three heroin-addicted mates, plus clean Tommy, arrive at Corrour railway station on the northern edge of the moor. They are trying to kick the drug habit, but are swilling beer and vodka.

"Now what?" asks Sick Boy, as the train pulls away.

"We go for a walk," says Tommy.

"What?" says Spud, incredulous. "Where?"

"There," replies Tommy, pointing to a snow-streaked ben. A few yards onto the moor, striding Tommy turns around after the other three pull up.

"Well, what are you waiting for? … It's the great outdoors! It's fresh air! … Doesn't it make you proud to be Scottish?" he asks.

"It's shite being Scottish!" says Renton, and they decide to go back on heroin.

Rannoch Moor did not make me feel anything in particular about being Scottish, but it was good to be in the great outdoors, hiking this sunlit track as it completed its rounding of the shoulder of Meall a' Bhùiridh—"hill of the bellowing". This mountain hosts the Glencoe ski runs on its north-facing slopes, but I believe the bellowing refers not to overexcited skiers, but to rutting stags. On completing its turn, the track also reached today's highest elevation (1,500 feet above the sea, much less above the moor). Views to the south opened up. They included a prominent ben toward which the track advanced for the next several miles. The ben had a high, conical peak and a lower, rounder top. A ridge ran between them. Farther down the track, a green crag came into view, nearer than the ben. It resembled a giant's ski jump off Meall a' Bhùiridh—the mountain his ramp, the crag his take-off. From the crag, the ben lay square ahead, a wrinkled corrie beneath its ridge, a burn shining on its western slopes. East, to my left, the scene was just as good. There was the narrowing funnel of the moor, the big hills squeezing it out from east and west. But there was still lochan, burn, and bog enough to glisten behind faint sunbeams.

I was able to find out only later that the ben was, in fact, two bens; the conical peak was Stob a' Choire Odhair, and the rounder top Beinn Toaig. At the same place where the Way had rounded the shoulder of Meall a' Bhùiridh, my Ben Nevis OS map had run out, and I did not have the next sheet. In Fort William, to save space, I had bought a map of the entire WHW. It was tough and waterproof, but it showed only a limited amount of country on either side of the Way. It could be as little as a few yards, or as much as a few miles, but it was never as good as OS. Stob a' Choire Odhair had been sacrificed for a box of Important Information in German (WICHTIGE INFORMATIONEN UBER DEN WEST HIGHLAND WAY). The map did tell me that the simple stone arch that I reached next was Bà Bridge, and the water rushing beneath it the River Bà. It was a gorgeous place. Upstream lay a horseshoe of mountains that collected the waters of the Bà and delivered them to the grassy flats around the bridge. On the horseshoe's arc were the flatiron mountain of Clach Leathad and a protuberant "nose" of Stob Ghabhar. Downstream, lined with birch whose leaves were beginning to yellow, the Bà cascaded around massive slabs of black rock.

I was covering the miles too quickly. I told myself there was no point in rushing through this bright and open country just to be the sooner within the walls of the Bridge of Orchy Hotel. But once you are used to a certain pace, it is hard to adopt another. The track didn't help either. It was excellent, a vehicle-width of small stones, with just a few rocks sticking out here and there to trip a misplaced boot. This vehicle-width was no coincidence. Most of the route today followed a road engineered by Thomas Telford in the early 1800s. It overlays an older military road for long sections, but by Telford's day carriages and other wheeled transport had become more important than marching redcoats. The quality of his road reflected this new traffic. Where the military road went high up a slope or directly over a ridge, Telford's followed gentler contours. Where soldiers might have used a ford, Telford put in a bridge. The road was part of a remarkable life that took Telford from shepherd's son in the southern Scottish hills to burial in Westminster Abbey. Along the way, he built an astonishing amount of British infrastructure, including 875 miles of roads in the Highlands alone.

Somewhere beyond Bà Bridge on this fast track I left the Highland council area and entered that of Argyll and Bute. As I have said, the council areas are now the divisions of Scotland for local government purposes; but they have existed only since 1996. There was another structure in place for the 20 years before that. But if I had walked my route as a boy, before 1975, I'd have walked through long-established counties. This particular boundary would have been between the counties of Inverness and Argyll, and I would have crossed it back at Kinlochleven. I suppose the changes of 1975 and 1996 were well-intended, but something a little cheeky has happened too. When you drive north from Glasgow today, you are welcomed into the Highland council area by a sign, a mile or two east of here on the A82. But it welcomes you—bilingually of course—to "the Highlands". Now, as any Scot worth the salt on her porridge will tell you, the Highlands begin 50 miles farther south. The roadside sign claims for a modern, and likely short-lived, administrative entity the centuries-old lands of Gaeldom—and it shrinks them. For me, it was too soon to leave the Highlands, and I was pleased that, whatever the bureaucrats may say, I would be in the *Gàidhealtachd*—the historical Highlands—for three more days.

The track descended past small conifer plantations, and emerged at a lodge set amid Scots pine. On the descent, a long shower fell, and for a while the walking felt eerily familiar. I decided the scene was harking back to my arrival at Clunes five days before—a loch down to my left; coming out of woods to scattered buildings; the same rain. My spirits fell suddenly, and I wondered if this melancholy was triggered by a subconscious memory of misery at Clunes. A single-track road led from the lodge to a small floodplain where an *abhainn* and an *allt* flowed down to the loch. When I had crossed the river, but not yet the stream, the rain and trees petered out to reveal the loch. It was Loch Tulla, and there appeared to be a stand of trees floating upon it. My map showed enough country here to identify the trees as Eilean an Stalcair—not in fact a floating copse, but a round islet 20 paces across. This isle was a crannog, an artificial island once used as a dwelling, hunting place, or refuge. And here the definition of "once" is wide indeed. Crannogs were in use for thousands of years, until as recently as 1700.

The road now crossed the stream on the far edge of the flood-plain, turned sharply east, and arrived at the Inveroran Hotel. By now my spirits had recovered as mysteriously as they had fallen. Although my own hotel was now less than three miles off, I went in to see what this one had to offer. It turned out to be a pot of strong tea and a cheese sandwich in the "Walkers Bar". I had the place to myself. Even the waitress popped in only to take and serve my order. She was Austrian, but preferred her adopted Highlands to the mountains of home. "I know the hills in Scotland are dangerous, but they *look* so much friendlier than those pointy, snowy Alps," she said. Take that, von Trapps.

Opposite the Inveroran Hotel, the West Highland Way left the road and began to climb the very un-Alpine Màm Carraigh, following a section of the military road discarded by Telford as too steep. It is just footpath today. It was only a 550-foot ascent to the summit, but the views on the way were varied and wonderful. Loch Tulla lay beneath the heathery hillside, partially screened by scattered Scots pines growing up the slope. Stob Ghabhar rose to the west, and got me pondering what the waitress had said. It is a decent-sized ben, its peak 3,576 feet above the sea, 500 fewer above its base in the glen below. It was a clear day, and I could see all its features—a far-off summit and long ridges running down from it; the corrie between those ridges; more ridges behind the ridges; the waterfall at the corrie's lip. The mountain was angular, rugged, and full of precipice. I would never call it friendly. It was accessible though; and I doubt there is a ben in Scotland that cannot, in reasonable weather and by the right route, be scaled with basic hiking kit, and have the climber back at his fireside for supper. Even the highest summits are within reach of the human world, not separate realms of eternal ice and thin air (it would need global *cooling*, though just a little, for glaciers to form again on Scotland's highest mountains). The Highlanders of old likely had no good reason to scale their peaks, but they would have driven their livestock to pasture high up the slopes, and hunted in the corries. I think this approachability, an element of friendliness, adds to the Highlands' appeal, but naturally does not diminish their grandeur in the slightest!

At the top of Màm Carraigh, I met a friendly and proper Scottish couple clambering around the cairn. They reminded me of an uncle and aunt of mine, as I remembered them 30 years ago or more. The man wore a white dress shirt. But since he was on a hiking trail, he'd rolled the cuffs up a couple of turns and undone his top button. They were going to the Inveroran Hotel, and asked where I would stay on my way to Glasgow. I reeled off my next four stops, and they picked up on The Drovers Inn, where I was booked tomorrow. I knew nothing about it besides its name and rough location.

"We'll not spoil it for you," he said, "but you're in for a treat!"

"Yes," she said, not very emphatically, "the food is really quite good. But, umm, shall we say the walls of the rooms are a bit thin?"

"Och, let's not bother with that," her husband cut in.

"Yes. It's not fancy, but you'll like the food, and the atmosphere is something different," she concluded. We chatted some more, before starting to edge away in our respective directions.

"Enjoy The Drovers!" she said. "The walls ... "

But her husband cut her off with his goodbye, and I was left to speculate on the trauma that befell them at The Drovers as I walked down the far side of the *mam*. At first, I imagined that their sleep had been disturbed by a party of feral Australians going at it all night long in the room next door, but then had the mischievous thought that perhaps someone had made a complaint about *them*. Aside from this matter, they had wrapped up The Drovers nicely for me, and I was anticipating what the package might contain when the path entered planted forest for the final descent to Bridge of Orchy. Here I met a middle-aged couple slogging up, and they communicated without saying a word that they were open to a chat (nearly everyone I met out on the trails was, and they said so through a combination of eye contact, expression, and the breaking of pace). Just a few sentences into the chat, he asked with a slight foreign accent where I was from.

"I was born here, but I live near New York now."

"Oh, I thought perhaps we could speak in Dutch." Except perhaps as a small child, my English has never been Scottish, and now it seemed it must have become so neutral, so uprooted, that it wasn't really British anymore either. I could, they thought, have been one of their own.

Where the path came out of the pines, a humpback bridge stood between me and the hamlet of Bridge of Orchy. The hamlet owes its name—its very existence—to this 260-year-old arch, another military project. There wasn't much to Bridge of Orchy—a few gray roofs and white walls clustered tightly beneath the steep, bare slope of Beinn Dorain.

# 18

# Long Trail
# to the Haunted Inn

I wanted to set out this morning right after an early breakfast. I'd had a good rest, taking early to my crisp-sheeted bed in the Bridge of Orchy Hotel's bunkhouse to catch up with *Kim*. At 19 miles, today's walk to The Drovers Inn at Inverarnan would be my longest on the West Highland Way, and the days were drawing in. Day was now shorter than night. Back at Blairmore, the sun had set after 8 p.m. Today it would go down a full hour sooner. Sunrise this morning had come an hour later too. Not that there was any question of seeing it. Rain was pattering on the skylight beside my bunk when I woke, and spilling down the restaurant windows as I ate breakfast.

I pulled my hood up and climbed the lane to the station, where an underpass led to the other side of the railway line. The Way turned south, keeping to a contour of Beinn Dorain a little higher than the tracks. A two-carriage train clattered by on its run to Fort William. Two glens met here. The nameless one I would

follow carried the railway, the A82, and the Way, though from this
hillside these routes looked no more than scratches on the moor.
The other was Glen Orchy, leading off through empty country to
Loch Awe. This loch, Scotland's longest, lay 15 miles away, and
was familiar territory. Our family spent three summer vacations
by its side a decade and more ago. The memory of them took me
momentarily away from my solitary slope, back to days filled with
the company of small girls—on forest walks; in crumbled castles;
puttering up the loch in an open boat. This place was nearby, and
unchanged I knew. But we had occupied it at a certain time, and
since then our changing—above all, their growing—had put Loch
Awe out of my reach even if I were to turn here and follow Glen
Orchy.

Back in the here and now, cloud drifted across even the low-
est slopes on the far side of the glen, as if the forest there were
smoldering, while I, much higher up my slope, walked for now in
the clear. Soon the Way re-crossed the railway—on a footbridge
this time—and slipped down toward a farm, announced by the
lowing of Highland cattle as they moved through a field to a burn.
A pickup was parked on the track ahead, and next to it a farmer
was whistling commands. His dogs were working sheep gathered
up the brae from the cattle. Twice I closed on the pickup, and
twice the farmer jumped into it and moved on a distance before
I caught up. I still thought we might get to natter, but he gave
a final whistle, and the collies jumped into the Toyota, and they
all sped off. The track through Auch Farm was now ever more
mucky with the waste of beasts until, hugging a stream on its way
out, it became a veritable minefield of country pancakes (except
they were shaped like Christmas puddings). Here I met a party
coming north. They had spent the night in Tyndrum, the village
now three miles ahead. We looked together at the cattle shit and
mocked our dainty steps to work around it.

Kim's lama friend, as my reading last night reminded me, walked with a big purpose. He was searching for the River of the Arrow and, through it, freedom from the "Wheel" of worldly concerns. The young Dutchman in Fort William had asked if I was seeking something big on my long walk. I said no, and then wondered if that was true. I wondered again now. I certainly was not seeking anything mystical or religious. Any self-transformation I wanted was only so that I could better order my worldly concerns, revolve more happily on the Wheel if you like. And, as I walked, I had made little progress on working out what I would in future do differently, my head instead full of routes, sights, and stories. Seeing the journey as meditation for the new direction I would take at its end had always been, I knew now, a thin alibi. What I sought was the journey itself, *this journey*. I have dreamed of grand journeys for as long as I can remember, but mostly the dreams proved idle and transient. I did not care deeply whether they came true or not. The dream of hiking across Scotland had been different. Since the idea came to me, up in Assynt three years ago, it had been remarkably constant, turning itself by its insistence into a plan. Walking away from Auch Farm this morning, I thought how that power derived from uniting in one desire different threads in my life—love of the trail, my unfinished business with Scotland, and the continued lure of taking off without much in the way of itinerary or responsibility. This walk was fulfilment, not seeking.

I wondered where that last thread had started. Certainly nobody among my family or close friends had set an example. I have heard that my grandfathers roamed, and it is possible that they were driven by something less hardheaded than a search for work or a place in the world. But I had scarcely known them, and if they infected me, it can only have been genetically. My father, for sure, never hinted at any interest in wandering. Life in the human troop is stressful. It can be complicated and dull at the same time. On this adventure, the task each day was simple, and accomplished in an ever-changing scene. Relationships were short-lived and in-consequential, without power to unsettle, frustrate, or chide. So my solitary takings-off (usually to places far from the thrusting, get-ahead parts of the world) were, to some extent, about putting myself at the edge of the troop, watching its disharmonies from a safe distance. But the same end is achievable by other means— immersing yourself in books, your garden, or whisky for example. What hooked me on wandering? A book may offer a clue. In my student years, I read and reread Laurie Lee's *As I Walked Out One Midsummer Morning.* Lee's walk through Spain in 1935-6 was, I decided, what journeying should be; independent, off-the-cuff, rough-and-ready, poetic. His was the kind of escape I wanted, es-cape with a beginning, an end, and an odyssey in between; a tem-porary, precious freedom from the concerns of the Wheel.

The Way, climbing gradually, drew ever closer to the A82 and the railway, until in the tight pass above Tyndrum, the routes ran cheek by jowl. Since Bridge of Orchy, the weather had been dis-mal but undramatic. As I neared Tyndrum, it began to bucket, to rain cats and dogs, to threaten the return of the Flood. In the vil-lage, I went into a snack shop for a cup of tea, and sat dripping un-til a puddle formed beneath my stool. Then I followed the WHW markers around the village, and came to a ford at a burn in spate. Maybe this was the place the woman on the Devil's Staircase had whined about—*that burn came right over our boots!* My sandals were in my backpack, probably still waiting for pick-up in Bridge of Orchy, so I had no choice but to pick my way over in boots. I couldn't stop the torrent flowing over their tongues and laces, but I kept it below their tops. The path emerged at Tyndrum Lower Station, which I now realized I could have easily reached on tar-mac through the village. The station serves the Oban line. Upper Tyndrum, a half-mile away, is on the Fort William line. Tyndrum is the smallest place in Britain with two stations.

For six miles the Way wound through Strath Fillan, the broad, flat-bottomed glen running southeast to Crianlarich. I left

Tyndrum through riverside woods, emerging at a patch of barren ground the color of ash. Lead was crushed here in the 1700s, so toxic that even now vegetation does not grow. The Way pressed on through scrubby woods and heather to a small loch, and soon after skirted the hamlet of Dalrigh. Here I saw a notice announcing a plan to develop a gold and silver mine in the nearby hills. Now, since before Tyndrum, I had been within Loch Lomond & The Trossachs National Park, so this notice surprised me, if not quite so much as if it were posted beside Old Faithful. Scotland's national parks—two so far—are a different concept from those in the US. They do not seal off large wild areas from human settlement. Instead, Scotland's parks are meant to be areas where conservation and sustainable development coexist. But a gold mine is more than a hole in the ground. It needs, as the notice said, a "service and production building, plant, storage area, Tailings Management Facility (TMF), recirculation pond and gauging station, diversion of burn, access roads, bridge and car parking". All this could make quite a mess of Cononish Glen.

I pressed on mechanically from Dalrigh, and arrived at a stony bend of the Cononish River. It was raining hard again after a letting-up since Tyndrum. A strung-out group of walkers came from the direction of Crianlarich, stoically cheerful and well kitted out—bar one. The stand-out was a teenager walking head-down without raingear of any description, his shoulders drooped inside a saturated sweater. The Way swung to the north side of the strath, passing underneath the A82 on a concrete path that was within inches of being inundated by the rising river at its side. The path came out to a lane, and a sign saying "SAC Auchtertyre Farm". The Scottish Agricultural College has its Highland research farms in Strath Fillan, and as a sideline runs Strathfillan Wigwams. They are holiday accommodation. But where there are wigwams there is usually a store called The Trading Post, and the one here provided a coffee break in the shelter of its porch. Two very tall German hikers were taking refuge too. Before I went out into the storm again, I looked up at them to chat. I said they might want to cut into Tyndrum before they reached the swollen burn. They thanked me for my advice, and the shorter of the two looked down to his faraway boots and chuckled—"but dey are already vet!"

Somehow comforted that even German boots leak, I followed the edge of the floodplain of the river now called the Fillan, and came to the ruins of Saint Fillan's Priory. It was 1:30. I still had half the day's hike to do, and the Germans had warned of a steep climb before Crianlarich. So I gave the priory a miss, though Saint Fillan rang a bell (as monks do) from my history reading. After I returned home, I browsed again Ronald McNair Scott's highly readable *Robert the Bruce*, and learned the significance of the site I now hurried by. In 1306, recently crowned King of Scots but hunted by foes both English and native, Bruce's flight brought him into the strath where once the saint had lived:

> *"This holy man of the sixth century was the most venerated of early Scottish saints, and it was not without purpose that Bruce had halted his little army beside his tomb. The sacrilege committed in Greyfriars church weighed upon Bruce's conscience and could shake with superstitious fears the faith of his followers. So here ... it is believed that, as his men gathered about him, he knelt for absolution before the Abbot of Inchafray and received his blessing for all to hear. He had little time to spare."*

It would do him little immediate good. The sacrilege was the murder of his rival for the throne, John Comyn, on sacred ground in Dumfries six months before. Shortly after the abbot's blessing, Macdougall kinsmen of Comyn fell on Bruce at Dalrigh, and inflicted on his army a second crushing defeat of the summer. Eight years of astonishing hardship and endless campaigning lay between this defeat and Bruce's final triumph at Bannockburn.

I had little time to spare either, and set off down a lane across rich, flat pasture grazed by black-faced sheep. In short order I re-crossed the river and main road, and entered planted forest. The climb was not so arduous, topping out 600 feet above the strath floor. The path rose through patches of mist, deepening the gloom and mystery of even a false forest. In my mind's eye I saw a black wolf come out of the dark to trot silently and watchfully among the trunks at the edge of the mist; and then I summoned up a sorcerer's cottage smoking in a damp glade. In the real world, there were tricky burns to cross. At one of them I met a north-bounder, German again, looking nervously at the scattered stepping-stones. I took the plunge first, though only figuratively, and saw her land safely on the far side before I pushed on. I came to a purple, heathery hillock in a clearing, and had a view through wispy mist across a broad glen, but could not tell if I had wheeled yet from Strath Fillan into Glen Falloch. Farther on, side trails led down to Crianlarich, and I knew that I had not. I baulked at dropping the 300 feet into the village even for a mug of tea. Soon a fresh southerly breeze announced Glen Falloch, and at this spot too I realized that I was halfway between Fort William and Glasgow.

Glen Falloch is not Scotland's most beautiful. Even seen from a hillside made suddenly comfortable by the passing of rain and the coming of a gentle wind, I could not overlook the power lines and pylons strung through it. There was a farm here too, always good for a change of sound and smell, usually to barking and manure. The Way was out on open moor now, slipping back down to the A82 and a new river, the Falloch. Before I reached them, I sat on a rock a while to dry in the air. There was a railway in the bottom of the glen too, and I went under it via a "cattle creep", a passage high enough for cows but not for the un-stooped walker. A couple came the other way through it.

"For coos," they said with German voices, inadvertently getting the Scots pronunciation about right too. I wondered if anyone at all was left in Germany. Ten minutes later, walking more mechanically than ever, I was woken by an exquisite chute where white water tumbled over black rock into the Falloch. I suspect it was a fleeting, storm-induced beauty, as I can find no falls there on any map. Then, as if to compensate for the sublime, I fell in with Wouter.

I saw him ahead of me, lounging and smoking at a trail junction. When I reached him, I wondered out loud which track was the onward WHW, and we decided together that the downhill path looked the more likely. Wouter was the only other north-souther I met on the WHW, and it was only this that made falling in with him even possible. He joined me on the downhill path, but it soon came to a dead-end, and we retraced our steps to the junction. I didn't really want company, but it would have been awkward to engineer a separation, and so I hiked with a buddy for the first time on my journey. The only problem was that Wouter was one of those famously ultra-conceited north European kids. He was from Ypres in Belgium, and liked to contrast the world's ignorance of his homeland with his own vast knowledge of the world. It mattered not a whit that I showed, I think, some reasonable knowledge of his neck of the woods. I mentioned the World War One battles of Ypres, and said that one of my great-uncles may well have perished in the third of them. "There are more dead people in my town than living," said Wouter, using up his quota of almost-humor for the day. I showed some understanding of Belgium's acrimonious language politics too, but to no avail. I foolishly admitted to having been to Ostend ("The only place the British go!"), and that I had not heard of the low-cost airport he had used to fly to Edinburgh ("the Americans only know Brussels!"). So Wouter went on, using up the mile or two we had together to offer proof that he was in the know, and that I and the whole benighted world were not. It was a relief to reach Beinglas Farm (more wigwams!), and leave the Way for The Drovers Inn.

Wouter went on to the "cottage" where he planned to sleep for free. "Jeez, Wouter, don't you know it's called a frigging bothy!", I wanted to call after him.

I walked in glorious silence over the flat bottom of Glen Falloch, crossed the river on a wooden bridge, and turned left onto the A82. The Drovers Inn came into view, a solid three-story stone building in different hues of gray. I could not imagine it anywhere else but Scotland. As soon as I stepped inside, it became clear that The Drovers was like no other hotel I had stayed in. The reception was jam-packed with stuffed animals in glass cases. Assorted heads and horns were nailed to the walls. Since many of the species on show do not, and never did, grace the wilds of Scotland, I did not take it all as a woeful attempt to fake a Highland castle or shooting lodge. Then there was the stuffed snarling bear, erect but chained to an iron ball and trap; and the suit of armor, similarly shackled. The receptionist was a kilted lass with an Australian accent. She wore a t-shirt that said "Scottish Pub of the Year ... 1705". I was getting the picture.

My room was the remotest in the hotel, at the far end of a corridor on the top floor. It had a dormer window, a few pieces of old furniture, and no bathroom. I suppose it was a bit spooky, but spooky was a quality that The Drovers cultivated assiduously (the building had looked haunted from outside too, like something from Scooby-Doo). The inn posted scary stories—the cold body of a girl drowned long ago that slipped into the bed in Room 6 from time to time; the family that perished in the snow and now appeared shivering in Room 2; and the ghost of a murdered drover by the name of Angus that wailed as it stalked the inn. And now I stalked the inn, condemned to wander its passages seemingly forever in search of a loo and shower. I finally found them on the other side of the building and down a floor. Then, since the inn had no drying room, I plugged in the heater in my room and hung my wet gear from the curtain rod across the dormer window.

I took my boots to the bar, and tried to dry them next to a grate that was too high and embers that were too low. Remembering the praise of the couple on Màm Carraigh, I looked forward to supper. When it came, the fish & chips were overcooked and dry. I sat at the bar manned by kilted Aussies, and decided that the best I could say for The Drovers Inn was that it did not take itself too seriously, and was unabashed that it provided entertainment above facilities and service. And with that I climbed the stairs, said goodnight to Angus on the landing, and fell asleep undisturbed by noisy neighbors or ghouls. Until, that is, I stirred in the middle of the night in need of the far-off bathroom, and dopily crossing my pitch black room walked right into my gear hanging cold from the curtain rod. "Ohhh, holy crap!", I wailed.

## 19

# Loch Lomond

├──────────────┼──────────────┤

It was a warm, dry morning, though overcast still. Last night, outside the inn, a bus driver told me it would reach 85° today. I thought he must have heard the forecast for somewhere farther south, like Marrakech perhaps. All the same, I set off back to Beinglas Farm wearing only one thin layer. From the wigwams, the West Highland Way climbed steadily through a mile of woods to Dubh Lochan. This little loch sat in flat, marshy ground between a knoll and the slopes of a bigger hill called simply Cruach (Gaelic for a heap or stack). Ahead, the land fell away to reveal slim, silvery Loch Lomond snaking south between wooded banks and the steep slopes of its confining bens. An islet floated near the loch's narrowest point. In the far distance, loch, hills, and clouds melded into a single vaporous gray. Lomond is Scotland's biggest freshwater loch. It would keep me company now for 19 miles and a day and a half, becoming ever broader as I hiked south. Best of all, the Way takes its eastern side, leaving the A82 and the tourists on the west. A mild breeze came off the water as the narrow path wound down to the shore.

The path reached the loch at Ardleish, and for the next four miles the going was often slow and tough. Although the Way kept close to the loch shore, there were sharp ups and downs that demanded clambering over rocks and sidestepping treacherous roots. Injury from a trip or slip felt a real danger. The loch was an elusive companion, glimpsed only now and then through the trees or from a rare clearing. There was a clearing at Doune Byre bothy, high above the loch, and I was relieved to find the place deserted, no Wouter smoking outside, ready to head south. In the woods beyond, I smelled a stink like goat cheese, and simultaneously caught sight of dark gray creatures chewing among the small birch and oak. I had read about wild goats on this section, and was not taken much by surprise. These particular animals were small and unthreatening. They bleated pathetically. But soon I ran into their dads, granddads, and uncles. One beast, armed with horns at least two feet long, blocked my path. He moved aside as I approached, but I decided against taunting him (stewed kid! cabrito asado!), as I might have taunted his ovine cousins. A bit farther on, I cricked my neck painfully, and stopped to massage it with eyes half-closed. When I opened them and raised my head, I was eye-to-eye with a huge billy standing on a rock. It was my turn to bleat pathetically.

The islet that I had seen floating, near where Loch Lomond is just a few hundred yards across, was Island I Vow. I was looking at it now from the south, a clump of woods in the gray water. It was its name that intrigued me. What kind of vow? A monastic one? Or was it a Highlander's vow, now that he was approaching the foreign Lowlands, to return home with the battle won or the cattle sold at a tidy profit? Alas, it probably has nothing to do with vows of any sort, but is an Anglicization of an uncertain Gaelic name. I suppose that when the OS map-makers came to this district in the 1860s, no one could provide the "correct orthography" of the island in Gaelic. Almost all the neighboring landscape has uncorrupted Gaelic names—the headland behind the island was Rubha Ban, the rocks above me belonged to Creag an Fhithic, the burns were mostly *allt* this or *allt* that. But even the earliest OS map calls this island "I Vow". A popular guess is that it comes from *Eilean a' Bho*—island of the cow.

I pushed on over more rocks and roots, and stepped at one point around a dead deer lying in the middle of the trail. Then there was a sign to Rob Roy's Cave. I didn't notice that the trail forked here, and followed the sign believing the way to the cave and the WHW were one and the same. The path grew ever more tortuous, turning into clambering ascents and on-your-butt descents of huge boulders. The area reeked of goat cheese. A tinny tour boat commentary drifted off the loch through the screen of trees. There was a cavernous pit next to one scramble, but I doubted it was where Rob hid from the Duke's men. "This can't be the bloody West Highland Way!" I said to myself, and went back to the sign. As for Rob, all that is widely "known" about him these days comes, naturally, from Hollywood, in this case the 1995 movie with Liam Neeson. And there is certainly no accepted version of Robert Roy McGregor's real life to set the movie against. He lived close to Loch Lomond from 1671 to 1734, and was a Jacobite soldier, a wronged businessman, and a Highland Robin Hood. Or make that a traitor to the Jacobite cause, a fraudster, and a racketeer. Take your pick. Either way, I had no interest in a cave he may or may not have known.

It was now a mile to the village of Inversnaid. It is the only place on the northeast shore of Loch Lomond that can be reached by road. In fact, it is the only place on the northeast shore of Loch Lomond. I knew it had a hotel, and I knew it was lunchtime. Casual walkers appeared on the trail. They clasped cameras and bottled water. Their sneakers were clean. When it came, Inversnaid seemed to consist only of the hotel and the car park in front of it. There were fine views over the loch, now a mile wide, to the bens beyond. I had long ago ceased to worry that the dirty walker faced rejection in Scottish hotels. They had all been welcoming, as well they might. But there was something about the Inversnaid that revived my fear. It looked like an old-fashioned seaside hotel, the kind of establishment that might have rules and "standards". As I peeled off my over-pants outside, I set up my defenses. This meant anticipating the moment of rejection:

"Could I order some lunch?"

"No. I'm afraid not."

"Oh, why is that?"

"I'm afraid, sir, you smell like a goat." And the hotel was rather formal on the inside, as well as spare and cavernous. The uniformed barman came and went, leaving me alone and unattended at the bar. He finally came over.

"Could I order some lunch?"

"Yes. Sorry to keep you waiting. We're short staffed today." And he said it without sniffing the air quizzically.

When I left the hotel after panini and two pints of Diet Coke, the sun was out. It was over 70° too, which in Scotland would be a scorcher even in July. I have said a lot about rain and wind on this journey, but next to nothing about temperature. That's because all the time, day and night, it was somewhere between 45° and 60°. It nudged a bit higher on the warmest of afternoons (and only that after Willie's Nubble springs to mind) and fell lower only in foul weather on high ground. But today became undeniably hot, if not quite the 85° forecast by the bus driver. The trail was much improved too, and I must have set about it with enthusiasm. Still in sight of the hotel I overtook a couple in young middle age. "Och look, we're being passed already!", they laughed.

The Appalachian Trail is nicknamed "the green tunnel". The walk from Cape Wrath had been nothing like that. Bare hills prevailed, with only short sections through trees, and those mostly in the linear forest of the plantations. But on the walk along Loch Lomond I began to experience something of the monotony of the Appalachian hardwood forest. It was not unpleasant, just that the horizon and much in the way of visual stimulus was shut out. Whether because of this or the easy going, I now drifted into daydreaming and telling myself stories more deeply and for longer than at any other time on the walk. Looking back later, this afternoon was like a night's sleep remembered only for moments of wakefulness. I recall some beautiful patches of sunlit woods, where the narrow path wound through mossy trunks and bracken thickets that were half green and half brown. A mile or two after Inversnaid the path came out to a view of "the steep, steep side o' Ben Lomon'". Ben Lomond rises more than 3,000 feet above this eastern side of the loch. It is the most southerly of the munros. Its summit was two miles away, too close for me to know whether I was seeing the very top or just a lesser ridge. Either way, the whole scene was very beautiful, and further lyrics from probably Scotland's most famous song fitted well with it[42]. The banks and braes were indeed bonnie, the sun did shine bright today, and down at the loch it appeared that "in sunshine the waters are sleeping." At least it did until two RAF jets roared over them.

I took breaks from sleepwalking through the clammy heat. One was on rocks by a small waterfall. The loch, hundreds of feet below, was sleeping again, a mile of empty water but for the white speck of a tour boat cruising the far bank. In the hazy distance, cloud drifted across the jagged peaks nicknamed the Arrochar Alps. Later, on a bench with another view down to the loch, I basked in the sun until my sweat dried and I was ready for the last miles to the SYHA hostel at Rowardennan. They turned out to be more miles than necessary. The OS symbol for a youth hostel is a red triangle. It is etched in my mind since youth. I saw a red triangle on my WHW map about half a mile beyond the village, and strode off toward it. The Way ran down to the loch, came to the Ben Lomond trailhead car park, followed a single-track road through the village, and finally turned back into the woods. Some distance along an undulating trail through big pines a hiker came from the south. You can guess her nationality.

"Can you tell me please how far is it to the youth hostel?" she asked.

"It's very close. That way," I replied, pointing to where she had come from.

"No. It is this way," she said, pointing to where I had come from.

"Look, there is a red triangle on the map here. It means a youth hostel."

"That is a red point. And it tells you it is the end of a mile." I took my glasses from my pack, and confirmed that she was absolutely right. My only defense was that the red dot was so positioned against other cartographic lines that it assumed triangular attributes. On the other hand, this map had its own symbol for a hostel (a tree beside a hut), and there it was a mile back, right beside the trail. I'd walked straight past it.

I waited for my big pack outside reception. If stuffy dormitories are the bane of hostelling, there can be spectacular compensation. Rowardennan Lodge could easily have housed an upscale hotel. A long drive wound up from the gate, and big windows looked over an expanse of lawn running down to the loch and premium views. It is the glory of the SYHA that any bum can stay in a place like this. Equipped, finally, with soap, towel, and a change of clothes, I took an ice-cold shower, and walked once again into the village. The track hugged the bank of the loch, where small oak and birch grew almost from the water. Yellows and browns were leaching into the woodland colors. I bought a pint in the

Rowardennan Hotel and took it outside. The midges could not spoil the pink-gray clouds of the approaching sunset, nor the view of Ben Lomond, which I knew I was seeing in its entirety now.

## 20

# Farewell to the Highlands

A t lunchtime today, after a walk of nine miles, I would turn my back to Loch Lomond. At the same place, I would say farewell to the Highlands. Considering the troubles and rewards they had given me for four weeks, I set out this morning with little feeling of occasion. Indeed, I set out with as much routine as I would once have left for the office. Getting up and walking was now just what I did. As if to prepare me for the coming Lowlands, the Highlands laid on the gentlest of walks. The big hills fell back from the shore, and the loch widened and filled with wooded islands, most with names that contained "inch" (from *innis*, another Gaelic word for isle). The West Highland Way went in and out of woods, climbed low lochside hills, and emerged frequently to share the single-track road that runs from Rowardennan down to Balmaha. I came down one hill through a pretty wood of well-spaced oaks, and arrived at a bay facing Inchlonaig. A breeze had picked up during the morning, and on this south-facing bay it was stiff, bucking the dinghies moored out in the loch. The weather was otherwise as mild as the trail, the sun and heat of yesterday replaced by overcast skies. From a place my map labeled Sallochy, but where I saw but two houses, visibility across the loch was good. I identified, or thought I did, more "inches" out beyond Inchlonaig—little Bucinch in front of Inchcruin; and perhaps Creinch four miles off, hazy behind tiny Ceardach. I am sure the locals always found uses for these islets, and some are glimpsed in the fog of history with greater or lesser clarity. Ceardach means forge, and the island may have been the site of smelting sometime after the arrival of iron-working 2,800 years ago. The yew trees of Inchlonaig are said to have been planted by Robert the Bruce to keep his busy archers supplied with bows. A travel writer of 1804 noted that Inchcruin housed "an asylum for insane persons".

Now and then I met hikers heading north. Two Scots lads, one with dreadlocks, the other with punky hair, both tattooed, stopped to talk, and did so with supreme eloquence and friendliness. They were planning to wild camp at the north end of the loch, they said, adding that it was forbidden on this southeast shore, where proximity to the Central Belt had led to abuse of camping rights. Later, I stopped near Cashell to chat with an elderly couple from Nantucket serenely edging their way to Fort William. Then the Way went back to woodland paths and single-track road until it brought me to Craigie Fort. I saw no sign of a fort atop this little hill, but it had fine views over the cloud-gray, miles-wide loch.

At the bottom of the hill was Balmaha. I bought a sandwich in the village store, ate it on the bench outside, and thought about the coming 1,000-foot climb around Conic Hill. It would be my first notable uphill slog since the climb to the Devil's Staircase, and the first hill on the whole walk with an English-sounding name. I set off, with little enthusiasm, to the trailhead, crossing on the way the car park of the National Park Centre. There, puffing at a bus stop, was a familiar figure. I talked with Wouter just long enough to be put in the know that Conic Hill would be hard work. And so it was. But after the trail came out of planted pines onto the moor, each stretch of slog brought new and rewarding views. At first, they were to the south, to an undulating tapestry of woods and fields in different hues of green. It was the most extensive farmland I had seen in four weeks. It was the Lowlands. As the path swung behind Conic Hill, through a saddle called Bealach Ard, the views switched to the north, all the way to cloud-topped bens on the far side of Loch Lomond. This was the Highland Line alright! And Bealach Ard would be my last *bealach*.

There was no sign to mark the frontier. Indeed, it was only I who decided it lay precisely here at Bealach Ard. I could not have been far off. As well as a historical cultural boundary, the Highland Line here is a geological and geographical one too, created by the Highland Boundary Fault. I could see the fault below, running across Loch Lomond as a tidy line of islands— Inchmurrin, Creinch, Torrinch, Inchcailloch. It came ashore at Balmaha, and Conic Hill seemed to be another of its topographical manifestations. At the risk of gross oversimplification, to the north and west of the fault the rocks and climate had combined to make the land unfavorable for cultivation. South and east of it the soils and weather were more suitable. These differences in physical geography had a huge impact on the societies that developed on either side of the fault, contributing to the cultural divide between the "wild" and "civilized" Scots that was well established 500 years ago. We cross some borders today, and little changes, not even the accent of our *barista*. For any Lowlander or Highlander who found himself, as Davie Balfour did, "on the wrong side of the Highland Line", just about everything changed—the look and use of the land; the identity and loyalties of the people; their dress, music, food, and language; the social order and its customs; and the force, or want of it, of the King's law. The Line was an east-west divide as much as a north-south one. From here, the cultural boundary ran northeast for 100 miles, following the line of the fault, but then it turned decidedly north, even northwest, to reach the Moray Firth not far east of Inverness.

The Way stayed close to the Highland Line for two miles, rounding and then descending Conic Hill. It felt good to be on open moor with unbroken views again. By now the big loch was disappearing behind Conic Hill, and the trail descending irrevocably into the Lowlands. It came to Garadhban Forest, a plantation in the midst of "harvesting". I walked on scarred trails, between long piles of logs painted with cryptic codes in primary colors— "CAL", "7-10". In a section of the woods not yet chopped down, I saw ahead an old dear in a pink jacket walking her dog. She seemed oblivious of my approach, and I halted for fear of startling her. Later, where the trail came out to a lane, she was driving off, sending a cheery wave in my direction. From this lane I saw the Campsie Fells to the southeast, half in faint sunshine, half in shadow. The hill called Dumgoyne stuck up from the sunny half, like an upturned, chinny face on the prostrate body of the other fells. The dum- prefix signifies a hill, or perhaps an ancient hilltop fort.

My map showed the WHW reentering the forest and circling back to Drymen, where I was booked for the night. But I rebelled, and followed the lane directly to the village. It turned out to be a fine shortcut, a downhill run lined with bracken and straggly woods that came to a rolling pasture dotted with black-and-white cattle. They were un-shaggy, un-Highland, *civilized* beasts. The pasture lay behind a dry stone wall whose topmost rocks stuck up like jagged peaks, some sheathed in forests of luxuriant moss. Soon I came to the tidy streets of Drymen, and then to the door of the Clachan Inn on the picturesque village square.

After cleaning up, I nosed around Drymen, or at least the part of it nearest The Square. From a closet in my brain I remembered that it is pronounced DRIM-en. My father was good at telling me things like that; that Wemyss is Weems; Dalry, Dal-RYE, and so on. Drymen was not like any other place I stayed on this walk. Its defining quality was a self-conscious attractiveness that spoke of affluent commuters, retirees, and weekend-breakers. Even photogenic Ullapool, with about the same population, had exhibited a utilitarian side of ferries and fishing. The Clachan Inn shared The Square—really a small green—with cottages that were now absorbed into the posh Winnock Hotel. Across from the Winnock was Drymen Pottery, which boasted a pub, shop, and café, but not apparently a pottery. I used a call box that looked out on The Drymen Village Shop, an old red pillar box in front of its whitewashed walls. All this was nicer than litter, broken glass, and dereliction, but it didn't charm me. With hindsight, my enthusiasm and attentiveness dipped on these last days on the WHW. It might have been that the Way had become too easy. I was still sweaty and footsore at the end of each day, but I knew that if I just kept to the red line on my map it would lead to the bed I had booked back in Fort William. There was no need for a compass now, or food rationing, or wading burns. Some of the edge had come off the walk, and Drymen symbolized this state of affairs— comfortable, but a bit dull. Anyway, all I wanted from the place was food, drink, and a seat to watch a football match on TV.

The football match was Celtic versus Udinese, an Italian side. It was in the Europa League, the poor cousin of the Champions League where Europe's elite compete. I entered the bar of the Clachan clutching my Celtic cap at my side, not wearing it on my head. Showing Celtic or Rangers colors in Scotland brands you as more than a fan of the team; it implies a religious affiliation and probably a certain view of the politics of Ireland. Although this sectarian divide is breaking down, a Celtic fan is still probably Catholic, and a Rangers fan Protestant. Now add Irish politics. Because many Irish, from both sides of the island's divide, have settled in Scotland over the years, and around Glasgow especially, many "Old Firm" supporters have ties to Ireland. A Celtic fan is more likely to favor the nationalist story of Ireland's past and future, and a Rangers fan more likely to affirm Northern Ireland's Britishness. Irish tricolors and Union Jacks wave at Celtic-Rangers games much more than Scotland's Saltire. Religion and politics had nothing whatsoever to do with my boyhood decision for Celtic. My family tree hangs heavy with Catholic Irish, but ties to the Church and to Ireland were broken for my parents long before I was born. At the age of seven I became a Celt because I liked their name. Out on a walk, my dad and I fell to talking about Scottish football, and he ran through the teams—Celtic, Rangers, Hearts, Hibs, Partick Thistle ... He did not steer me, and if he also mentioned that Celtic had recently reached the top of their trade by winning the European Cup (and that, in the words of their greatest manager, they did so "by playing football. Pure, beautiful, inventive football"), that likely influence on a boy's mind has been wiped from my memory.

I did not seriously fear assault, hostility, or even gentle mockery in cozy Drymen, unless perhaps the ladies' lawn bowls club had a feisty Orange section. But it seemed wise to be discreet, especially now that I was approaching Glasgow. The game was already underway when I entered the bar. It was 6:15, and the place was far from busy. Not everyone was paying attention to the TV either. But those that were rose from their barstools when Celtic threatened to score, and flopped back down groaning when the attacks were thwarted. I placed my cap squarely on my head. Celtic were winning 1-0, but it was not a thrilling game. No one was expecting "pure, beautiful inventive football" but Celtic seemed short of drive too. Even so, it looked like they would hold on, until in the dying minutes Udinese equalized from a penalty kick. I stayed in the bar to watch more football and down more beer. When, eventually, I went around to the courtyard at the back of the inn to get to my room, a kitchen worker was loitering there. He looked at me and said "no passion!" I was bewildered until he nodded at my cap, and then I had to agree with him.

The next morning, in the same yard, I readied the Big Bastard for action. AMS would have taken it on to accommodation at the end of the WHW in Milngavie (Mull-GUY), but I planned to stay in central Glasgow tonight and so had to walk fully laden. Scarcely out of Drymen, I could not believe that I had carried the pack from Cape Wrath to Fort William, even at times ceasing to notice its weight on my back. Now it felt leaden and ill-fitting. It was a humid morning, unseasonably warm again, and I wondered how on earth I would manage the 12 miles to Milngavie. But I pressed on—across the main road to Stirling, through a swampy field, and out to a tight country lane. The lane ran straight at first, then swung and rolled through the fields to Gartness, a name given to a pretty row of cottages beside the bucolic Endrick Water.

Across the Endrick, the Way struck out toward the lump of Dumgoyne on a straight and level path, once the Aberfoyle & Glasgow railway. My pack was sitting lighter now, and the old railway bed gave me an easy ride, remembered only for dog-walkers, a cyclist's warning ding, and a cow that nuzzled its calves toward me. At the village of Dumgoyne—beneath the 1,400-foot hill of the same name—the path arrived at the Beech Tree Inn. Gathered around an outside table was a group of hard-looking men messing with gear. They had crew cuts, tattoos, and muscled arms. One of the items they were messing with was an artificial leg belonging to one of their number. They asked if I'd come from Fort William, and I asked in return if they were headed there. They were, but I hesitated to ask next about what I suspected, that they were soldiers helping a comrade to recover on the WHW some of what he had lost in Afghanistan.

I continued along the railway bed in the valley of the Blane Water, taking aim at Dumgoyach—Dumgoyne's smaller, woodier, and more precisely conical twin. I passed the white buildings of

Glengoyne distillery and spied in the haze ahead the gray towers of Duntreath castle. But before I reached them, the Way curled around Dumgoyach and rose onto an open brae. Dumgoyne, seen now from the south, was reshaped, rising across the strath beneath a window of blue sky. At the top of the brae, the WHW joined a country road for just long enough to find a path into patchy woods. A mile later, reedy Craigallian Loch appeared.

There was a notice beside the loch, homemade and low to the ground. It began: *Here Burned the Craigallian Fire.* I had not heard of this fire, and had to kneel, as if at prayer, to read the remainder of the text:

> *The 'Eternal Fire' was a beacon which attracted those industrial working-class Wanderers who wanted to escape from the stone jungle of Glasgow into the countryside during the Depression of the 1930s—and during which, it was said, the Fire never went out. From here, the Highland of Freedom and all Scotland beckoned them: the Fire was the cradle for all the other fires which warmed Wanderers in howffs, dosses, bothies, and caves as they explored further north.*
>
> *Some remained in the hills or at the Fire most of the week and only returned to the city to claim their dole money from 'the buroo'. Within its glow, philosophy, socialism and hill-lore were discussed at length and the fire-flickered woods echoed songs which were sung well into the night.*
>
> *The Ptarmigan, Lomond and Creagh Dhu Climbing Clubs were all born here and many who sat round the Fire fought in the Spanish Civil War (1936-39). Several Wanderers who used the Fire would be notably instrumental in fighting for the freedom of all people to enjoy the Scottish countryside through the development of such things as our Rights of Way and National Parks.*

I liked this text because it was about people who helped to make it possible to roam the places I had just spent a month roaming. I also liked some of its words—*howff* (a haunt, a rude shelter), *buroo* (the unemployment benefit office). But mostly it conjured up my paternal grandfather. I doubt he ever sat at this fire or wandered the Highland hills to escape hard times. He was a bricklayer with five children to support when the Great Depression came. From what has trickled down to me about him, he wandered in search of work, and would have approved wholeheartedly of the fireside talk of socialism. I knew here by Craigallian Loch—still three miles from Milngavie and ten from the city center—that I was leaving scenic Scotland for now, and entering the industrial landscape of my forebears.

## 21

# Glasgow Gloom

├──────────────────┼──────────────────┤

I left the birdsong of Craigallian Loch and set off for the nearby pines and the city. An aircraft going to or coming from Glasgow Airport hummed overhead, but signs of the city were otherwise absent yet. In less than a mile I came to Mugdock Country Park. It abounded in footpaths, all signposted to Milngavie. "It's that way!", a dog-walker called out as I stood perplexed at a junction, wondering which path was the WHW. Later, I saw a man with a pack coming toward me, and looked forward to a hikers' natter until I saw that the pack contained his sleeping child. Then the path came out to a brow that overlooked houses and an industrial estate from which the dull thump of machinery rose. I was close now. But the end of my West Highland Way trek fizzled into anticlimax as I navigated uncertainly through backstreets, eventually emerging onto Milngavie's main street from the backside of its shops. My eyes were drawn to the coffee shop with the sidewalk tables, and my thoughts to a large Americano; but I had a plan for tonight, and went directly to the railway station.

Milngavie is the end of the line, and the train was empty for the first stops. Rattling through Hillfoot and Bearsden I wondered if this was the line that ran at the bottom of the garden of my first home. It had been a tiny garden, perhaps 50 feet from house to tracks. When we took the train, my mother stood an inflatable Yogi Bear in the back bedroom window for Jackie and I to wave at from the carriage. I sat now on the left of the train to look for that window; but when we pulled into Partick I knew that my old home must abut another line. And sitting on the left meant I was missing the River Clyde as it made its appearance on the right. "Glasgow made the Clyde, and the Clyde made Glasgow," the saying goes, referring to the engineering of the river that made it navigable by big ships right up to the Broomielaw[43]. More than most cities, Glasgow is inseparable from its river, and for the next eight days I would be inseparable from it too, until we both disappeared into the Southern Uplands.

The train went underground, and soon I was gliding up into Glasgow Central on an escalator. There was a barrier at the top, and ticket collectors. I thought I had left mine on the train, I said, truthfully. "Aw'right then," said the collector, "bit keep it wi' ye nest time". I took a taxi to the SYHA hostel on Park Terrace, and blethered with the driver about our shared liking of the hills. Then Afghanistan intruded again. His son looked after army helicopters, and was going back for another tour of duty. He said his wife coped with their son's situation by avoiding news of the war, but that he himself devoured it for the same reason. When we stopped outside the hostel, I wished his son a safe return, and tipped well for the blether. But a Glasgow cabby does not look you in the eye and shake you firmly by the hand, as this man did, just because you add a few quid to the fare. In Edinburgh maybe.

I knew that the big city, after a month of villages and just one
town, would test my nerves, and my plan was to go now where
I might find quiet, and little in the way of excitement. Firhill
Stadium is home to Partick Thistle Football Club. Poor Thistle,
also known as The Jags, or even "Partick Nil". My father never
declared for Rangers or Celtic, and I think this was because, in
his heart, he was a Jag. It would have been natural. The house on
Salmona Street in which he was born is 500 yards from the goal-
posts of Firhill Stadium, and once upon a time his father had lived
just across Firhill Road from today's stand for away supporters.
The Jags were on my dad's turf. Tonight's game against Greenock
Morton ("The Pride of the Clyde") was Thistle's experiment with
Friday-night football, and I had plenty of time before kick-off at
7:45. I used it to walk to the City Centre for pizza before heading to Partick. Except you don't head to the district of Glasgow
called Partick to watch Partick Thistle. Poor Thistle are named
for a place they have not played in for a century. Since 1909 it is to
Maryhill that you go to watch The Jags. But when the time came
for me to go, I was mysteriously apathetic. It was the beginning of
my "Glasgow slump", a pervasive three-day gloom that lifted only
rarely. Whatever its cause, it was only the fact that I had nothing else to do that pushed me into a taxi up the Garscube Road.
Almost as soon as I stepped out of it, and joined the spread-out
groups flowing through the murk toward the stadium, a soaking
rain came on. Poor Thistle, I thought, it's pouring on their Friday-
night football parade.

This was not Yankee Stadium I was entering. Tonight's game
would be graced by only 3,380 fans. Even so, I felt the special
thrill that comes from emerging out of the bowels of a stadium
to see green, green grass bathed in floodlight below. Morton
kicked off, and Thistle fans began to scold their team ("keep ra
baw, Thistle!"). After two minutes, the Thistle goalie hoofed the
"baw" up the field, where a header, and then a nifty touch, put it at

the feet of O'Donnell. He drilled it past the Morton keeper, and stifled the scolding for a while. Poor Thistle, 1-0 up against the First Division leaders. The First Division is, in fact, the second tier of Scottish football, sitting beneath the Premier League; and this game was a world away from the glamour contests periodically enjoyed by the big boys. For a start, the players were almost entirely Scots, with just a leavening of Irish and English (Morton had somehow come by a French midfielder, but their glamorous-sounding forward di Giacomo was solid Glaswegian). I expected kick-and-run football, slack passes, and crunching tackles, "blood and snotters" stuff; but The Beautiful Game came to Maryhill when that man O'Donnell directed the perfect pass for Doolan to slide home on 29 minutes. It was still 2-0 when I went for a pie at half-time. Poor Thistle, my foot!

Returning with a Scotch pie, I took a new seat rather than ask everyone to get up so I could reach my old one. It was nearer the action too. So near that I promptly made the save of the game (one-handed, half a pie in the other) to stop a stray ball from smacking me in the kisser. Behind my new seat, I realized next, dwelt Firhill's most unrelenting cheerleader, booming praise, advice, and insults at players and referees alike: "Good save, Foxie!"; "C'moan, son, keep it tight!"; "Yer a Thistle reject, Smyth"; "Well done, Sinkie." Sinkie was Aaron Sinclair, and it was his free kick that led, with a lavish dollop of luck, to Thistle's third goal. There were still 15 minutes to play, but the Morton fans began to leave. Certain victory did not quiet the cheerleader. One of the assistant referees was a woman. Ms. Clark called an offside in Thistle's favor. "Well done, hen!" he bellowed with greater than usual enthusiasm. Defeat became rout when Thistle added two more goals in the final ten minutes. "C'moan, Jags, finish it off," our man was still yelling seconds before the final whistle.

I decided to walk back to the hostel. I had a rough idea of the way, and the rain had stopped. There were no taxis, and I didn't want to have to figure out the buses. It was 10 p.m. The City Centre, a mile or two away, would be in full swing, but by the time I shook off the knots of fans and turned onto Maryhill Road, this part of town was surprisingly empty. Even the footsteps from my rubber-souled boots echoed off the flags. But I was not feeling low. I'd been entertained, and had joined the select group of football fans who can say "I saw Partick Thistle win 5-0".

The buzz of Firhill Park did not last. In the gray morning, I walked again into the City Centre, leaving the park-lined streets and fine sandstone houses around the hostel for the inner grid of streets on the other side of the sunken M8 motorway, which wraps the Centre like a moat. A seedy length of Sauchiehall Street—divey pubs; betting shops; fast food places to sell revelers something solid to throw up on the bus home—gave way to its pedestrianized section, and here the leaden sky melted into pouring rain. I trotted into a store to buy a flimsy umbrella and felt my gloom return. It was a gloom of emptiness and purposelessness, in which little pleasures were not. In City Gents on Renfield Street, a pleasant girl took a half-inch off my hair and beard. Normally, that alone would make me feel sharp, but today it gave me no lift. The urban rain helped make my mood, but I think the sense of purposelessness came from leaving the trails and the easy meaning they offered. I did not know, either, when and how I would return to them.

It was October 1st. For a month I had concentrated on getting to Fort William and then on to Glasgow. When I thought at all about southern Scotland, it was somehow lodged in my mind that there were 100 straightforward miles of it. Now, as I faced up properly to this final leg, I began to doubt that Portpatrick really could be so close, and I took this nagging thought from the barber's shop to Waterstones bookstore, hugging Glasgow's walls to supplement the meager shelter of three feet of cheap umbrella. Waterstones' maps and guidebooks quickly confirmed my fears. My intended route up the Clyde and along the Southern Upland Way was nearer to 160 miles. In the southwestern region of Dumfries & Galloway especially, it would be anything but a simple hike in settled country. One guide warned that rollercoaster hills, isolation, and scarce accommodation made this stretch "a far more serious proposition than the West Highland Way". At my normal pace, 160 miles would take 11 days. My flight home was booked for October 15th, and I was adamant I would not reschedule it. That left things tight, even if I departed Glasgow right now and took no more days off. I needed a new plan.

I wandered the City Centre, blankly it seemed, but probably my brain was whirring unnoticed on the matter of the route. I went to Costa Coffee, cut off from the soggy city by the glass roof of Central Station. I roamed Saint Enoch mall. I had lunch at Subway. I spent 20 pence to use the gents at the station. I was half a mile from where I was born, resting after a long walk and planning to see relatives. Yet I felt that I had no business here, that I was shuffling around the wrong film set, unnoticed among the city's lively performers. Surely I should be where I had a part? And this desire to be homeward bound showed itself as a recurring image of being comfortable in my own kitchen, quietly making mugs of tea. Instead, I was killing time in a grubby, _dreich_ place. It crossed my mind that I could end here. It would still have been a worthwhile adventure, a pleasing line drawn on the map. I was glad to have my relatives to see before this idea grew.

On January 21st 1878, a 30-year-old widower was married at Saint Margaret's Chapel in Kinning Park, a district of artisans

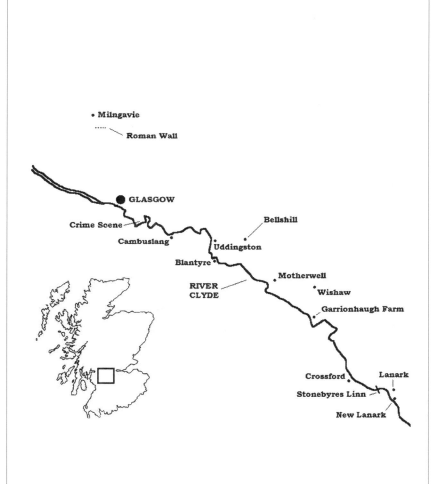

Map 5: Glasgow to Lanark

and laborers southwest of the city center. He was a contrac-
tor's carter, and could not sign his name in the marriage registry.
His bride was a domestic servant called Margaret Cullen, seven
years his junior, and able to sign her name. They were both from
Ireland; he from County Londonderry in the north, she from
Dublin. They were wed that winter Monday "after Banns according to the Forms of the Roman Catholic Church". They left the
chapel Mr. and Mrs. Francis McWilliams. People emigrate for all
kinds of reasons, but there is little reason to doubt that this set of
my great-grandparents came to Glasgow with the same objective
as hundreds of thousands of their compatriots of the time—paying work. They had come to the right place.

Glasgow emerged late to its position of primacy among
Scottish cities. Throughout the Middle Ages it was of much lesser
importance than places like Perth, Saint Andrews, and Stirling,
which are today just small cities at best. In the 1500s and 1600s,
the River Clyde was as much an obstacle as an asset, its shallowness
preventing large trading vessels from reaching the city. Glasgow
anyway faced the wrong way for the prevailing North Sea trade.
By the early 1700s, out of a national population of about a million, there were something like 15,000 Glaswegians—a big city
for Scotland at that time, but half the size of Edinburgh. If the
Clyde eventually made Glasgow, so too did the Atlantic. Even before union with England in 1707, Scots had traded, illicitly, with
the English colonies in North America. After the Union, a tiny
elite of Glasgow merchants came to dominate the transatlantic
tobacco trade. As early as the 1720s, a traveler from England took
note of them:

> "Glasgow is a city of business; here is the face of trade ... The
> Union has answered its end to them more than to any other
> part of Scotland ... ; I am assured that they send near fifty
> sail of ships every year to Virginia, New England, and other
> English colonies in America, and are every year increasing."

The traveler was Daniel Defoe, author of *Robinson Crusoe*. He noted Glasgow's manufacturing too—sugar refineries, a distillery, linen mills, muslin factories. The tobacco ships did not sail to America with empty holds. A century after Defoe's visit, Glasgow was Scotland's biggest city. The census of 1821 totted up 147,043 inhabitants to Edinburgh's 138,235. Glasgow's absolute population, and its size relative to Scotland as a whole and to other Scottish cities, then continued to grow rapidly throughout the 1800s. By 1911, Glasgow had 784,496 citizens—one out of every six Scots, and much more than the *combined* populations of Edinburgh, Dundee, and Aberdeen. And this was Glasgow narrowly defined. If one considers the concurrent population explosion all along the Clyde between the Lanarkshire coalfields and the port of Greenock, the immensity of change can be seen. But, beyond numbers, what kind of change?

Glaswegians increasingly had roots elsewhere. Lowlanders moved in from the countryside, and so did dispossessed Highlanders and starveling Irish. Nineteenth-century Glasgow must have felt much like booming mega-cities today—a place where everyone was from somewhere else, and somewhere else was usually rural and alien. The Irish came in large numbers. By 1861, a decade after the Great Famine, the census noted 62,084 Irish-born Glaswegians, 15% of the population. Many more Irish would have been Glasgow-born. Immigrants flooded into Glasgow because changes in its industry created jobs for the unskilled. In the early 1800s, artisan weaving of linen and woolen cloth was yielding to steam-powered cotton mills. By mid-century, fueled by iron and coal from nearby Lanarkshire, heavy industry became the motor of growth—iron, steel, machine tools, locomotives and, above all, shipbuilding. By now, the Clyde had long been dug wide and deep enough for ocean-going ships to reach the wharves and jetties of the Broomielaw. This was Glasgow as the workshop and second city of the British Empire. In 1878, Francis and Margaret could expect work; but also low wages, long hours, overcrowded housing, dirty air, and disease. Economic growth was not an ever-climbing graph either. The year they married, the City of Glasgow Bank collapsed, putting the city's economy into a spin. It is perhaps not surprising that they left Glasgow for a while, perhaps back to Ireland, certainly to the Liverpool area. They were back on Clydeside in time for the 1891 census. When he died (of cancer, 50 or possibly younger) Francis was a chemical work laborer. Margaret lived on until 1929, to the grand old age for her time and place of 74.

The Glasgow Subway is a single, circular line joining 15 stations. It is sometimes nicknamed the Clockwork Orange, because of the color of its carriages and, presumably, rather rinky-dink nature. At Saint Enoch this afternoon, football supporters in Rangers gear were going down into the station to catch the train to Ibrox Stadium. One of them asked a passerby which platform he should use. Then he leaped onto the down escalator, shouting back "I'm from Northern Ireland, you see!" in beery explanation, and promptly fell hard on his backside. My Celtic cap zipped firmly in my bag, I rode with the Gers fans only as far as Shields Road, and there waited outside the station for my cousin to drive by. Bored in the City Centre, I had arrived way too early. Bored now, I crossed the street to a handsome building with what looked like a school playground behind its railings. It turned out to be a museum of Scottish schooling. Here was my chance to find out what my dad's wartime secondary schooling had *really* been like. It had come down to me as all academic rigor and the sting of the strap. Maybe, in fact, he had made daisy chains all day. I'll never know; the museum was closed—flood damage.

My cousin, her husband, and their teenage daughter and son pulled up at Shields Road station and we drove along the M8 to visit dad, granddad, and uncle united in the person of Peter McWilliams, the last of my father's four siblings. Uncle Peter was three years older than my dad, and therefore had to "do his bit". The bit was duty on landing craft during the Italian Campaign and the invasion of southern France in 1943-44, service that qualified him now for a room in the Erskine home for veterans. He had grown thin and appeared fragile, but the teasing twinkle in his eye had not aged. He grew chirpy and funny, talking about the war, and family, and the Scottish hills. In Italy he once chased a local boy off a landing craft, he said. The boy shouted back at him "you're going to Anzio!", and Peter thought "well, if he knows, the Germans surely do". We looked at old photographs. Uncle Peter made a point of showing me one of him, in his 60s maybe, on Ben Lomond's snowy summit.

The Arlington bar stood on the corner of its namesake street and Woodlands Road. It was five minutes from the hostel, and became my local during my time in Glasgow. This is to say I made three visits, trying each time to be out before the live music drew in crowds. There were no bouncers at the door early on, and it was quiet enough within to have a chat or write up my notes. The Arli had few frills, but its friendly staff and assortment of customers made it a comfortable place for a stranger to hang out. By Sunday evening this stranger wanted to be close to people again. Firhill Stadium had felt intimate, everyone together with a common purpose. I had been happy with Uncle Peter too, and afterward over dinner with my cousin and her family. Today I had felt adrift again, haunting the dripping city and Waterstones' maps and guides section. Now, my back to the door of the Arli, I felt a cold hand on my head.

"Now that's a nice wee shiny head," said a female voice. I turned, expecting to see a crone. I saw instead an attractive young woman, neither visibly intoxicated nor deranged.

"Don't mind her," said one of her companions "she does weird things like that." Mind? I went back to my calculations noticeably uplifted by her touch, almost as if it had been a benediction. The calculating concerned a problem chalked up on a board by the Arli staff. "You are a farmer at market to buy animals. There are three types of animals—horses for £10, goats for £1, and ducks at eight for a pound. You must buy 100 animals for £100, buying at least one of each. What combination allows you to do this?"

"It wid drive ye nuts, wouldn't it?" said the woman to my right. She and her husband were also valuing farm critters. Her speech was slurred, but her faculties seemed otherwise intact. She, and I, went on to proclaim "I've got it!" several times over the next half-hour, but we never had. Not until a young fellow, probably from the School of Mathematics of the nearby university, came in, thought for a few moments, and said "seven horses, 21 goats and 72 ducks".

On a wall of the Arli, behind the musicians now tuning up, there was a wooden panel illuminated by a picture light. The panel was covered in text with the title THE STONE OF DESTINY. Beneath the panel lay a chunk of gray stone. It is preposterous, on the face of it, that the hallowed rock upon which kings of Scotland were crowned until 1292 would end up in an unremarkable Glasgow pub, but that is what the text claimed. The Stone of Destiny, or Stone of Scone, is a 335-pound block of sandstone about the size of a pillow. It is believed that kings of Scotland sat upon it for their inauguration since the very birth of the kingdom in the 800s. The stone resided at Scone Abbey near Perth until 1296. In that year, Edward I of England ("Longshanks"), with Scotland briefly under his control, took the stone from the abbey and placed it in another, 450 miles to the south. In Westminster

Abbey the stone became part of the coronation ritual of English, later British, monarchs, lodged in a wooden throne called King Edward's Chair. And there it stayed for 700 years, apart from four months after Christmas 1950. Then it had returned to Scotland, seized from Westminster Abbey in the dead of night by nationalist students from Glasgow University. The official story is that, confronting an intense police search, the students gave up the stone, leaving it at the altar of Arbroath Abbey wrapped in a Saltire[44]. This stone was taken back to England and its perch in Longshanks' chair. But the Arli held to a different version of events. Back in Glasgow with the stone, the students hid it in the bar, giving up only a replica in the abbey (a "shitey copy" as the barmaid put it to me). In which case, it was the shitey copy that was ceremoniously given back to Scotland in 1996, and placed in Edinburgh Castle. And it was the real thing hidden behind the amateur performers in the Arli tonight.

In the morning, the buses on Woodlands Road were full of serious faces. Glasgow was returning to work. Perhaps if I did too, I would feel better. So I set off for Milngavie, to cover on foot the miles I had ridden on ScotRail on Friday. I walked The Great Western Road, dead straight from the City Centre to Anniesland Cross. It was lined at first with four-story terraced houses, occupied at street level by shops, pubs, and cafés. At intervals ahead, slender church spires rose into the gray sky. On the bridge over the River Kelvin, a hold-on-to-your-cap wind blew unchecked up the river valley. Joggers pounded the riverbank path below. A dad walked his uniformed tot to Glasgow Academy. Soon the houses became grander, terraced still, but set back and screened by trees. Beyond the Botanic Gardens, the road reached the top of a rise, and green hills far to the west came into view. By the time the

Great Western Road went beneath the metal truss of Anniesland station bridge, it was becoming a highway, and the West End was beginning to look like suburbs.

I turned onto Bearsden Road, where terraced housing soon gave way to detached homes in hedged gardens. A road sign marked the end of Glasgow and the beginning of East Dunbartonshire. I felt out of place; a wind-rumpled, clammy walker in neat, motorized Bearsden. It did feel better to be walking with a goal again, but I couldn't escape the thought that today I was walking *away* from my finish line, getting no nearer to making cups of tea in my own kitchen. I planned to walk right up Milngavie Road, but at Boclair Road there was an unobtrusive sign: ROMAN WALL 800 YARDS ON LEFT. I followed it, and found only big houses and a cemetery. I turned onto a path skirting a golf course. There was a groundsman at work. At first he acted as if my addressing him was quite the last thing he wanted today, thank you; but when I mentioned the Roman wall he grew enthusiastic. "It's in the graveyard! Right among the stones!" He was right too. On a hill in the cemetery, a rectangle of chunky stones lay surrounded by grass. They looked like a rough cobbled road more than a wall, and did not appear ancient. But a plaque affirmed that they were indeed a section of the base of the Antonine Wall.

On the wall of my boyhood bedroom hung a magazine give-away map of Roman Britain. It showed the roads, towns, villas, baths, and garrisons of Britannia—and how they abruptly ended at Hadrian's Wall in the north of England. Scots said that the mountains and tribes of Caledonia[45] were just too wild for the Romans to subdue. According to *The Eagle of the Ninth*[46], they swallowed whole legions. But these were just satisfying myths. The Romans were far more active in the land that became Scotland than my map suggested, and their annihilation of thousands of Caledonians at the battle of Mons Graupius around 83 AD showed that the northern Britons were not too wild for them at all—nae bother, in fact. So why didn't the Roman Empire incorporate the whole island of Britain? It was not for want of trying, at least periodically. In the early 70s AD, Petilius Cerialis, governor of Britannia, led the legions perhaps as far north as Inverness. They built military roads and forts as if intending to stay, but then seem to have quickly abandoned their conquests. Another governor, Agricola, marched to the Forth-Clyde line in 78, and again built extensive military infrastructure. In 81 he marched into the north—a campaign that reached its climax in the slaughter of Mons Graupius, and what was perhaps a near-genocide of the Caledonians in its wake. Surely now Rome would hold on to Caledonia, or at least that part of it that would later be called the Lowlands. But again, within a few years, the legions were back holding a line near today's Anglo-Scottish border. But the northern tribes were a pesky lot. They lined up with their southern brethren to make trouble for Roman Britannia. The Emperor Hadrian thought he had the answer. The wall that bears his name was begun in 122. It ran 70 miles from the Solway Firth to the North Sea, dividing Britain emphatically into Roman and barbarian parts. But this massive complex of wall, ditch, fort, and road does not seem to have cowed and divided the tribes as thoroughly as Hadrian hoped. So, after 138, the Romans again moved north. Now they built a second wall, named for the new emperor who had sponsored this latest invasion—Antoninus Pius.

The wall that Antoninus built was inferior to Hadrian's. For a start, it was half as long, running 36 miles from the Firth of Forth at Bo'ness to the River Clyde west of Glasgow. And it was made of turf instead of stone. It must nevertheless have been an imposing sight—a line of ditch and rampart, bolstered with a fort every mile or two. Then the Romans did what they always did—they left. Within little more than two decades the wall was abandoned. The Romans came back in the early 200s with punitive expeditions, but thereafter they mostly left "Scotland" alone (and from this quiet, a people they named *Picti* would emerge). The last Romans in uniform to see Scotland seem to have departed for much the same reason as Cerialis, Agricola, and the legions that patrolled the *Vallum Antonini*—there was something more important going on elsewhere. Troops were needed to fight rebels and barbarians in more vital parts of the empire. Glory might be won by conquering Caledonia, but in the final analysis the prestige was not worth lasting trouble. So Caledonia was saved not by its wildness but by its insignificance; and its catastrophic dealings with Rome for 150 years brought little benefit to either party. A lot of trouble for nothing.

My business in Milngavie was done the moment I set foot on its main street and could, therefore, say I had walked between the West Highland Way and Glasgow City Centre, even if in the wrong direction. But since I was here I might as well find out what happened to The Black Bull Hotel. I had not seen it on the approach to town, nor now in the center either. I picked out a man of appropriate years. He was carrying a plastic grocery bag on Mugdock Road.

"Excuse me, have you lived here long? I'm looking for a pub called the Black Bull."

"First of all, I don't live here. I live in Bearsden." He was smiling as if I had made a very foolish move at chess, and now he had taken my queen. The smile inquired, "so what's your next move?" I said that this was my first visit to Milngavie in 23 years, and I wanted to revisit the hotel where my dad had gathered the family to celebrate his retirement. The old man put down his bag and warmed to the topic.

"Och I see. We held our daughter's wedding reception there. Let me think. They knocked it down before my wife died. I'm not sure, but it must be about ten years ago. There's a Marks & Spencers there now." I bought a sandwich at the Marks & Spencers and sat outside to eat it. I felt buoyed by my chat with the old man, and realized I had been lonely in Glasgow. I felt further from my loved ones than before, my connectedness to them draining away unrefreshed by living contact for a whole month now. With the city about me, solitude no longer felt natural or comfortable. Surely the purpose of cities is for people to draw on one another? Here, I did not want to be invisible at the edge of the troop. But as Glasgow's people worked, shopped, and partied around me, they were a reminder that my troop—the people who knew me—were nearly all elsewhere.

I rode the train back to Glasgow Central, and Waterstones. The temptation to end the journey here had not taken hold. Although a walk from Cape Wrath to Glasgow would have met many of my goals, I was driven to continue, and chiefly for the same reasons that had steeled me when I hurt my ribs back at Bealach na Croise—vanity, and fear of what jacking it in would do to my confidence for the tasks facing me when I returned home. If I wanted to believe that I could overcome discouragement, better not to surrender to a little loneliness now. There was also the matter of wanting to see what the trails and byways of southern Scotland had to offer. At Waterstones I made a decision. I would walk as planned to the headwaters of the Clyde, but then head south to the Solway Firth instead of southwest to Portpatrick. This brought the remaining mileage close to the 100 miles I had imagined. The first 40 would follow the Clyde Walkway—another long-distance path, but without the fame, hiker traffic, or services of the WHW. I was unsure what lodgings would be available in the industrial towns that sit back from the Clyde along its first 25 miles upstream from Glasgow, but came up with what I thought a clever solution, starting tomorrow with a walk to Uddingston. This plan gave my evening focus and purpose, and I avoided the aimless emptiness that had threatened to descend once again. The city, in contrast, was still wrapped in gray.

# 22

# A Body by the Clyde

I walked beside a gray, shiny Clyde to Glasgow Green, an emblem of Glasgow's popular history. The Green was the city's first public open space and had earthy uses. In the 1700s, it was used for grazing cattle, bleaching linen, and drying fishing nets. In 1732, it became the site of the city's first "steamie", or washhouse. My walk took the Green's edge, meandering with the riverbank to an area called Fleshers' Haugh. There were rowers on the river this morning, keeping up a tradition of recreation. In the 1700s, Glaswegians bowled and golfed on the Green, and swam from its banks. It is said that four young rowers caught the football bug from a game played on Fleshers' Haugh in 1872, and went on to found Rangers. The less said about that the better, but I won't leave the Green without saying something about the "great proletarian celebration". Glasgow had held a summer fair since 1190. It was conceived as a place to trade. But by the 1800s entertainment overshadowed commerce, and the Green hosted a week-long carnival of fiddlers, pipers, dancing, "whisky palaces", waxworks, freak shows, "strumpery", and penny theaters. It was more and more a working class event, as those who could afford it began to take holidays "doon the watter" on the Firth of Clyde. In 1870, the city fathers could take no more and banished the fair from the Green. "Glasgow Fair" is still the name of the July holiday in the city.

Foul odors from tanneries and slaughterhouses once disturbed strollers on the Green. Today the sweet smell of a whisky distillery wafted over the Clyde from the Gorbals. The Gorbals had a black reputation. Whenever I tell Englishmen of about my age that I was born in Glasgow, they suck in air and say "The Gorbals!" They are thinking of hard men and razor gangs. This notoriety dates from the interwar years, when the Gorbals was home to teeming slums, high unemployment, and more than its share of gangs. A 1935 novel—*No Mean City*—turned Gorbals violence into a byword for working-class Glasgow generally. The area's reputation survived its transformation in the 1960s from a tenement slum to a high-rise slum. But the Gorbals, like Glasgow as a whole, has since enjoyed a renaissance. As I rounded the bend in the river that bounded Fleshers' Haugh, I was thinking about this rebirth, and snorting at the people who had said "The Gorbals!" Then, somewhere near Rutherglen Bridge, it began to rain. I stopped to put on my jacket. The footpath here occupied a thin fringe of trees along the riverbank, behind which shabby industrial yards seemed to lie. When I was about to resume walking, a cyclist came from the other direction. He stopped, and told me the police had sealed off the path 500 yards ahead. There was a crime scene, he said.

The news put a spanner in the works. My plan today had been to follow the Clyde Walkway to Uddingston, then ride the train for one stop to Bellshill, once my mother's home and still her sister's. After a wee visit, I would ride back to Glasgow for a last night, and resume the Walkway from Uddingston in the morning. Now I faced hanging about in Glasgow until the crime scene was cleared, or walking to Uddingston on busy roads I did not know. So, in stubborn hope, I continued along the riverside path. My hopes rose when I crossed broken barrier tape, and again when it felt that I had walked much more than 500 yards. The fringe of trees now hid a sewage plant. Then, ahead, under the arch of Dalmarnock railway bridge, was a seated figure in a yellow emergency jacket. He rose as I approached, and walked toward me.

"I'm afraid no one can go through. There's a grave site beside the path." The policeman was friendly, but a grave site leaves no room to wheedle special treatment.

"Do you know if there's a way to get around?" I asked.

"Sorry. I don't really know this area," the bobby replied.

On my way back to Rutherglen Bridge, I met a man striding toward the crime scene. It was my turn to jam a spanner in the works.

"Is that still there?" he said, in disbelief and frustration. He was meant to be doing repairs on the bridge, and had been prevented from getting to it before. I asked if he knew what happened.

"They found a body burning by the river. The poor man had been stabbed and shot." I didn't think any more about Glasgow's renaissance as I retraced my steps. The day had acquired an edge and a pall. At Rutherglen Bridge, I climbed to the street. It looked on my OS map as if a fairly simple road-walk would take me beyond Dalmarnock railway bridge, where with luck the Walkway would be open again.

After the closed-in riverbank, Glasgow's East End felt wide open—an effect of vacant swathes of land and low-rise buildings on the flat floodplain. It was a patchwork of decay and renewal. There were isolated remnants of tenements and warehouses, and neat new brick homes. But mostly this was an area of untidy industrial premises, a zone of lock-up garages, parked trucks, and piled-up cargo containers. There were few pedestrians, and I was glad not to be carrying my big pack to add to my conspicuousness ("Look at that *eejit*. He thinks he's in the *Hielands!*") I walked along French, Swanston and Strathclyde streets, and began to feel pleased with myself for navigating out of trouble. At least, I did until I saw the police van at Dalmarnock road bridge. It was parked where the path led down to the Clyde Walkway. The fence at the start of the path was decorated with flowers and football gear. There were scrawled messages on the scarves and shirts. The gear was mostly in the royal blue of Rangers, but there was green and white in there too. A policewoman stepped out of the van—a young blonde.

"I'm afraid the path is closed."

"What happened?" I asked, hoping for new information.

"A local man was killed." Then, nodding at the fence, "People are paying their respects."

"Was it anything to do with football?" I asked. The gear had made me wonder. Football-related violence is not unknown in Glasgow, though this would have been extreme.

"No, it had nothing to do with football." I explained about my walk to Uddingston, and asked if she knew a way around the closed path.

"I'm not sure, but do you know where the Celtic Supporters Club is on London Road?" she replied.

"Yes," I said half-truthfully, knowing only London Road.

"If you go down beside it, the river path might be OK there."

Dalmarnock Road led to Springfield Road, and to a glimpse of Paradise. It is a nickname for Celtic Park, the largest football stadium in Scotland, and home of course to Celtic. The team's first home, in 1888, lay 200 yards from today's stadium. It had bordered a graveyard. A move across the road in 1892 to much finer premises prompted a journalist to quip that it was like "leaving the graveyard to enter paradise". The name stuck. It must have felt like paradise to Celtic's early fans too, a brief escape into unity and excitement from the harsh reality of East End immigrant life. But

I turned my back on Paradise today to walk east along London Road. The two would not be confused. After a few hundred yards, the Celtic Supporters Club came into view. It was a square, ugly, unadorned building. Its street-level windows were barred, and those higher up not much more than slits. As the policewoman had promised, there was a path next to it that led to the river—and no bobbies were guarding it.

Where the path came down to the river, a chubby, gray-haired man was loitering, his back turned to me. When I said good morning, he turned to face me, and looked utterly bewildered, as if my greeting were just too much to deal with. He might have been hungover, senile, or up to no good. He nodded vacantly as I passed, adding to the sadness that had descended on the day like a fog. But it felt good to be striding in the right direction again, along the wooded fringe of the meandering Clyde. The sadness began to lift gradually, pushed aside by simple, sane things. There was the man and his collie. They often walked here on his day off, he said. Sometimes they saw deer. We were still just three miles from the City Centre, as a George Square pigeon would fly. A little farther on, from beneath a motorway bridge, there was a surprisingly bucolic view up the Clyde, its eddies and ripples reflecting a bright patch of cloud wherever the riverbank trees did not cast their shadow on the water.

At no point this morning had I questioned my safety on the Clyde Walkway. Whatever befell the victim, I felt certain he was not set upon while walking out to Bellshill to have tea with his auntie. Back in Glasgow that night, I went online to try to discover what had happened. There were two BBC reports. The first was posted about the time I was walking through the heat to Rowardennan last Wednesday. It said police were treating as suspicious the death of a man whose body was found by the Clyde that morning. The second report, from the next day, added that the man had been violently attacked, and his body set on fire. He may have been killed elsewhere, police said, naming him as Brian Faulds, 29 years old. This was all I knew until I returned home. Since then, the Glasgow newspapers have told the story. Police made arrests. Two brothers confessed to killing Mr. Faulds, carrying his body to the Clyde in a "wheelie bin", and setting it on fire. They were jailed for life, about 20 years in practice. Reports said that the murder followed a row about drug money or a stolen phone. Alcohol was a factor. Faulds and his murderers were recently minted friends. There was a snap on Facebook to prove it. Faulds himself was "known to the police", and had been to prison. His nickname was "Nightmare". The killers had previous convictions for unspecified crimes too. I was glad not to have been in Joseph McQueen's boots, walking along the river at about 8 a.m. last Wednesday. "I thought it was rubbish that was burning," he said. I relate these details because my path through Scotland brushed against this gruesome event just as it stumbled on happier things. And the scraps of information about the lives of Brian Faulds and his murderers are glimpses of a Glasgow that exists as surely as the smiling city of the Arli, Firhill Park, and almost everywhere else I went. Glasgow's murder rate is twice London's. But let's keep things in perspective; Glaswegians are murdered, relative to their numbers, barely half as often as New Yorkers, and the city is just a tenth as murderous as Detroit.

At Cambuslang, a footbridge crossed to the south bank of the Clyde and so into Lanarkshire. As it had been all morning, the Walkway here was a National Cycle Route too—NCR 75, Firth of Clyde to Firth of Forth. It was broad, tarmacked, and dry. Looking north, back across the river, a factory chimney streamed white vapor against dark-gray clouds. To the southwest, identical-triplet tower blocks sprouted from Cambuslang. I pressed on east, passing a wire sculpture of a nesting heron set atop a tall post. Soon after, the Walkway and the cycle path diverged. My OS map didn't show this. It showed them running together into Uddingston, mostly on minor roads, and that suited me just fine. Now a sign directed me down a real footpath. It went beneath a disused railway bridge, and became narrow, slimy, bug-infested, and obstructed with undergrowth. I wondered if a local joker had adjusted the sign for the fun of seeing walkers lose themselves in riverside marsh. Two gray-haired ladies came from the other direction.

"Oh yes, this is the Walkway," they said. Then, perhaps sensing my lingering skepticism, added: "We've walked in from Blantyre on it this morning." A mile on, climbing an exposed slope above the river, it felt suddenly like the countryside. A fox darted across the path ahead of me. A hawk circled a small wood. The west wind drove rain across the hilltop. I realized here that my overpants were giving up the ghost, splitting along an inside leg. I was getting muddy on my way to tea, and felt oddly cheated of the clean, tarmacked path to Uddingston. The mucky path I was on now descended to a burn called the Rotten Calder, went beneath a railway line, and emerged at a farm track. Next to the track was a mountainous, reeking midden abuzz with flies. Starlings flocked overhead against a somber sky.

The Clyde, hidden from view since the fox and hawk, had made a sharp turn south, and the footbridge over to Uddingston crossed to what was now the river's east bank. Here I left the Walkway, and reached Main Street by way of the Grammar School and a neighborhood of solid homes set behind solid walls and well-tended shrubbery. On Main Street, I went into a convenience store. There was a young South Asian man behind the counter.

"Nice day to be in!" he said with a good Scots tongue. I didn't think I looked at all like I had been in.

"It would have been, but I've been out. Walked up from Glasgow."

"From *Glasgow?* That's amazing! I didn't know you could do that." He seemed utterly, genuinely incredulous, and I dared not mention Cape Wrath.

Bellshill was five minutes on the train. When I arrived, school was out, and around the station knots of kids ambled and horsed past billboards and shabby pubs. I wondered if my once-removed cousins might be among them. Uddingston gets "Britain in Bloom" and "Beautiful Scotland" awards, but Bellshill is grittier. It was once a coal-mining town, its production peaking a quarter-century either side of 1900. On a Wednesday afternoon 90 years ago, when the heyday of its pits was starting to wane, a miner died at Old Orbiston Colliery. It stood then a few hundred yards ahead of where I walked now. *The Scotsman* reported the next day, September 22nd, 1921, that "James O'Reilly, fireman, Main Street, Bellshill, was killed by a fall of stone from the roof. He leaves a widow and family". They got his name wrong. He was James Reilly, 51, and another of my great-grandfathers. The family he left behind included 15-year-old Margaret, known to Jackie and I as Gran Bellshill. We called our grans after the places they lived. Gran Stepps—Isabella—rarely smiled. But Gran Bellshill did, false teeth in or out, and she seemed forever soft and approving. She lived with Granddad Bellshill—a man for the horseraces—in Glenmore Avenue when we were little. It was a terraced house, with a covered passage between front and back. We liked to run through this tunnel, shouting and stomping, savoring its stony echo of our voices and footfalls.

In matters of kindness, Aunt Margaret is in every way her mother's heir. Today, as usual, I walked right past her gate and, as before, she sprang to her front door and called down the street after me. We spent a nice few hours. I won added kindness from the Bellshill womenfolk by saying how much I was missing my own. Aunt Margaret talked about gran and granddad. I nattered with my teen-age girl cousins. One had come in from school with a black eye, but it turned out to be a cosmetic one, painted on as classwork. I nattered with my boy cousin about Celtic. He was "scunnered" with the team's manager after defeat to Hearts on Sunday. And I nattered with his mom about job prospects for Bellshill kids, and the task of keeping them safe from crime and drugs. Then, after Aunt Margaret, her scunnered grandson, and I ate a tea of cottage pie and *champit neeps*, it was time for me to get the train back to Glasgow.

# 23

# The Urban Clyde

The next morning, working stealthily so as not to wake the dormitory, I carried my gear in installments down the grand staircase of the hostel. It was a relief to be leaving the dormitory for good. It was not that anyone had been unpleasant. But mostly the room was occupied by university students who had not yet found digs. It was cluttered and stuffy, as you would expect of a space containing three bunk frames, a shower, a loo, five students, and an old fart. And the students kept, well, student hours. One night the door opened and the lights went on around 2 a.m. Voices came in, one talking tipsily and excitedly about success with a Glasgow girl he'd met at a club. I had seen the voice's owner earlier—a quite extraordinarily ugly Canadian—and marveled again at the wonders worked by drink. Now, on an expanse of floor at the foot of the stairs, I spread my stuff out and meticulously packed it into the Big Bastard. Then it was the familiar walk to Central Station. On the way, I mailed maps home from the post office at Charing Cross, and went into a sporting goods shop to look for tape to patch my over-pants. An assistant helped me find a bulky reel of wide duct tape. He said, "These are two for one today!" I said there was barely room in my pack for one. A few moments later, at the cash register, he tried again; "Are you *sure* you won't take the other one?" It is a nice thing about Scotland that people take care of your money as if it were their very own.

On the train back to Uddingston, the ticket collector noticed my pack and gave up his pointless walk through the empty carriages to take a seat and a deep interest in my route. Fifteen minutes later, I climbed the steep steps of the Uddingston station footbridge, and returned to the Clyde by the same tidy streets I had arrived on yesterday. It was morning break at the Grammar School, and students were milling about near the river. They wore carefully disordered uniforms, and appeared unruly themselves, but they looked me in the eye and said bright good mornings. The walk south beside the Clyde was not especially attractive. The riverbank was edged with straggly woods, and the footpath littered unbeautifully with leaves that had fallen still green. There were only glimpses of the river, flowing the color of a strong *café au lait*. At a bend in the river, a massive ruin appeared suddenly. Bothwell Castle sat on a low bluff tight by the water, its roofless sandstone walls seeming as one with the rocks they stood upon. After the Battle of Bannockburn, some of the foremost nobles of England fled here, pursued by Edward Bruce, the King of Scots' brother. The castle was still in English hands, but commanded by a Scottish noble, one Walter FitzGilbert. FitzGilbert had not taken Bruce's side—not yet, anyway; "*When Sir Walter heard from his distinguished guests the reason for their presence, his duty immediately became clear. His men removed their arms and made them prisoners, and on the arrival of Edward Bruce at the castle gates, Sir Walter handed them over to his keeping with protestations of loyalty to his brother.*"[47]

Glasgow was my place of birth, and the place where my ancestors of recent generations had spent much of their lives. So this morning, escaping the city's gravity on a sometimes dull path, I tried to sort through my visit. I knew I would have seen Glasgow differently if I had not been born there. It would have mattered less then. But I felt about Glasgow maybe like an adoptee who gets to know his birth parents only later in life—a distance and intimacy simultaneously, and decades of lost time to make good. I had wanted to come to grips with the city, to understand what it is like, and how it got to be that way. I only got to scratch the surface. Glasgow is the work of generation upon generation, each one hundreds of thousands strong for centuries now. Each generation built, remodeled, neglected, tore down; and not just the physical city. A city's people are surely also the work of generations. You can't grasp a legacy like that in days, and I walked away still feeling my ignorance. But things were going in the right direction. Long ago, I passed through Glasgow as a university student to march against the nuclear-armed submarines that were, and still are, stationed in the Gare Loch west of the city. We were given a floor to sleep on in a trade union building on the Broomielaw, and I remember looking across the Clyde from its windows.

"Pretty dire, isn't it?" offered a fellow marcher.

"Believe it or not," I answered, "I was born here." It wasn't a rebuke. I felt the tenuousness, irrelevance even, of my link to the city. Now, after two decades of occasional reacquaintance, I had been struck by the solidity of that link. The city had proven full of stories and mental images of people I hardly knew, or knew not at all, but with whom I was indissolubly connected. But what about my gloom? I was certain now that it had nothing to do with Glasgow. I could have spent the weekend in any city, even a warm and sunny one, and would have felt no better.

After Bothwell Castle, the Clyde meandered again, but the Walkway did not follow it, cutting instead across the bulge of land. Where path and river rejoined, an imposing white building stood on the far bank. I knew very well what it was. I was taken there as a child, and took my own children a few years ago. A footbridge strung high above the river led across to it—the David Livingstone Memorial Bridge. I stopped in mid span to watch the Clyde slide gently over an upstream weir. The still water behind the weir glimmered silver-gray between densely wooded banks. On the far side, I made my way to the white building, a tenement called Shuttle Row. Dr. Livingstone, missionary and explorer of Africa, was born here in 1813, and Shuttle Row is now his museum. The visitor center was not busy at all, but the young man in charge was not at his usual job, and managed only by trial and error to operate the cash register and sell me a ticket. I left my pack and poles with him, and went over to the museum. It was a simple, unfussy record of Livingstone's extraordinary life. On my childhood visit, I had been captivated by an illustration of Livingstone being mauled by a lion. I was just as captivated today.

Later, in the visitor center café, where I was having tea and sandwiches before returning to the trail, a woman in her late 60s, dressed in Victorian attire, came over and sat at my table.

"What brings you to Blantyre, may I ask?" she asked. I explained about my journey, and then the childhood visit that made a big impression.

"I did that too when I was young, with our church. We came here from Falkirk." Then she smiled. "You know, we drove all the way home afterward, and then found a little boy who didn't belong with us. He came from another place altogether! He got on our bus by mistake, and nobody noticed!" I thought about a distant time with few telephones, and said: "Oh dear, what did they do?"

"Oh, I don't remember now, but he was just fine." There was a pause, and I went back to what brought me to Blantyre.

"Nowadays," I said "we don't much admire people who went to Africa to change it. But Livingstone seems to have liked Africans, doesn't he? And what amazing adventures!"

"I think he did, and I didn't see that they think of him as just an imperialist. I lived a while in Malawi, you see." Like Ken and

Hester at the Tomdoun, I thought; Malawi, where the second city is still called Blantyre.

Livingstone left Scotland for London aged 25, and sailed for Africa two years later, in 1840. There, ostensibly a missionary, he "discovered" and named Victoria Falls, and crossed the continent ocean-to-ocean at the latitude of the Zambezi. Later, he reached Lake Malawi, and would spend the last seven years of his life crisscrossing a vast territory around that lake and Lake Tanganyika, often hungry, ill, and close to destitution. He was famously found in 1871 by Henry Morton Stanley of the New York Herald ("Dr. Livingstone, I presume?"). He died, in what is today Zambia, 35 years after leaving Scotland, and having returned only for a few short visits. At the height of his success, he was lionized (poor word choice!) by Victorian society. With the trumpets of empire growing louder, he could have taken on imperial attitudes, but kept instead to the values of his upbringing. Though hard indeed by modern standards, it had been happy. He had a strong family. He attended the village and mill schools. He roamed the Lanarkshire countryside, poaching salmon from the Clyde. Aged 23, he took advantage of Scotland's egalitarian university system to enroll at Glasgow's Anderson's College.

Livingstone later applied principles of equality to others, notably—and unusually for the time—to Africans, in whose company alone he spent nearly all his final years. There is a uniquely Scottish dimension to his view of "savagery". He was well aware that his great-grandfather had died at Culloden, fighting for a people that others called barbarous and tribal. A generation later, it was the failure of a subsistence economy that forced Livingstone's paternal grandparents to the Lowlands from the little western island of Ulva. Livingstone remembered listening to Grandfather Neil's stories of the old Highlands, "many of which were wonderfully like those I have since heard while sitting by the African evening fire." He remembered his grandmother's Gaelic songs too. So

while Livingstone saw the *condition* of Africans as savage, he did
not see Africans themselves as backward. Nor was a bettering of
their lives to be sought through colonization, but through commerce and Christianity alone. In 1795, Robert Burns—Scotland's
national poet—had written "A man's a man for a' that", a song of
brotherhood. We are told that Dr. Livingstone hummed it as he
tramped the heart of Africa.

In the heart of Lanarkshire, I set out for Bothwell Bridge, a
mile and a half that became the most unpleasant segment of my
entire journey. The Clyde Walkway reentered woods, and was decent for a bit. Then it grew slimy and indistinct, and rose to an
embankment where once a viaduct bridged the Clyde. Now there
was just a shabby clearing, and a line of useless pillars marching
across the river. It was a scramble to get down from the embankment. I read later in a Clyde Walkway pamphlet that "from here
the route is currently very informal". No kidding! I could find no
route at all. The rain came down hard. I picked across a piece of
torn-up wasteland that contained flooded pits I could not account
for. Then, coming down a slope, I saw a figure ahead of me. I was
not wearing my glasses, and the motionless human remained indistinct in the gloom of trees. Getting closer, I saw that it was
stooped, half-crouched with hands on knees, as you might position yourself to catch your breath. It was side-on to me. Then I
saw that he—clearly a he now—was looking between his bare legs
as six inches of turd dangled between them. It was too late to turn
back, and there was nowhere to turn back to. So I scurried past
this dosser in his camp, and hurtled down a dark track. I hurried
from disgust more than fear. Even if he had been inclined to assault me, he was just a wee bit indisposed the minute. The strange
thing is that, as I approached and hurried by at a few paces, he
kept his gaze between his legs, moved not at all, and uttered not
the smallest noise—not so much as "Could you pass the paper?"

The orderly scene at Bothwell Bridge reassured after the un-
nerving wasteland. There was sidewalk and a neat riverside park.

The bridge had old-fashioned street lamps and lots of traffic. At its far end stood a stone pillar and plaque. The plaque read BOTHWELL BRIDGE 22nd JUNE 1679. It had been a battle of religion. On one side were the Covenanters, Presbyterians opposed to the episcopal organization forced on the Scottish church when the Stuarts came back after the Cromwellian military occupation; on the other, the Scottish royal government. The Covenanters took a pasting. Beside the monument, the Walkway plunged into woods again, where I was vigilant—*my glasses on*—for dossers' camps. The hum of traffic was everywhere, though the trees kept the roads unseen. The track went under the A725, and then followed it at a discreet distance to the M74 motorway. This is the main highway from Glasgow to the south. A sidewalk took me beneath it, but I had to cross busy ramps. Traffic signals made this easy enough at the off-ramp but, 150 yards farther on, vehicles were streaming onto the on-ramp unchecked. And the drivers drove as if they no more expected a pedestrian than a moose. I was left to time my ungainly trot to a fleeting break in the traffic, and reached safety barely ahead of an onrushing white van.

A measure of dignity returned to my walk in Strathclyde Country Park. The park is part of a sliver of less developed land between the industrial towns of Hamilton and Motherwell occupying the hills to either side. The path—tarmacked, and marked out for walkers and cyclists—ran on a spit of land between the Clyde and Strathclyde Loch. The loch surface was as flat and gray as a sheet of Motherwell steel, and indistinguishable from the sky. On its far bank, a Ferris wheel, roller coaster, and other amusement contraptions rose above the trees. During interludes in the rain, Motherwell tower blocks appeared beyond the loch's southern end. Despite the poor weather, there were walkers and joggers out, and I was very glad of their company. I did not have it for long. At the end of the loch, the Walkway returned to a fringe of riverside woods. I met two workmen at a bridge pier. The pier was slim and tapered, its ascent conjuring up Jack's beanstalk. Whatever it carried over the Clyde and the treetops looked very far above. One of the workmen had climbed a little way up the pier. The other was below, holding what looked like signs. He called to me when I got close.

"Dae ye know where this bridge goes?"

"No idea. I'm sorry."

"Nae bother, pal." If I had thought to bring out my map, we could have seen together that it carried the railway from Hamilton to Motherwell.

My plan was to take a ride on another railway line later this afternoon—part of my clever solution for accommodation along the Clyde. A train from Wishaw would take me to Lanark and an SYHA hostel. But Wishaw stood back from the Clyde on higher ground, and I wasn't sure where to leave the river. When the path came to a nature reserve called Baron's Haugh, I checked the map. It showed I could continue by the river for a couple more miles, or cut away from it now and head for road. Ahead, the trail toward the road looked broader and firmer than that beside the river, and I set out along it. In three-quarters of a mile, I came to Dalzell House, where it was bucketing. I stood at an information board trying to work out where to go next. A small car pulled up, and a tall, muscly man of about 40 stepped out. He came toward me, wincing from the rain. I could see a woman behind the car's frantically waving wipers.

"Where do you need to go?" the man asked.

"I'm going to Wishaw, but ... "

"Come on, we'll give you a lift."

"Thanks, thanks very much, but I need to walk." He looked at me as if I were nuts or, worse, didn't like the look of him.

"I'm walking across Scotland. All of it. Started at Cape Wrath." He offered his hand as smartly as a salute, and gave me directions that he said would lead through the park to Netherton—wherever that was.

I didn't fully grasp his directions, and just followed the broad park track that seemed to lead in about the right direction. It kept to damp woods until, very abruptly, a gatehouse appeared ahead and, just as unannounced, a high-rise that soared above it. I walked around the tower block and up a short path lined with red railings. It came out on a divided road where tower blocks stood all about. They were not grim and gray as they are meant to be in Scotland, but well-kept, each painted in light browns and yellows. A woman sat hunched up in a bus shelter. She looked fed up and lethargic. I pointed along the road toward the next cluster of towers and asked if Wishaw was that way. She nodded and said "aye". Since leaving the river, the walk had been uphill, on and off, often imperceptibly. Now the road completed the climb, leveling out 250 feet above the valley floor. Even amid the urban sprawl, this modest ridge felt exposed, without shelter from the drenching squalls coming from the west. I had reached that point now when a walk becomes pure chore. All I wanted was to swap the cold rain for a hot shower and find a friendly place for dinner. Two young women came nattering along the sidewalk. I stopped them. They smelled of cigarettes.

"Can you tell me how far it is to Wishaw station?" I asked.

"Oof, it's a long way," replied one. "You'd be better off going to Shieldmuir."

I didn't know if Shieldmuir had direct trains to Lanark, and anyway, surely Wishaw could not be so very far off. I tramped on along Shields Road, as I now knew it to be called. It seemed to go on forever, lined with well-kept housing of all types and eras, until at last it came to a place called Netherton. I expect the big-hearted man at Dalzell House thought he had sent me here more directly than I had managed. On the last mile from Netherton to Wishaw my aches grew—ankles from pounding pavement, and shoulders from the weight of my pack. I knew how to get a little relief for my shoulders, and held my trekking poles horizontally behind my back and used them to lift the pack as I walked. I had no trick for ankles. In Wishaw, it turned out to be much easier to find railway tracks and railway bridges than to find the railway station. I took a fruitless excursion down Glasgow Road before backtracking to find the little station off Alexander Street instead. But my timing could not have been better. The half-hourly train to Lanark clattered and screeched to a halt seconds after I flopped into the platform shelter. On my map, Wishaw was at the edge of the big tan splotch of Glasgow and its surrounding towns. After Wishaw, the splotch gave way to brown contour lines on white paper, and green patches here and there—open country, woods. And on the train the truth of this cartographic world was proved, as the Central Belt faded in 20 minutes into a landscape that was again more country than town.

My preoccupation now was dinner, and it posed a problem. I knew from a previous visit that the New Lanark hostel stood beside the Clyde, and beside the Clyde meant at the end of a long descent from "old" Lanark up on the hill. Old Lanark would have the pubs. I could dine there, grubby and early, or buy something in a store to heat up at the hostel. Climbing back to Lanark to eat later was out of the question. I didn't reach a decision before the train reached the end of the line. Since I had to go *somewhere* from the station, I set off irresolutely toward New Lanark. If there had been a bright pub with a decent menu before Lanark fizzled into fields, I might have stopped. But there wasn't, and I reconciled myself to, at best, a frozen pizza bought at the hostel. At first, the descent was on gentle Braxfield Road, where gray cottages, solid as castles, looked over the cleft of the Clyde Valley. Then the descent became ever steeper, ending as a path that came out just above the tenement blocks of New Lanark. New Lanark is a UNESCO World Heritage Site, preserving a notable cotton mill settlement of the late 1700s, so its tenements were not, so to speak, run-of-the-mill buildings. The hostel occupied one of them, named Wee Row. On my way to it, to my delight, I noticed a building I had forgotten from the earlier visit. It was a spinning mill in the 1780s, but now housed the New Lanark Mill Hotel, which surely would serve dinner. My joy increased at the sight of my room in Wee Row. It was, in most respects, exactly like the dormitory in Glasgow. But it was clean and tidy, and cool fresh air blew in through an open window. Best of all, it was empty.

# 24

# The Rural Clyde

In the morning, still in bed, I listened to the weather forecast on my radio. It was wretched. Rain and gales would be nothing new; hail and thunder sounded ominous. I thought of staying indoors today, but then flattened my waterproof pants out on the dormitory floor and stuck duct tape on the growing gash along the right leg. In my heart, I knew this fix didn't have a prayer. Then I packed my day-pack and headed up the hill to Lanark. The wind and rain were already on, and my hopes for the day quite modest. At Morrisons supermarket, the checkout lady said "I don't like thunder when I'm not at home." I went into Frasers on Bannatyne Street. It was a small outdoors store, every inch jam-packed with gear. I couldn't move without knocking a pack off its peg or clattering into a rack of shirts.

"Can we help you with something?" asked the manageress.

"Yes. Do you have waterproof pants? I mean waterproof trousers."

"We do," and she led me down a constricted aisle.

"This pair has an elasticated waist and side zips. The Regattas are breathable, and have a bottom leg zip so you can put them on over your boots. Those over there are more expensive. They're ultra-light with articulated knees. Now, if you are planning to be out in the cold this winter, you'll want a lining … "

"I think you've got what I need," I said, and promised to return tomorrow. Tomorrow was a day off, and now I was looking forward to having it in Lanark. Not only did the town have a fine selection of over-pants, it looked handsome and old-fashioned too.

The sun put in an appearance on the train ride back to Wishaw, bathing the countryside in watery light. A few minutes out of Lanark, the smooth outline of the Tinto Hills showed six miles to the south, dominated by the bulge of Tinto itself, at 2,333 feet the biggest hill since Loch Lomond. Its name may be Gaelic in origin, and signify fire; likely the hilltop bonfires of ancient Celtic signalers and revelers. The train swung sharply west. As far as Carluke—the only stop—the hilly countryside was an attractive mix of fields, scraps of woodland, and farmhouses the same gray as Braxfield Road cottages. This country looked, broad-brush, idyllic for hiking, until you looked closely at the puddles, mud, and dripping undergrowth that would be at your feet. Soon after Carluke we were back in the Central Belt. At Wishaw station workmen were unloading road salt. It wasn't for today of course, but it added to the portents of bad weather. For now, the storms held off, and I followed a straight suburban road to Gowkthrapple.

I have found no authoritative explanation of Gowkthrapple's name, so my dad's musty, disintegrating old dictionary will have to do. It is a dictionary of English, but was printed in Scotland about the middle of the last century and includes many Scots words. It says that a *gowk* is Scots for a cuckoo or a fool, and that *thrapple* is Scots too—for the throat, especially of an animal. To thrapple is to strangle. So, a place for wringing the necks of cuckoos or fools?

It seems unlikely. Was Gowkthrapple just where the cuckoos sang? It was, anyway, where I sought a way to the Clyde. My first attempt ended in a U-turn when the track swung too far west. Back at the road, opposite a pair of tower blocks, I found a lane leading downhill toward, said a sign, Cambusnethan House. It was a pretty, tree-fringed lane, without a building in sight. It came to a dirt track where an expanse of open field tipped down the side of the valley. In this exposed place, there was a flash of lightning, followed quickly by a crack of thunder and a squall ripping across the valley. I had no choice but to take my cue from the cows, and go fatalistically about my business—"whit's fur ye'll no go by ye."[48]

The lightning spared me this time, and the squall fled as fast as it had come, and the track ran down toward the Clyde through pleasant woodland. In the bottom of the valley, woodland track became farm track, the Clyde Walkway again. My hopes for the day were rising, and somewhere hereabout scenic Scotland definitively reappeared some 30 miles after fading into Mugdock woods. Lush, luminous-green pasture sloped down to the Clyde, which here was a slender gray line behind a screen of spindly trees. Fields just as bright, and dotted with sheep, sloped up the far bank. Although the sun shone, black cloud hung over the braes to the west. Moments later, a towering wall of black loomed like a giant wave about to break over Garrionhaugh Farm. In the end, this squall flashed across the valley behind my back.

After Garrionhaugh Farm, I put away the Glasgow OS map and pulled out sheet 72—"Upper Clyde Valley". It took me first around an angular turn in the river to a bright meadow where a knot of horse-chestnut trees were dropping their seeds, or conkers. I do not know if British boys still play conkers, but they did 40 years ago. You skewer a hole through a sturdy-looking nut, and pull a knotted string through it. Then the objective is to smash other boys' conkers to smithereens. Your opponent dangles his threaded seed, and you try to strike it with yours, using strong, precise downward swings. I bet there is an app for it now. The Clyde was full here, a swirling green-brown stream 40 yards across. Another bend, and it was spanned by the low arches of Mauldslie Bridge, at whose end stood a turreted gate lodge. There were people out and about—dog walkers, kayakers, and a wading fisherman floating a yellow and red lure on the current. The path climbed into the riverside hills, steep and cut by burns. The walking was up and down, in and out of woods. I remember a clearing that sloped steep and even, and in it a lonely tree, plump and green like a broccoli stalk. Back down on the river, stir and eddy still sparkled in sunshine, but another wall of black menaced ahead, and this one would not miss.

The afternoon divided into deluge and dry. The squall broke on the path to Crossford, but brought no lightning or hailstones. In a gloom that it brewed with the trees, I met a couple coming the other way. They looked like farm folk—ruddy, shabbily dressed, indifferent to the rain. Their dog was well-behaved, as if it worked for a living. The man wore a frayed flat cap. An unlit pipe hung from his mouth.

"Nice weather!" I said. He took his pipe down, and smiled with brown and missing teeth.

"Aye, and it won't get better until tomorrow." But at Crossford, the sun came back, lighting up the turning foliage, and turning drips into crystal.

It was a slog to the waterfall—sometimes in rain; mostly uphill; sloshing, slimy, or squashy underfoot. The Clyde was invisible down to my right. Broad pastures rose to my left. Run-off from their trampled margins added to the path's murky cocktail. The grazing cows divided into two camps—those who came to the wire to inspect me, and the *fearties*[49] who lurched away as fast as their hooves would carry them at my very sight. Below, the Clyde was growing younger. This morning, by Garrionhaugh Farm, it had finally reached 100 feet above sea level. By the end of today's

walk, at New Lanark, its waters would have to fall 325 feet before
they lapped against the Broomielaw. It was not yet an upland torrent exactly, but it was getting noisy and, when glimpsed below,
swifter and whiter than before. I came to a power station, where
the valley was tight and the Clyde thundered. It was a hydro station, driven by water dropped through invisible pipes from above
the waterfall now just upstream. A waterfall is a *linn* in Scots,
and this was Stonebyres Linn, the most downstream of the four
Falls of Clyde. I did not see anything of Stonebyres Linn until,
upstream of it, the path swung across the weir that directs water
down the pipes. Here I hung my pack on a fence, and lingered to
watch the remainder of the Clyde foam and surge between luxuri-
antly dressed slabs of rock—and then vanish over the brink where
a fountain of spray marked its unseen fall.

It didn't look difficult on the map. The red diamonds of the
Clyde Walkway led off to New Lanark from a point on a very
short stretch of road in Kirkfieldbank. My problem in the real
world was that the only track going anywhere from this bit of road
was barred by a wrought iron gate. On the gate hung a warning
that security cameras were in operation—24 hours a day! And
indeed it looked as if the track was private property. I searched up
and down, even along the nearby main road, to see if I had missed
a trailhead. I had not. Then I had the revolutionary idea that
this gate and notice did not amount to "Private Property—No
Trespassing". They would have said that if they could, wouldn't
they? So I lifted the latch on the wrought iron gate and walked
through. Nobody yelled "jist where the hell dae ye think you're going, pal? Aye, you with the ripped troosers." After that, the last mile
to New Lanark was a mixed bag—a climb past the sewage works,
a walk between clipped hedges on tight Saint Patrick's Road, and
finally a down-and-up section through pinewoods on a bend in
the river. Coming out of the bend, there was a view upstream to
New Lanark's mills and tenements lit by the lowering sun. There
were black clouds behind the village, but they were fleeing.

On Friday morning I puffed up the hill to Lanark. A cool, drying breeze blew beneath a cloudless sky. Halfway to town a sheep was striking a pose. Her hind legs stood in her field, but she had placed her front hooves squarely on the wall dividing her pasture from New Lanark Road. There she surveyed the world like the Lion King on Pride Rock, unaware that her bleating and overall sheepy-ness turned majesty to comedy. Across the rolling fields behind was Lanark on its hilltop, steeples rising into the blue— slender Saint Mary's; white Saint Nicholas; Saint Kentigern's and Greyfriars in the west. It brought to mind a Tuscan town with a thick Scottish accent, and after breakfast I went out to fall in love with it. Lanark sits compactly on its hill, a country town tightly wrapped in farm and wood. A stroll down the lanes south of the broad High Street brought views to green and yellow-brown fields beyond the Clyde. North of the High Street, the town was a maze of lanes, closes, and shaded nooks. Look up and you saw tall chimneys and the tower of Saint Nicholas. On sunlit walls the sharp shadows of gables were cast.

Lanark is full of medieval history. It has a Castlegate, Broomgate, and Wellgate. There is a Friar's Lane and a Tolbooth. All this might be expected to draw tourists—not to mention an Edinburgh Woollen Mill—but Lanark seemed to exist for the locals. They were shopping this morning at Morrisons supermarket for sure, but also at the butchers with the pies in the window and the other High Street shops. Shoppers were blethering in tea-shops, and it seemed a chatty town altogether. They were chatty with me in Frasers when I bought my new waterproof pants (elasticated waist, bottom leg zip, side pocket openings). The Indians who ran the post office were chatty when I went in for stamps. Most of all, I had a right good natter with the lady at tourist information (she wasn't busy). Most tourists, she said, came for New Lanark. I told her about my travails on the Clyde Walkway, and she gave me a packet of pamphlets, one for each of its stages. They had maps, sunny photographs, and text describing the route. At first I thought "well, these would have been handy". Then I realized they just presented a third version of the Walkway, on top of the one on the OS maps and the one erratically indicated by markers along the way. They all differed in significant ways. The Walkway, I realized, was a work in progress. But, my goodness, that's better than no trail at all.

There is another reason why Lanark should be on the tourist trail—its association with William Wallace. Sir William, of course, had an enormous reputation in Scotland long before *Braveheart*. But the movie gave his name—and a highly fictionalized account of his life—worldwide publicity. In Lanark, there is an 1882 statue of Wallace on the steeple of Saint Nicholas. Then, just across Castlegate, there is a plaque marking "the site of the house reputed to be the marital home of Sir William Wallace and Marion Braidfute". It continues: "It was at Lanark in 1297 that Wallace first drew sword to free his native land." At the east end of town are the ruins of Old Saint Kentigern's Church. Its roofless walls and exquisite arches stand against a backdrop of fields. It is a romantic place. And here, it is said, William and Marion married (presumably it had a roof back then). Add to this that Wallace may first have drawn sword after the English occupiers killed Marion, and you have a marvelous story of love and war that happened here in Lanark—if it happened at all, that is.

We know almost nothing for certain about William Wallace, least of all about the roughly 27 years of his life before he erupts, briefly and fitfully, in the historical record. *Braveheart* has him as a ragged boy among the snowy bens of the Highlands. This, at least, we know to be fiction. Wallace was born around 1270, probably on what is today the western edge of Glasgow's conurbation; and

he was the son of a landowner, albeit a minor one. He was no
raggedy-ass Highlander. Whatever the real Wallace did as a youth
and young man, it prepared him for war. In 1297, with Scotland
seemingly firmly in the grip of Edward "Longshanks" of England,
he appears suddenly as a standard-bearer of revolt—and he does
so by killing the Sheriff of Lanark. Four months later, Wallace
pulls off (with Andrew Moray, a noble from the northeast) a sen-
sational victory over superior English forces at Stirling Bridge.
But the following year brings catastrophic defeat at Falkirk, and
Wallace returns to the mists of history until his betrayal to the
English in 1305. Betrayal was followed by a quick trial and a gory
execution in London. There is no evidence at all to support the
Gibson version of his last word, a tortured cry of "Freedom!"

Wallace has been a sought-after brand ever since his death.
An early admirer was Blind Harry, author of an epic poem[50]
composed 170 years after Sir William's execution. It may be as
full of whoppers as *Braveheart*, and indeed the source of many of
the movie's fictions. For Harry, Wallace was a powerful weapon
against the pro-English drift in Scottish affairs in his own time.
More recently, Wallace became the upstanding patriot for every-
man, uncompromising beside the vacillating nobles like Bruce.
His cult has not always been seemly; witness spats over his place
of birth, and the Mel Gibson-lookalike statue that for a while
adorned the car park of the Wallace Monument near Stirling. This
made Lanark's muted celebration of him the more commendable.
And what about Marion? Harry has her marrying William and
bearing a child. The Sheriff slays her when she tries to hinder his
pursuit of Wallace. Wallace returns and cuts the Sheriff to pieces.
True? We know for sure that Wallace killed the Sheriff of Lanark.
If he did it to avenge his Marion, we shall never know.

I would have stayed longer up in Lanark, but I had a route
to plan and chores to do, and both required the facilities of the
New Lanark hostel. As I have said, New Lanark is a World
Heritage Site. It is centered on the early-19th century work of

Robert Owen to give mill workers decent living and toiling conditions. You can, with a ticket, visit Owen's house, workers' homes, a school, and something called the "Annie McLeod Experience ride". I passed them all up. New Lanark also boasted a half-museum-half-souvenir-shop store, and workers in period costumes. It was Disneyesque after Lanark. Then I saw The Edinburgh Woollen Mill, and was pleased to have laundry to do. In the hostel's basement laundry room, I threw my old over-pants into the garbage bin. They deserved better—Taps and a stiff salute at the very least.

In the morning I fretted that I would climb above the remaining Falls of Clyde and be able to advance no farther. On my map, where the Clyde Walkway ended at Bonnington Linn, a footbridge was shown crossing the river to meet a farm track; but I feared—simply because this sort of crap happens—that the bridge might be private and barred. Yesterday, I asked the girl at the Scottish Wildlife Trust in New Lanark if you could continue on above the falls. "Definitely," she said, but I still fretted. Normal weather had resumed, and it was a wet, uphill slog with the Big Bastard. I had no Plan B if it was all in vain. The slog was not unrewarding. Pausing to catch my breath, I looked down into the wooded gorge, and saw a gray-white bird of prey—a peregrine falcon perhaps—circling menacingly. At Corra Linn, the highest of the falls, water the colors of coffee-foam tumbled in two steps through a green chasm. But the din of rushing water pressed on me, and began to jar. It was a relief to pass Bonnington Linn and find the Clyde flowing placidly again—and to see a footbridge free of barriers. Halfway across I looked downstream to the current slipping over the linn, and the mist swirling in the pines above the drop.

All at once the country was flat and open. If the day had been less *dreich*, there would have been a big sky and a horizon. It was liberating even so. The track became a straight country lane that led away from the Clyde. Woods gave way to fields. Only the solitude was unchanged. I followed a sign for Sandilands, and walked a deserted road down to a river. It was not the Clyde. It was the Douglas Water on its way to join the big river a half-mile downstream. I rested my pack, still upon my shoulders, on the parapet of Douglasmouth Bridge. Upstream, the water meandered through a misty valley of the gentlest slopes and lushest pasture. There was a cottage at one end of the bridge, but no people anywhere. I began to feel like an intruder in a wary land. Ten minutes later, approaching Sandilands Farm, the narrow road turned to cow shit, and looked like it might terminate altogether at the farm buildings. There was a worker ahead maneuvering machinery between sheds, but he drove inside as I drew near. Climbing gently to the next farm, I saw another figure. He came out onto the road ahead, and turned his back to me. But he walked fitfully, pausing here and there to stare into the fields. I gained, and soon caught up.

"So, is the walking easier with two stakes?" he asked. He had just the one walking stick himself; and a scruffy overcoat and flat cap. His tone was jocular.

"They help me along," I replied, jocularly. He asked where I was going, and I said Abington.

"There's a farmers' road to Abington through Howgate Mouth," he offered. Before I could reply, he added, "Now, where are you from?"

"I live in America," I said. But he waited for more, so I added "I was born in Glasgow, and went to England when I was small." He snorted at the mention of England, a country now just 60 miles down the motorway.

As much as I loved the name Howgate Mouth, especially the way the Anglophobe farmer had said it, I would have needed to retrace a mile of steps to pick up the route. I continued on my course. At a cluster of houses and farms, joinery work was underway in a cottage doorway. A carpenter called out "not the best day for a walk!" as I passed by. My route turned southeast here, and crossed a main road where pungent smoke wafted from a bonfire in a lonely industrial yard. I climbed gradually into a misty, blurred world of rough pasture and pine. Within a mile, for the first time since Conic Hill, I was 1,000 feet up. There were no views, just mist. Every so often a van hauling a motorcycle overtook me, until, on the descent from the summit, Tinto Park Moto appeared on the hillside. It was silent. Whoever had arrived to race their motocross bikes had vanished into the vans and scattered prefabs on the bare slope. The country was lonely and the inhabitants fugitive again. The only life that took an interest in me was the bull near Little Galla Farm that rose to its hooves to see me out of town. Howgate Mouth was off to my left now, a cleft between steep braes, dramatic even behind the sheer of mist and drizzle. I wished I had walked through it. The turn for Roberton was here too, beside a single cottage. Coal smoke came from its chimney, leaving a delicious perfume hanging in the motionless air.

The signpost said three miles to Roberton, and I could see the first of them from right here, winding up through sheep and cattle to a clouded, forested ridge. These cattle were neither single-minded *fearties* nor bravehearts. They rushed excitedly ahead to a corner of their walled field as if to greet me, but then fled before I got near. Their pasture was crossed by a little stream called the Garf Water. Was this Garf the Gaelic *garbh* (rough) corrupted when this region switched to the Scots language? Its timid flow argued otherwise. And certainly the landscape immediately about was now more Scots-English than Celtic in its names. The hills were hills; or laws, rigs, knowes. There was not a *tom* or *meall* anywhere. There were waters and burns, but no *allt*. The names of some of the bigger hills looked Celtic—Dungavel, Lochlyock—but most hill-names needed no deciphering. There was Ewe Hill (two, in fact) and Blackstane Hill; Little Law and Jack's Law;

Priestgill Rig and Bent Rig. The villages had easy arrangements of letters too—Wiston, Rigside, Newton.

I stopped at a high crossroads between pinewood and fields. It was lunchtime, and I propped my pack against a farm gate, and paced around munching the usual stuff. Farther on, at the highest point of the road, it felt as if the views would be magnificent if only the mist cleared. Tinto stood three miles north, but the Great Fire of London could have been raging on its top and I would not have known. For the first time on this journey, I deeply wished the weather were better. Dark brooding is not such a Lowland thing. It seemed as empty here as in the Highlands. Not a car had passed since Tinto Park. Now, descending, I marched undisturbed right down the middle of the lane. It fell 250 feet in half a mile, and arrived at Nap Bridge, a single speckled-gray arch spanning Roberton Burn. An old-fashioned wooden signpost stood at one end of the bridge pointing to Roberton and farms named Fallside and Maidencoats. It was a timeless scene, and beautiful even in the gloom.

I stepped delicately across a cattle grid, and walked through Roberton's string of cottages to a main road in a wide valley. Minutes later I was reunited with the Clyde, placid and undiminished among these big hills, 700 feet above the Broomielaw now. The main railway line south ran beside the river. A London-bound passenger train whooshed by, preceded by a sound like thunder and a screech. A long freight train ground sedately north. All I desired was to get my boots off. When I saw my hotel across a field, there was no footpath leading to it. I wasn't surprised. This would not be a walker's kind of place. Pushing on to a roundabout, I wheeled into Abington Welcome Break motorway services, and found my Days Inn behind the gas station and parking lots. After the receptionist checked me in, I asked her if the hotel had a restaurant.

"No, but there's food over in the services." Then she looked at me more carefully.

"If it's a pub you're after, there's one in Abington, but we don't usually recommend it." Perish the thought. Days Inn was a characterless place of course, but free beer would not have dragged me from my clean room and huge bed. There was abundant, steaming, peat-free water for the tub, and hot radiators to dry my clothes. I bought a newspaper and a burger in the services, and hunkered down.

## 25

# Dods, Laws, and Cleuchs

I went across to the motorway services to buy breakfast. The new day looked exactly like the one before. Featureless gray cloud sat just above the surrounding hills, and looked as if it would start dripping at any moment, like a saturated sponge. I bought a breakfast as out of tune with my journey as the Days Inn—coffee and pastries from the only Starbucks for 35 miles around. Then, as soon as I had packed up my gear and set out for Abington village, the rain began. There were no announcing blasts of wind, no darkening sky, no thunderclaps or rainbows; just a leaking of cloud into air, as undramatic as it seemed inevitable. I walked on past the pub that Days Inn did not usually recommend. It looked alright but maybe had I gone last night I'd have a bandaged *heid* or the *squitters* now. To my left, mostly hidden behind trees and cottages, was the Clyde. At the end of the village it swung southeast. I swung southwest; and that, strictly, was the end of our acquaintance. The headwaters I expected to cross tomorrow would no longer bear its name. But that is just labelling, and I refused to say goodbye just yet.

On the bridge across the motorway, I removed my cap for fear the wind would lift it into the traffic below. The motorway was not unattractive for six lanes, the big green hills it wound through cutting it down to size. The cars speeding south would be in England in an hour; but I was taking a B road into the Lowther Hills and would need rather longer to be done with Scotland. The Lowthers are part of the Southern Uplands, the great swathe of hills that run across southern Scotland from sea to sea. The region is, touristically, a poor cousin of the Highlands, neither as rugged nor romantic. It is for most people a drive-through zone, and that had been my experience of it too, until today.

The B road climbed gradually, following the hillside above a burn called Glengonnar Water. I put a line of transmission towers behind me, then stopped at the brow of a hill and took out my map. Across the glen, bare hills rose behind the winding burn, colored in greens lower down, and browns as they climbed higher. The nearest hill was called Craig Dod. Behind it, stood Ravengill Dod. In fact, there were dods everywhere—Coom, Wellgrain, Brown. And when these blunt hills were not dods, they were rigs or laws, as well as plain hills. So what's the difference? I have been back to my father's old dictionary. A dod—a Scots word—is "a rounded hill-top, esp. a shoulder of a greater hill". Law, also Scots, means "a hill, esp. rounded or conical". A rig is a ridge. Brown Dod stood off the road ahead, behind the settlement of Lettershaws, which its bulk made look insignificant. I went that way now and soon arrived at a knot of cottages, sheds, and trailers. Lettershaws really was insignificant, little more than a campsite by a smelly farm.

The road resumed a gentle climb, and at the top of a rise, where a pinewood appeared on the left, I graduated again to a new OS map, this time the "Nithsdale & Annandale" sheet. The pines, planted of course, ended neatly after two miles; and thereafter the

Map 6: Lanark to the Solway

valley—1,150 feet up now—felt bleak and exposed. The wind drove a cold rain horizontally into my face, and I was glad my hike today would be a short one. The kiss of sweet Scottish rain! Hah! Ahead, low stone walls appeared on either side of the road, marking where a burn ran beneath. When I reached the walls I saw white letters painted on one of them. They were faded, but quite legible—ENGLISH GO HOME.

Leadhills did not look much. Its long main street was all dug up and dirty. For a quarter-mile, there were rows of cottages but nowhere to get me out of the weather. The village's name proclaimed what had once been mined here but, looking up, you could fancy it dug from the very sky. I found a bus shelter that shut out the driving rain, but it left me cold still. I pulled up my hood and crossed Main Street to The Hopetoun Arms. The landlady was opening the door for me even before I reached it. Inside, I hung my wet jacket and cap on a hook and sat at a table. A fire was being lit, a cloth draped in front of the fireplace to improve the draw. I ordered a pot of tea, which arrived hot, strong, and enough for four. I decided to stay for lunch. Then, after pie and chips, I decided to linger some more over the last of the beer I had ordered to accompany them. The landlady said, "Are you putting off going out in that rain?"

Of course I was; but not for very much longer. And by the time I was walking out of Leadhills en route to Wanlockhead, the rain had stopped anyway. When I was planning this adventure, Wanlockhead figured prominently. It was where I would join the Southern Upland Way (SUW) for the final push to Portpatrick. The plan had changed, but I'd still join the SUW in the village, but to hike east instead of west. A mile from Leadhills, the road reached its height, and a sign welcomed me to Dumfries & Galloway, the last region of my journey. There are 32 "council areas" in Scotland, so it surprised me that in crossing the whole country I had touched but eight[51]. The height was a natural border too.

Beyond it, the burns flowed eventually into the Solway Firth, off
to the south, instead of swelling the young north-flowing Clyde.
A short descent brought me to the edge of Wanlockhead and
another sign: HIGHEST VILLAGE IN SCOTLAND (1531
FEET ABOVE SEA LEVEL).

Emily's B&B was called The Garage. It occupied a cottage
beside what looked like an old mechanic's shed. GARAGE was
painted on the shed's rust-colored roof in big white letters, which
had made it easy to find. Emily was waiting outside, ready to guide
me to the cottage. She had not told me, when I phoned from New
Lanark to book, that she would have to reopen after the end of
her season to put me up. Now she said that I was her 199th guest
this year. I hoped number 200 would come by before she closed
irreversibly, but I was her only guest tonight. Emily was a warm
and efficient granny. She showed me what was where in her sin-
gle-story place—my room, the bathroom, the breakfast room at
one end of the corridor. There was a picture of the Last Supper on
the breakfast room wall, and Charles and Diana mementos by the
fireplace. My room was snug. I put gear everywhere to dry; hung it
from drawer knobs, draped it over the bedside lamp, spread it over
one half of the bed. I lay on the other half, and dozed until woken
by my own abrupt snore. Then I stared out the window, toward
what was making me anxious to a degree I had not been since
the Northwest Highlands. Tomorrow's hike would be 15 miles
at least, and up and down over ground higher than anywhere else
on the walk. And looking out now toward Lowther Hill, there
seemed to be an excellent chance of doing it all in mist and rain. I
asked Emily for an early breakfast.

There was half-light outside my window at 7 a.m. Cloud sat as
low and thick on the hills as ever. Over breakfast, Emily said the

weather was supposed to improve later on. But it was raining when I stepped onto the Southern Upland Way, and raining as I managed to stay on it without a hitch for all of 300 yards. At a junction of tracks at the village edge, I chose left. It looked the most long-distance-path-like. I walked for five minutes before changing my mind and returning to the junction. Now I went straight ahead, and found myself soon on the waymarked track, up among the heather. Still, I'd lost precious time and composure on a day that seemed long on miles and short on hours of daylight. I turned to look back at Wanlockhead, nestled in its sodden valley, slate-gray cloud sitting on top of slate roofs. Then I followed a dead-straight path into the mist. My only company was flitting grouse until, a mile uphill, a Range Rover came suddenly out of the fog as if gliding on heather. There was a road, of course, hidden from view. The Way soon came out to it, and thereafter road and trail crisscrossed as I climbed. Radio masts and then a radar station appeared above. The radar station was atop Lowther Hill, and when I was atop it too, its broad summit was socked in, windswept, cold, and surreal. The radar station was a giant's golf ball set on a fat tee, the tee attached to a long hangar. Toadstool-like structures edged the hangar. These buildings were blurred in the mist, and hardly different from it in color. A single lamp burned at one end of the hangar like a tiny, weak sun. I circled the buildings, looking for the onward SUW to the sound of their alien hum. This was the highest point of my whole journey—at 2,378 feet, higher here in the Lowlands than anywhere I trod in the Highlands—and it felt like a sci-fi set much more than a Scottish hilltop.

I had to retrace my steps a short distance down the road—now clearly the access road for the radar station—to pick up the SUW and follow it off Lowther Hill on the southeast side. To my surprise, the mist and wind did not accompany me. By the time I had dropped 500 feet to a saddle between summits, my immediate surroundings were again in sharp focus. The saddle was a bare place of rough grasses and heather, a watershed where burns were born. Again, those born on one side would join the Clyde, those on the other tumble to the River Nith and eventually the Solway. The map showed Enterkin Burn and Loch Burn, but also watercourses labelled cleuchs—Rough Cleuch, Smidding Cleuch, McBride's Cleuch. I liked this Lowland word. It is pronounced *clooch* with a rasping Scottish "ch". The English equivalent is *clough*, and both mean a ravine or valley. Now I crossed what looked to be the beginning of Loch Burn, little more than a ditch in the moor, and began to climb the hill called Cold Moss. The rain was long gone and the mist ascending to the sky. There were astonishing views. The Dalveen Pass lay 1,000 feet below, hemmed in by steep green hills cut by deep *cleuchs*. The path descended gently enough from Cold Moss to Comb Head, but then I saw it drop away ahead at an absurd pitch. I felt a flash of unreasonable annoyance. Why on earth had they routed the SUW down *this?* But I eased down with pigeon steps, zigzags, and just one oh-Christ-I'm-slipping dance, and arrived in one piece at another saddle. Here, there were open views over a patchwork of green and brown vegetation clothing steep but rounded hills and the valleys between—dods, laws, and cleuchs all in one scene.

Next came Laght Hill. Coming off Comb Head, Laght Hill had looked like a long, steep climb. But it took 15 minutes, and from the top I could see back to the golf ball on Lowther Hill, now perfectly free of mist. I could even make out the wee toadstools. To the north, there was a large patch of blue sky. Clouds snagged only the very tops of some hills in the remotest distance. Between me and those hills the land was an undulating expanse of greens and light browns, darkened here and there by ruler-edged pine forests. There was another kind of forest too. It spread over most of the hills in the middle distance, maybe four miles end to end. This forest was not dense, but it dwarfed the pines in height and looked as out of place as the golf ball. The scene would certainly have

been prettier without it, without its white trunks and propeller
branches. But the wind farm had a certain grace.

It was a short, steep descent over greasy ground from Laght
Hill to a farm called Overfingland and the main road. Overfingland
was screened from the SUW by pines, and dogs howled from behind them as I passed. The path met the road just north of the
Dalveen Pass, putting me in South Lanarkshire again for a while.
There was little traffic, and I walked through a handsome high valley, surrounded by bald hills with solid names like Pin Stane and
Meikle Shag. The wind farm had receded with my descent, and
only a few forestry scars now marred the scene. After ten minutes,
road and SUW parted company at a bridge over the Potrenick
Burn, and I followed Way and burn over rough fields to where
they met another stream. This was the Potrail Water, which two
miles downstream—and off my route—would arrive at a place
called Watermeetings. There it would join the Daer Water, and
together become the River Clyde. I crossed the Potrail Water on a
footbridge and began to climb into forest. In a scrubby area of new
plantings, I halted to catch my breath. I turned to look back, and
saw the most magnificent rainbow arcing over the shining hills
that give birth to the Clyde.

For a few miles the SUW became a fine track with gentle
grades, first through the forest and then on open moor. Where
the moor ended, there was a signpost. It pointed both ways and,
beneath a white thistle symbol, said SOUTHERN UPLAND
WAY. I worked out that this was almost exactly the Way's midpoint. If I followed it west, back the way I had come this morning,
it would take me to Portpatrick in 106 miles. Ireland would lie 20
miles across the sea. If I walked east for 106 miles, I'd end up in a
village called Cockburnspath on the North Sea, not far from John
Muir's birthplace of Dunbar. And walk east I did, soon meeting
a single-track road. It rose toward a brow, above which thick gray
clouds were reoccupying the sky. When the road flattened out,

a gray parapet appeared ahead, then a sloping wall of turf, and finally the shimmering surface of the Daer Reservoir. To my pleasure, I saw next that the SUW was routed over the dam. It was a half-mile of soft, slick path, the parapet and water to my right, the grass-covered dam wall sloping steeply away to my left. At the base of the dam, the Daer Water slipped away to Watermeetings, and I accepted that this, now, was goodbye to the Clyde.

I was flagging and hungry, and promised myself a long break before starting up Sweetshaw Brae. I sat on a rock and ate cheese and dried fruit. Across the reservoir, the hills were a thin layer of dim green, sandwiched between massed gray clouds and rippling silver-gray water. Well short of a long rest, the compulsion to move on kicked in, and I snapped myself into my pack. Sweetshaw Brae and the heights that followed it had looked easy from the dam, but they became a slog. From the Brae, the whole reservoir could be seen, contained in its bowl of hills. The scene recalled the Highlands. The slopes were gentler, for sure, and the summits lower and less pinnacled. But other things were the same; there wasn't another person, dwelling, or unplanted tree in sight. And as in the Highlands, I was at peace with this solitude, a comfort that had returned, it seemed, as the densely peopled Central Belt had fallen away behind me.

On the way to Hods Hill, I got a close-up view of the wind turbines and then found something mysterious. I called it "spawn like ice" in my notes. From a distance, the stuff looked like the very last remnants of an old snowfall, hand-sized bits of gray ice surviving in the rough grass. Up close, it looked like the jelly part of frogspawn. But neither ice nor breeding amphibians was a good explanation on an October moor. Hmm, I thought, and didn't think any more about it until I returned home. Then I googled "strange jelly on Scottish moor", and discovered that I was not alone in having been perplexed by it. It had been spotted that autumn across the border in northern England, and in Scotland two

years before. *The Daily Mail* had asked if the "mysterious translucent jelly" came from outer space. Oh come on! But when I read
on, I learned that "star jelly", "star slime", even "star snot" had, in
the popular mind, been linked to meteors for centuries. After the
2009 outbreak in Scotland, scientists tested the goo. They decided
it was *not* algae or fungi, but offered no positive explanation. An
old theory is that it is the remains of poisonous frogs consumed
by other animals and then spat out on the moor. I can't come up
with anything better.

On Hods Hill—1,850 feet up in a battering wind—the SUW
turned south. As it did so, I caught sight of an indistinct, light-
brown squiggle across low-lying land in the far distance. The
squiggle gave off a dull shine. The Solway! And were those faint,
shadowy humps behind it the fells of the English Lake District?
The firth, my finish line, was perhaps 40 miles away by path and
road. I felt a flicker of anticipation and relief, but—like looking forward to the end of term when exams still loom—quickly
returned to the tasks at hand. Right ahead was a steep descent,
along the edge of a pine forest that was emitting wisps of mist like
smoke from goblins' hovels. Or could it be real smoke from the
fireplace of a bothy? The map showed two buildings in the forest,
labeled Brattleburn and Rivox. The map did not say so, but I knew
they were bothies. The village of Beattock was nine miles away,
and close by it the town of Moffat. They offered the prospect of
a soft bed and rich food. Just like in the Highlands, a battle began in my head between roughing it and comfort. Roughing it offered the chance of an uncommon experience, a story to recall and
recount; but it offered little in the way of instant gratification. I
came off Hods Hill, crossed Beld Knowe, and veered off the moor
and into the forest. Here the trail descended even more steeply on
slimy ground, toward a stream named the Cloffin Burn. I slipped
and fell for the third time on this journey, another reminder of
the Highlands. The Cloffin Burn springs from the watershed

and flows into the Evan Water and then the River Annan to the Solway. I was sliding into Annandale.

I crossed the Cloffin Burn, put my pack down beside the trail, and set off unladen along a side path to Brattleburn bothy. I examined the bothy from a distance, and it did not invite. I conjured up damp and midges within its white stone walls. There was, really, no way it could have invited, not without lights, sheets, and the smell of cooking. It was too early to stop anyway, even though I was tired. Even gradual climbs were hard work now, as hard in the contemplation as the climbing. On Craig Hill, the SUW was particularly sodden and thankless. "Southern Upland Waterway!" I muttered, and reached for my map. It told me I didn't have to follow the SUW to Beattock. I could take a mile-long track down to a road beside the Evan Water, and walk to the village on tarmac. I was out of the forest in no time, arriving at the bottom of a broad valley at the hamlet of Middlegill. It was a pretty valley, but used—used by my road to Beattock; by the railway beside it; by transmission lines; and by the M74 motorway across the river. The three miles to Beattock were flat and dry, but tedious. The tedium meant I felt my sore feet and my journey coming to an end.

It was getting dark as I walked into Beattock. There was no hotel at the top of the village where the map showed one. I walked on, thinking I would need to find a bus to Moffat. Then, where cottages began to line the road, I saw The Old Stables Inn & Restaurant. I went into the bar and found a ruddy-faced woman.

"Do you have a room for one night, maybe two?"

"I do," she answered with an English accent, "but I'd need to move the laundry that's piled up in it." She said this as if it would be a bloody nuisance, but her teasing look said otherwise. So I had a scalding shower, and came back to the bar for lamb casserole and beer. I thought guiltily of how much better this was than damp and midges, even if they would make a better story.

# 26

# *Annandale*

————————|—————————

I decided before breakfast to take the day off. My legs were tired after yesterday's 20 up-and-down miles. But I had a bigger reason. Scotland would play Spain tonight in a match that would decide their participation in the 2012 European football championship, and I knew I could see the game at The Old Stables. I decided something else before breakfast too. When I changed my plans in Glasgow, I saw myself ending the journey at Gretna, the town on the English border at the eastern end of the Solway Firth. Everyone in Britain has heard of Gretna. It—or more precisely the adjoining village of Gretna Green—was notorious from the 1700s on as the place where English couples eloped to marry, exploiting Scotland's looser marriage laws. But Gretna was also where the motorway crossed the border, and if I walked to it from Beattock, I might be always in sight and sound of traffic. So I decided to stay farther west, and meet the Solway at Annan, as Annandale itself would.

Beattock's main street possessed some well-kept cottages, but otherwise the village was a plain place, left to itself by busy people speeding past by road and rail. It wasn't always a backwater. Until the 1960s, the main road from England to Glasgow ran right down the main street. My family drove through back then, but I remembered nothing of the village. The place I did remember from those trips was Beattock Summit, a pass a dozen miles north. Impossibly steep hills had crowded against the road, bare but for grass and chewing sheep. Those hills were very dramatic for a boy accustomed to the modest curves of Surrey. I saw hills this morning from the bus stop opposite The Old Stables, but they were dressed in the pine forests that had burgeoned only in my lifetime. A pretty girl was waiting for the bus to Moffat with me, pulling deeply on a cigarette in preparation for the five-minute ride.

Had the girl told me that Moffat was a spare, forsaken place, I would have believed her. I had no picture for it at all. So when the bus pulled onto the High Street, the prettiness of Moffat came as a surprise. The High Street was broad, its median marked out with trees and decorated with a bronze ram celebrating the town's old wool trade. The buildings that lined the High Street were handsome and housed businesses that looked like they did a handsome trade. It brought to mind a south-of-England market town. Then, as I wandered around, it became clear that Moffat nowadays was a tourist town. There were hotels from the modest to the ivy-clad and beflagged. There were B&Bs galore. There was, of course, an Edinburgh Woollen Mill. The town center seemed to cater to short-breakers, as once it thrived on those who came to "take the waters". At the edge of town stood Moffat Mill, a store behind an acre of parking that sold quick souvenirs to coach bus tourists before they left Scotland on the motorway. I judged Moffat unkindly at first, but later nosed around the lanes off the High Street. They were attractive, just as attractive as Lanark's.

It's just that they were hamming it up for someone other than the Moffatonians.

That evening, in the bar of the Old Stables, decently busy but hardly abuzz, Spain swiftly killed Scotland's hopes. There was a funny man among the group intently watching the game, another Willy. With Scotland outclassed, he cheered little triumphs. "Look, we've won another throw-in!" His lines were dry and well-timed. "Why is he bringing on Don Cowie?" he asked nobody in particular when the Scotland coach made a substitution. "I don't like Don Cowie. I don't like his *faither* or his *maither*." Willy told me afterward that he was proud of the team despite the failure.

"So, Willy, will you support England now that Scotland is out?" I asked. England had qualified from their group by a country mile.

"Yer joking? The Romans didn't build that wall high enough for my liking," he said, referring to Hadrian's Wall, 40 miles southeast, and shorthand for the Anglo-Scottish border. But it was a lighthearted, footballing animosity. Willy was a regular in this English-run pub, rubbing along with the English locals, who had not gloated when Scotland fell short.

In the morning, Mrs. served me breakfast. Mrs. was how I had come to think of the ruddy-faced woman who had moved her laundry to give me a bed. She had cooked me Full Scottish Breakfast yesterday too, and I had felt it was a lot of trouble for an only guest. In the evenings, she served in the bar. Mrs. was the personification of Keep Buggering On, a weary but ultimately positive resilience in the face of life's trials. I told Mrs. that when I hiked into Beattock I had feared I would need to go on to Moffat to find a bed. She sighed a keep-buggering-on sigh, and said that the most popular guidebook to the Southern Upland Way said that Beattock offered no accommodation.

"If you're publishing a guide, you would think you'd bloody well check, wouldn't you?" she added. You would, so I will report that I enjoyed my stay at The Old Stables Inn & Restaurant, Beattock, Dumfriesshire, and that Mrs.' world-weary humor played no small part in that.

Drizzle moistened my cheeks as I walked out of Beattock. In no time, I was beside fields and the soft rain had given up. I joined the main Dumfries road for a few hundred yards, then turned onto the B7020. The sign pointing down it read "Lochmaben 11". I had booked a room in Lochmaben. The road was a quiet lane through trees and fields. A mile onto it, a rich aroma announced Stockholm farm long before its sheds and stacked bales of plastic-wrapped hay came into view. A cock pheasant strutted in a nearby field. The farmer, moving bales around with a tractor, gave me a wave. Almost always on this journey, I had looked forward each morning to the scenes that surely awaited. Today, I had not looked forward to anything much, except reaching Lochmaben and being just a day's march from the Solway. But beyond Stockholm, I looked between two sturdy trees beside the road and felt a surge of pleasure, the better for being unanticipated. Away to the northeast, there were high hills still, gray-brown where they were not hidden in cloud. But in the foreground rolled a gentle, green valley of copse and pasture. The two miles between me and its other flank contained a railway, a motorway, several lesser roads, and the River Annan; but I could see none of them, only lazy, fat cattle in fat fields.

Sometime during the morning, a flock of hen pheasants took flight in a field beside the road ahead. A Land Rover was parked close to them, and a dog was moving in the field too. The driver of the Land Rover saw me, and waited as I approached.

"We've been shooting," he said, "chasing the pheasants back where they belong." He spoke as I imagined a doctor or lawyer in these parts might; clear, precise words, in an accent still unmistakably Scots. He was dressed well too, no farmer's scruffy overcoat or frayed flat cap. "They like the beechnuts and other mast they find down here; not so much the firs and pines up there, where they are meant to be," he went on, pointing to the planted forest at the top of the field. It did not occur to me to ask why the pheasants belonged there, but not here. I guessed only later that he ran shoots for an estate, and was chasing the birds back to where his clients could more easily hunt them. As we were talking, the dog—Nicky by name—jumped into the back of the Land Rover and curled up beside a dead pheasant.

"I see you have one for supper," I said.

"It was hit by an electricity van back there," he replied. "Feel it, it's still warm." I did, and it was; and feeling its feathers provoked a memory. When I was in my early teens, my father came by a brace of pheasants somehow. They hung in our garage to "ripen", and then I was given the task of plucking, gutting, and skinning them. I'm sure dad helped. Afterward, I looked at the tiny bodies that were left, and thought what a lot of stomach-turning they had caused for so very little meat. They shrank further in the pot, which was just as well; I had little appetite to eat them.

The lane went gently up, then gently down, always due south, mostly free of traffic. It ran between farmhouses, and thick, old trees that lined and dotted the broad pastures to either side. Somewhere on this stretch, I gazed at a dozen cream sheep standing atop a green brae against a gray sky. A rabbit darted under a farm gate. A small flock of starlings put on a show. At Chapel Wood I stopped for lunch beside a stout tree in a hedge. There were hills away to the southwest. They were not high enough that their green ever gave way to brown, but they rose conspicuously above the intervening lowland. I checked my map, and decided they were Hightown Hill and Barrs Hill, five miles distant. Both, the map said, showed the marks of earthworks from Celtic forts, strongholds that would have had a dominating view of the goings-on of Iron Age Annandale.

I pressed on. A little after a farm called South Greyrigg the road crossed a slender burn, a low wall to either side where it did so. On an impulse, I rested my pack and poles against one wall, set my camera on the other, and dashed back across the road to pose beside my gear. It's not a bad picture—a green field for background, and me wearing the same cap, jacket, and boots as when I last turned the camera on myself near Ben Nevis. Only the waterproof pants have changed, and they only from black to dark blue. I did not know it then, but this wee stream—the Black Burn—was 400 miles from Cape Wrath by my peculiar route and rough calculations. Half a mile later, I paused again. Moffat and Beattock had been hard by the Southern Uplands, but now I looked at those same hills across ten miles of flat valley floor. They were big, bald lumps, the summits of the highest merging into the unbroken sheet of cloud. But in every other direction I looked, the country was rolling and gentle. Scotland had finally run out of hills.

At the Crown Hotel in Lochmaben an elderly man wearing a pinstripe suit showed me to a room at the back, overlooking Kirk Loch. This was no dark, hill-bounded water, plunging to monster-inhabited depths. It was more of a pond. In my room, I had to squeeze between the furniture to move about, but the place was clean, and had a shower like a piping-hot Niagara. After supper, I strolled past the lochside caravans and golf course, and out to where Lockerbie Road[52] and the High Street met. Lochmaben was a bigger Beattock, tidy but unadorned. Back at the Crown, I lay on my single bed, straining to watch the tiny TV on top of the wardrobe. I went out again later to call home, and found a phone box near a statue of Robert the Bruce, but it was missing its door, and youths in the adjacent bus shelter were letting out shouts of uncertain meaning. The street was dimly lit. I gave up, and marched along empty streets to look for another call box. Finally, I said "sod it" and called on my cell. The line was bad, and

Charissa's words were soon cut off. At that moment, I wanted to be home right now. Back on my bed, I watched a TV show that revolved around police videos of the stupid things drivers do on British motorways, and reproached myself that this was not what I had come to Scotland to do.

When I got dressed the next morning, I put gel on my thigh and pulled on my thigh support, as I had done every walking day for a month. The injury had healed long ago, but as long as there were rough paths to contend with, I had feared a relapse. Today, with the big hills behind me and a B road ahead, these precautions felt like an empty ritual. In truth, the end of the rough paths and big hills had taken away more than a need for care. It felt as if other staples of my walk were gone too: challenge; risk; discomfort; remote places that seasoned both solitude and company; effort that sweetened the idleness that followed. The sudden absence of these things had left me empty, watching garbage on TV. I felt better this morning. I had a finishing line to reach, and 15 miles was a trek even in gentle Annandale.

The road to Dalton—the B7020 again—left Lochmaben along the shore of Castle Loch. There was a footpath through the fringe of trees between road and loch, and for a mile it took me off the tarmac. Scattered along the path were wooden sculptures of creatures of the neighborhood. I recall a heron among sculpted reeds, a standing otter, and a fat owl. Castle Loch was a more imposing body of water than Kirk Loch, but there were only glimpses of it through the trees. Finally, from a jetty, I looked out on the water in the company of a man with a bouncy pup. He wanted to go sailing later, he said; but the morning was dead calm and the sky gray. Boating on the loch has a history. The remains of logboats chiseled by ancient Celts have been pulled from the water, as well as bits and pieces of crannogs to which they may have been paddled. The path returned to the road, and I walked a mile to a crossroads. On the way I saw an astonishing number of pheasants, and crossed the invisible boundary onto the "Carlisle & Solway Firth" OS map—my last. At the crossroads, there was a sense of height. A sign pointed left to the village of Hightae, unseen behind the brow of a hill. But elevation is relative; the road had climbed 60 feet from the loch! Another sign said "Dalton 3", and that was the way I went.

At the Crown, the landlady had asked where I was from; or rather, as they say in Scotland, where I *belonged*. Good question. For ever more of us on this mobile, globalizing planet the answer is not straightforward. For me, "I'm from Connecticut" would be true, but only to a point, and the accent with which I answered would raise the doubt. Saying Glasgow or Surrey, instead, would also be true but incomplete. So I gave the landlady my pat answer—born in Scotland, grew up in England, live in the United States. But, walking now to Dalton, I thought how it really is a pat answer, especially when you consider that Scottish way of asking the question. If belonging means where you fit in, where the locals would say "he's from around here" and you yourself feel like a native, then I belong nowhere. I can't say this troubles me, maybe because it has always been so. I could have belonged in England; but, as I have said, something held me back as a boy from feeling native. I had, I think, already latched onto the wild-seeming, colorful country where I was born as the place I wanted to belong. I didn't, of course, not in the born-and-bred way; and I didn't interrupt my life as it unfolded to change a sentimental attachment into the real, everyday thing. It would have demanded a one-way ticket "home". But my years of occasional reacquaintance, and this long walk, had left me with a feeling of belonging that suited me quite well, neither misty-eyed romantic nor taken for granted. You can be American and something else, especially when that second identity is a harmless source of roots and inspiration, and in the here and now your feet are planted solidly in the New World. Instead of belonging nowhere, I should count myself fortunate to belong to different places in different ways.

Yesterday, the pheasant-hunter mentioned the Annandale Way, which I had not heard of. It was up in the forest, he said, up where his pheasants should have been. In Lochmaben, I picked up an Annandale Way booklet at the Town Hall, and tried to study it to see if there was a more interesting route to Annan than my B roads. But the booklet was fussily organized, and the Way was not marked on my OS maps. Part of me, anyway, did not want to be distracted from my quick-and-easy route. On the road to Dalton, there were low hills to the southwest again, and I suspected the Way ran over them. Now another part of me wanted to be up there, feeling a little challenged and uncomfortable. But the lane sped me on, and Dalton appeared after the hills fell away. It had two churches and the ruins of a third. Otherwise, there was a well-tended graveyard, a row of cottages, and a pub. The Murray Arms flew three flags—the Saltire; the Lion Rampant of Scotland; and of course the red, white, and blue of the … Kingdom of Thailand. The pub advertised "authentic Thai cuisine", and I imagined a son of the village—a Murray perhaps—returning from his globetrotting with a Thai bride who now made Tom Yum soup to serve with the Belhaven beer.

Annan was seven miles away by the B7020, but where Dalton's cottages ran out I turned onto a smaller road, toward Hoddom Castle. Halfway down this lonely byway, a square structure came into view on a hilltop in the distance. It was not quite as tall as the pines beside it. It had to be the "Repentance Tower" marked on my map above Hoddom Castle, itself still hidden at the hill's foot. The tower is named for a single word carved in a beam above its entrance. But repentance for what? The most likely story concerns one John Maxwell, second son of a local lord in the mid-1500s. At that time, more even than usual, the Anglo-Scottish border was in turmoil. Henry VIII of England and, after Henry's death in 1547, the regent for young Edward VI, had mounted a series of invasions of Scotland to encourage it to accept a marriage between

the infant Mary, Queen of Scots, and Edward. The wars became
known as the Rough Wooing. By 1547, the wooing had put
Annandale under English control, and the young John Maxwell
had pledged himself to the English cause. That this pledge was
forced can be presumed from the hostages taken from among his
kin to be held in England as guarantee of good behavior. It did
not work. In February 1548, Maxwell and his men marched with
their English allies into the southern hills to engage the Scots. At
a critical moment of battle, Maxwell switched sides. The English
campaign failed, and its commander retreated to Carlisle to hang
his hostages. Maxwell may not have been motivated by pure patriotism. The story goes that he had been promised the hand of
Agnes of Herries in return for switching allegiance, and Agnes
was a route to lands and titles. The decades that followed seem
to have treated John Maxwell very well. He and Agnes were wed.
He became Sir John. He acquired new lands and built Hoddom
Castle upon them. His country put him in charge of its western
border. But it is said that his conscience was troubled by the inno-
cents slain on his account, and when he built a watchtower to keep
the English out of Annandale, he showed his remorse on a lintel.

Beneath Repentance Hill, there was a parking area for
Hoddom Castle. It had moss-covered picnic tables, and I stopped
for lunch. Sir John's castle was some way off through trees, and I
never did catch sight of it. As I ate, I wondered where to go next.
Annan, obviously; but there were three options to get there. A sign
across the road said the B723 would take me there in four miles.
According to the fussy booklet, the Annandale Way followed the
east bank of the River Annan downstream to the town, but no
footpath was marked there on my OS map. There was, however,
the dotted line of a path along the west bank, and it started right
across the road from here. It became my plan.

The path began as a broad track, and soon came to a bluff
above the River Annan, flowing gray and deep between confining

wooded banks. The arches of Hoddom Bridge stood a quarter-mile upstream. Next to the path stood a sign:

*Access not recommended beyond this point.*
*Please keep to waymarked paths.*

I found this notice annoying. To me, it said, "There are paths, but we do not suggest you use them, for reasons we will not deign to give." I pushed on into the woods my map called Woodcock Air. These deciduous woods became very pleasant, and the path very waterlogged. I clambered over a broken stile, crossed a field of sheep where flies buzzed on droppings and rabbits hopped, and arrived at Turnshawhead farm. Its yard, and the track leading away from it, were swimming in a sludge of very dubious content. Above the mire, a Saltire flew. Its pole was set at an angle, hinting at forward motion or perhaps a strongpoint. The angle of slope was away from the border, ten miles to the southeast here as a heron would fly. My own forward motion appeared stymied. I could not see a way ahead to Upper Brydekirk, the next farm. Fearing a fruitless tramp through the unsavory sludge, I gave up and went back to the sign that perhaps I should have heeded. Perhaps; but I felt curiously rewarded by the shitty, out-of-the-way farm, and its very private show of patriotism.

The escapade had added two miles to my day, but now I was striding along the B723. It rose slowly for a while, then levelled out for a long straight. Somewhere on the straight, the Solway—silvery this afternoon—and the fells of Cumbria appeared again, three days after Hods Hill. The road fell. I rested at a burn lined with trees bent by a Solway wind that was quiet today. Ducks took off quacking from a puddle in a nearby field. At the next rise in the road, I saw traffic stalled on the A75 outside Annan; and soon, rounding a bend, the town appeared, starting cleanly on the far side of fields and its namesake river. I walked onto the High Street and found a room at the Corner House Hotel. I dumped the Big Bastard and my heavy boots in the room, and set out to find the Solway.

I walked through Annan's sandstone buildings to its railway station, took the bridge over the tracks, and soon was once again on a lane between fields. The lane climbed to a built-up knoll—Annan Hill—from which bungalows looked down over grazing cows to the Solway. A footpath led down to a fringe of green, lumpy land, cut by rivulets. I crossed this narrow *merse*[53] until it met the saturated sand-mud of the foreshore. The tide was out, and the mud stretched for some distance, reflecting a faint pink from a layer of clouds touched feebly by a sun sinking otherwise invisibly. The mud eventually slid into a channel of mirror-still water. On the far shore—a mile and three-quarters off—I could make out houses and trees, and far beyond them, blurred gray fells. It could easily have been more of Scotland. But the map said that a national boundary ran in mid-channel, and the houses and trees were in Bowness-on-Solway in England, where Hadrian's great dividing wall meets the western sea. The map showed too that, over there, they put up monuments to Edward "Longshanks". I could walk no farther, and since I could not, I turned around and walked back to Annan as soon as I had lingered long enough to dignify the moment. It was not long; the midges saw to that.

# *Epilogue*

I did not punch the air or do a jig when I reached the Solway sand. It was not how I felt. I was pleased the journey was over. Now tomorrow would bring a change from the preoccupations and tasks of six weeks. Now I could head for home, starting with a train that would take me—dry and seated—back over the southern hills to Glasgow. Above all, I was pleased that I had done what I had set out to do. I had a trove of stories, not just one about how I jacked it in when rain, pain, and strange beds got the better of me.

But the journey had meant too much to celebrate its end. When I set off into the rough grass and bog cotton at Cape Wrath, I thought I knew Scotland pretty well for a half-stranger. Now that I had put my boots down hundreds of thousands of times on its coarse vegetation, winding roads, stony paths, muck, and sidewalks, I felt simultaneously that I knew my birth-land better than ever before and less than I had thought. Thanks to six weeks of footsteps, and voices, and new scenes at every bend and bealach,

I fully grasped what John Muir had meant by "quick and living contact" with a native land. Like him, I didn't feel like a stranger anymore either. But intimacy had bred a desire for more. I hadn't ticked an item off a bucket list to flit joyfully onto the next. I did not do a jig on the Solway in part because, though this particular journey was over, there were still paths all over Scotland that I wanted to follow, routes of inquiry as well as routes in the dirt.

An end is a new beginning; and I sensed my new start, strongly, as I walked back into Annan. I had a family and home to return to, but no career. I needed to find my new way of making a living, the one with space for what really matters. Thinking about this took me back three and a half weeks. I had just waded the River Loyne. All the way to the river, I had focused on the crossing. Would it be possible? What would it mean if it were not? Then I found myself, suddenly, on the far bank with no way forward. I hadn't thought about what would happen on the other side. It felt like that now. I had hoped on my journey to think about the future, but I'd thought instead about miles, trails, my boots, and keeping the sweet Scottish rain from trickling down my spine. Now, all of a sudden, I was on the other side of my walk, seeing that there was no onward path conveniently marked out for me. But perhaps the journey had taught me something. Now, at its end, the hardships had become as precious to me as its untroubled moments, the memory of limping into Strathcarron as treasured as the sunny views from Willie's nubble. I felt sure that my future would work the same way. There would be setbacks, self-doubt, ordeals. But now I could almost look forward to them, because I knew they would sweeten whatever rewards might come my way, and in time would seem inseparable from them.

# End Notes

1. A narrow strait.

2. A ben is a mountain or hill.

3. Soccer.

4. Tiny biting flies.

5. The Celtic language once spoken in most of Scotland. *Beinn* is the Gaelic form of ben.

6. A stream or brook.

7. A *lochan* is a small loch (lake).

8. A walkers' hut.

9. Toilet, restroom.

10. Pronounced *gyoh* not, as I at first assumed, *gee-o*.

11. A cracker made from oats.

12. Collapse was not entirely improbable. Three weeks later, a geologist in southwest England filmed thousands of tons of cliff as they slid into the Atlantic. It became a YouTube hit.

13. The Viking tongue, a forerunner of modern Scandinavian languages.

14. My authority here is *Place-names of Scotland*, Iain Taylor 2011.

15. From Latin *Picti,* the "painted" or "tattooed" people.

16. A speaker of a Celtic language, so here either Pict or Gael.

17. The extinct Scandinavian language of the Orkney and Shetland islands. These northern archipelagoes remained fully part of the Scandinavian world until their acquisition by Scotland only in the 1400s.

18. An arm of the sea.

19. Ordnance Survey (OS) Landranger series, numbers 9 and 15 respectively.

20. Food in a tent was an unaccustomed luxury, permitted by the extinction of Scotland's bears a millennium ago.

21. Pronounced *byal-ach*—with "ch" as in the Scottish loch.

22. Mountain amphitheaters, cirques; from the Gaelic for cauldron.

23. A shepherd's summer hut.

24. "Big mountain of Assynt".

25. "Bh" in Gaelic is pronounced "v". *Bheinn* here means the same as "ben", though pronounced as "vein".

26. Often written, and always pronounced, Stack Polly.

27. A broad valley.

28. The gathering and burning of seaweed to create an ash used in certain manufacturing processes.

29. Pronounced approximately *mee-yall doo*.

30. *An cha-loch*, more or less, with loch pronounced the Scottish way.

31. The Loch an Nid river. *Abhainn* is pronounced more or less *avin*.

32. Those supporting *Jacobus*, or James, the deposed James VII / II and his heirs.

33. Almost certainly a legend. King Robert the Bruce, hiding from his enemies in a cave, watched a spider try and fail to weave a web. Over and over it tried, until at last it succeeded. King Robert followed its example.

34. The broad, 60-mile glen between Fort William and Inverness, a natural travelling route.

35. I carried the 1:50 000 scale maps, not the 1:25 000 series.

36. Scotland's flag, a white Saint Andrew's Cross (or saltire) on a blue field.

37. *Lairig* (pronounced *larick*) is another word for mountain pass.

38. The murder too is a historical event, and James of the Glen

was hanged for it in November 1752, his bones left to swing in the wind for three years. His conviction is widely recognized as a travesty of justice. The true perpetrator—the wielder of the gun I'd seen in the Fort William museum—is unknown.

39. Kinlochleven is 18 miles by road.

40. Scots for drenched, soaked.

41. The Battle of Bannockburn, June 1314, led to grudging English recognition of Scotland's independence; Scotland's Yorktown perhaps.

42. You know the one. The chorus goes:

*O ye'll tak' the high road, and Ah'll tak' the low road*
*And Ah'll be in Scotlan' afore ye*
*Fir me an' my true love will ne'er meet again*
*On the bonnie, bonnie banks o' Loch Lomon'.*

43. The street along the Clyde in the City Centre, once home to quays.

44. The home of the Declaration of Arbroath was surely carefully chosen, the place where in 1320 the Scottish barons declared that they fought the English not "for glory, nor riches, nor honours… but for freedom—for that alone, which no honest man gives up but with life itself."

45. The Roman name for the northern parts of Great Britain beyond their frontier, and now a poetic name for Scotland.

46. A 1954 novel by Rosemary Sutcliff, made into a TV series in the 1970s.

47. Ronald McNair Scott, *Robert the Bruce*.

48. The gist is "Whatever is meant to be, will be."

49. A *feartie* is a fearful person (or, here, a fearful cow).

50. *The Wallace*; or, more fully, *The Actes and Deidis of the Illustre and Vallyeant Campioun Schir William Wallace*.

51. In order, Highland; Argyle & Bute; Stirling; East Dunbartonshire; Glasgow; North Lanarkshire; South Lanarkshire; Dumfries & Galloway.

52. The town where Pan Am 103 came down in 1988 was four miles east. I remember hearing the news of the attack on the radio in Hong Kong. The impact was greater because I'd received postcards from Lockerbie over the years. It was one of my parents' weekend-break places.

53. Scots—the flat, alluvial land by a river.

# About the Author

ROBERT MCWILLIAMS was born in Glasgow, Scotland, but moved with his journalist father's job to the south of England at the age of three. Rob graduated from Wadham College, Oxford, with a BA Hons. in Modern History. After university, he worked as a tour guide and English teacher in France and Spain, before joining Reuters news agency in London. Rob spent 16 years at Reuters as a business manager in Hong Kong, Japan, the US, Venezuela and Brazil.

For nearly 20 years, Rob has lived in Connecticut with his wife and daughters, and is now a US citizen. Tired of corporate life, he quit his job to fulfill a stubborn ambition to walk the length of Scotland. He has contributed the *Taking a Hike* column to local newspapers every month for five years. *Taking a Hike* placed second in the general column category of the 2017 Connecticut Press Club awards. Rob has also written for *A.T. Journeys*, the official magazine of the Appalachian Trail, and *Ctvisit. com*. *The Kiss of Sweet Scottish Rain* is his first book.

Rob enjoys hiking, and travel off the beaten track. He does consulting work on information privacy, and volunteers with the Nature Conservancy, Appalachian Trail and other outdoor causes.

# HOMEBOUND PUBLICATIONS

*Ensuring that the mainstream isn't the only stream.*

At Homebound Publications, we publish books written by independent voices for independent minds. Our books focus on a return to simplicity and balance, connection to the earth and each other, and the search for meaning and authenticity. Founded in 2011, Homebound Publications is one of the rising independent publishers in the country. Collectively through our imprints, we publish between fifteen to twenty offerings each year. Our authors have received dozens of awards, including: *Foreword Reviews'* Book of the Year, Nautilus Book Award, Benjamin Franklin Book Awards, and Saltire Literary Awards. Highly-respected among bookstores, readers and authors alike, Homebound Publications has a proven devotion to quality, originality and integrity.

We are a small press with big ideas. As an independent publisher we strive to ensure that the mainstream is not the only stream. It is our intention at Homebound Publications to preserve contemplative storytelling. We publish full-length introspective works of creative non-fiction as well as essay collections, travel writing, poetry, and novels. In all our titles, our intention is to introduce new perspectives that will directly aid humankind in the trials we face at present as a global village.